The Truth About Port Arthur...

E. K. Nozkin

Nabu Public Domain Reprints:

You are holding a reproduction of an original work published before 1923 that is in the public domain in the United States of America, and possibly other countries. You may freely copy and distribute this work as no entity (individual or corporate) has a copyright on the body of the work. This book may contain prior copyright references, and library stamps (as most of these works were scanned from library copies). These have been scanned and retained as part of the historical artifact.

This book may have occasional imperfections such as missing or blurred pages, poor pictures, errant marks, etc. that were either part of the original artifact, or were introduced by the scanning process. We believe this work is culturally important, and despite the imperfections, have elected to bring it back into print as part of our continuing commitment to the preservation of printed works worldwide. We appreciate your understanding of the imperfections in the preservation process, and hope you enjoy this valuable book.

THE TRUTH ABOUT PORT ARTHUR

First Edition . . . April, 1908.
Second Impression . May, 1908.

GENERAL SMIRNOFF.

Frontispiece.

THE TRUTH ABOUT PORT ARTHUR

BY MONSIEUR E. K. NOJINE
ACCREDITED RUSSIAN WAR CORRESPONDENT DURING THE SIEGE

TRANSLATED AND ABRIDGED BY
CAPTAIN A. B. LINDSAY
2ND KING EDWARD'S OWN GURKHA RIFLES
TRANSLATOR OF 'THE BATTLE OF TSU-SHIMA,' ETC.

EDITED BY
MAJOR E. D. SWINTON, D.S.O.
ROYAL ENGINEERS
AUTHOR OF 'THE DEFENCE OF DUFFER'S DRIFT'

WITH MAP AND ILLUSTRATIONS

NEW YORK
E. P. DUTTON AND COMPANY
1908

PRINTED IN GREAT BRITAIN

PREFACE

THE siege of Port Arthur was the event of the late war in the Far East which most attracted the attention and interest of the rest of the world. There were other military operations, it is true, of equal if not of greater importance to the ultimate issue of the struggle; but, owing to their complexity, their slowness, and the absence of definite advance information, their progress and purport were not easily grasped by any save military students. The case of Port Arthur was different. The long drawn-out agony of the siege was continued before the eyes of the world for many months,[*] and, while the imagination was touched by its romantic side, the point at issue was at once apparent.

Even so, there was much mystery about the conduct of the defence and the eventual fall of the Fortress; for, owing to its remote position and almost complete isolation by the enemy, the available information almost entirely consisted of that supplied by correspondents with the Japanese, and was, therefore, information from the outside, and more or less a history of *results* alone. In 1907, or between two and three years after the culmination of the siege, the inevitable disclosures—the aftermath of defeat—which sometimes help to an appreciation of *causes* began to be made in Russia.

More than one book has recently been written by

[*] One hundred and fifty-four days after the close investment.

Russians who saw the defence from inside the Fortress, and who therefore claim to be in a position to give the inner history of the tragedy.

'The Truth about Port Arthur' was published in Russia last year. M. Nojine, the author, by whose permission this abridged translation has been made, was the accredited Russian war-correspondent in Port Arthur, and as such went through the greater part of the siege. He had exceptional facilities for collecting material for his work, for he was all through in close contact with the 'fighting' leaders of Port Arthur, and had access to official documents and diaries, and, having been an eye-witness of much, and possessing the trained observation of a journalist, his testimony should carry weight. His book is one long indictment of the then régime in Russia, and of some of the officials connected with the defence of Port Arthur.

By the time that the English translation was completed, in the autumn of 1907, it was announced that some of the senior officers who conducted the defence were to be tried by court-martial. In fact, from the copy of the official indictment then published,[*] it seemed as if it might almost have been framed upon material furnished by M. Nojine's book. It was therefore decided to delay publication whilst matters were *sub judice*. The trial is now over, the result is known to the world, and there seems no reason why the English version of the account by an eyewitness of what went on in the ill-fated Fortress should not be given to the public.

The translator and editor disclaim all responsibility for the statements made and the opinions expressed, which are the author's own.

If he has sometimes been carried beyond the limits of a strictly judicial impartiality, it is, perhaps, in the

[*] See Conclusion, p. 336.

circumstances, comprehensible. His patriotism must have been again and again outraged by the existing maladministration, while his personal feelings were probably embittered by the treatment which he and those who bore the burden of the defence received.

Though the author, as will be seen by a perusal of his book, is not sparing of censure and is distinctly outspoken in his conclusions, yet he is capable of giving praise when he considers it to be due. Indeed, it is a relief, amongst so much that is depressing, to read his opinion of Generals Smirnoff and Kondratenko amongst others, and his whole-hearted championship of the stolid, dogged Russian soldier who, weighed down by the incompetence of many above him, struggled through those weary months of defeat, privation, and suspense.

Amongst much in this book which gives food for thought there are two or three matters described by the author which are truly extraordinary. For instance, it is difficult to believe that when, after so much threatening, the storm eventually burst and war broke out, Port Arthur—that outpost of the Russian Empire—was so far from being ready that on January 14, 1904, only eight guns of the allotted armament were mounted on the land defences. And yet there is official authority for this statement (see Appendix II.). It is also remarkable that even before the place was finally cut off by complete investment in July, 1904, the troops had to be put on short rations; this seems to have been caused by the subordination, even in war, of the military to other requirements. General Fock's theory also upon fortress warfare (p. 227) is strangely at variance with the practice of his great countryman Todleben, who defended Sevastopol for 349 days, and his reasoning is difficult to follow. Finally, the action of the senior officer of a beleaguered fortress, in disobeying and concealing the official messages which

...ered his recall and appointed his successor, seems inconceivable.

Undoubtedly, if a proper organization had existed upon the outbreak of hostilities instead of the inadequate product of a nation's false economy, Port Arthur might have held out for a considerably longer time than it did; but speculation upon the possible results of this is beyond the scope of this preface. Without labouring the morals pointed by this siege, it is clear that policy should wait on military preparedness, that now as of old the internal jealousies within an army are as dangerous to it as the enemy, and that it is still the moral factor that counts most.

In the translation there has of necessity been some abridgement; but an endeavour has been made all through to convey the writer's meaning and, wherever possible, to use his exact words. The chief interest of the work for British readers seems to be in the picture presented of the general conduct of the defence and of the state of affairs in the Fortress rather than in the more technical accounts of the actual fighting, which are very like each other. To those not engaged, the description of an attack on one point bears much resemblance to the descriptions of attacks on other points. It is with this feeling that the necessary curtailment has been made. Some, also, of the author's picturesque writing, which would probably appeal less to the Briton than it would to the Slav, has been eliminated.

All military history must to a certain extent lose in interest for the non-professional reader from the continual occurrence of the names of small places which are only of importance to the military student, and which, even without necessitating a reference to the map, rather break the continuity of the narrative. This is especially so in the case of the recent war, where the majority of the localities referred to are obscure spots, possessing names of Chinese origin which not only are very long and uncouth, but also have a confusing resemblance to each other. Added to this, they have been as a rule spelled differently in every account or on every map. It has, therefore, been decided in this translation to give, wherever possible, the English equivalents of the Russian instead of the Chinese or Japanese names of places, forts, or positions. They are shorter, convey more meaning to the British reader, and therefore so far tend to simplification. This has been thought to outweigh the disadvantages of the fact that they are comparatively unknown, for the Chinese or Japanese names have so far been almost exclusively used in England.

To this rule there are three exceptions. Three localities at Port Arthur possess non-Russian names, which are now almost historic in the English tongue, and for which it would be confusing and almost pedantic to use the Russian equivalents. These are 203 Metre Hill, North Fort Chi-kuan-shan, and Fort Erh-lung-shan, which would not be recognized under their Russian names of High Hill,* Fort No. 2, Fort No. 3. For these three places the names already so well known have been used, except in Appendix I. and the table of Appendix III.

As regards the accounts of the fighting and the numbers engaged, it must be borne in mind that the organization of both the Russian and Japanese infantry is different to that existing in the British army, and that where a regiment is mentioned in the text it means three battalions. Thus a division of the East Siberian Rifles (as well as a Japanese active division) consisted of two brigades of two regiments of three battalions each, or twelve battalions.

* There is another hill called High Hill, on the eastern flank, which has been left as such.

Finally, a short description of the defences of Port Arthur will, perhaps, elucidate the author's narrative. At the outbreak of war the land defences of the Fortress consisted of the following:

The Chinese Wall, which was a continuous earth rampart extending for some distance round the north of the place.

Five principal permanent works of large size and great strength, arranged in a rough semicircle from sea to sea. Of these, one, No. 5, was not finished at the outbreak of hostilities. Another, No. 6, which was to have completed the girdle on the west, was not commenced. These works are called in the text 'forts.'

Five subsidiary works in the intervals between the principal 'forts.' These were not of such strength as the latter, and were for the most part completed but not armed at the commencement of hostilities. They are called in the text 'fortifications.'

Certain of the batteries on the land side, and a few auxiliary works—such as redoubts, etc.

After the outbreak of war the existing permanent and semi-permanent works were supplemented by a large number of batteries and closed infantry works, in some of which guns were emplaced. These were sited between the other works, or, in some cases, upon special points, and are called 'redoubts' and 'lunettes.' There were also a few open infantry works constructed for the special purpose of 'flanking' others, or for firing over ground in front of them not covered by their own fire. These are here called 'open caponiers,' and should not be confused with the masonry structures called 'caponiers,' placed at the bottom of the deep ditches of the larger works for the defence of those ditches.

Round, between, and behind the forts, fortifications, redoubts, lunettes, etc., a maze of trenches grew up for fire, shelter, and communication, and numerous bomb-proofs, magazines, dressing stations, were also built. In front were wire entanglements, live electric wires, land mines—every obstacle that ingenuity could suggest.

To assist in identification a table has been prepared in which the Russian and the other names (where available) of the localities mentioned are given. A chronological table of the principal events of the siege has been also added.

LONDON, *March*, 1908.

TABLE OF NAMES

List of Principal Places mentioned, giving their Russian and in some cases their Other Names.

Russian Names.	Other Names.
Principal Works—'Forts.'	
No. 1 Fort (S.E.).	Paiyin-shan Fort; South Fort.
No. 2 ,, (N.E.).	North Fort Chi-kuan-shan; Fort Kitohadai.
No. 3 ,, (N.).	Fort Erh-lung-shan; Fort Nirusan.
No. 4 ,, (N.W.).	I-tzu-shan Fort.
No. 5 ,, (W.).	Tayanko North.
No. 6 ,, (S.W.).	
Subsidiary Works—'Fortifications.'	
Fortification No. 1 (S.E.).	South-east Chi-kuan-shan Battery.
,, No. 2 (E.).	Dangerous Mountain.
,, No. 3 (N.).	Sung-su-shan Fort; Shozu-shan Fort; Shojusan.
,, No. 4 (W.).	South An-tzu-shan Fort.
,, No. 5 (S.W.).	Cha-kua-tzu.
Intermediate, Temporary, and Field Works.	
Takhe Redoubt (S.E.).	South-east Redoubt.
Rear Redoubt (E.).	
Kuropatkin Lunette (N.E.).	'Q' Work.
No. 1 Open Caponier (N.E.).	
Redoubt No. 1 (N.E.).	East Pan-lun-shan Redoubt; East Banrusan.

Russian Names.	Other Names.
Intermediate, Temporary, and Field Works (continued).	
No. 2 Open Caponier (N.E.).	'P' Work.
Redoubt No. 2 (N.E.).	West Pan-lun-shan Redoubt; West Banrusan.
No. 3 Open Caponier (N.E.).	'G' Work; Hachi-maki-yama.
Water Supply Redoubt (N.)	Fort Kuropatkin.
Rocky Redoubt (N.).	Railway Redoubt; Lung-yen.
Temple Redoubt (N.).	
Pan-lun-shan Redoubt (N.W.).	
Flat Hill, No. 1 Redoubt (N.W.).	
,, No. 2 ,, (N.W.).	
,, No. 3 ,, (N.W.).	
,, No. 4 ,, Stone-broken (N.W.).	
Double Angle Lunette (N.W.).	
New Lunette (N.W.).	
Fougasse Lunette (N.W.).	
No. 5 Redoubt (W.).	Quarry Battery.
No. 4 ,, (W.).	
Timber Redoubt (S.W.).	
Salt Redoubt (S.W.).	
Quail Hill (centre).	
Land Batteries.	
Cross (S.E.).	
Dragon's Back (E.).	
Dragon's Head (E.).	
'A' (E.).	
'B' (N.E.).	
Zaliterny (N.E.).	'R.'
Little Eagle's Nest (N.E.).	'M.'
Eagle's Nest (N.E.).	Bodai; Wang-tai.
Zaredoubt (N.).	'H.'
Howitzer (N.).	
Wolf's (N.).	'I.'
Tumulus (N.).	Sung-su-shan Auxiliary.
Cemetery (N.W.).	Cemetery.
'C' (Sapper) (N.W.).	
Jagged Hill (N.W.).	

Russian Names.	Other Names.
Land Batteries (continued).	
Howitzer (N.W.).	
Obelisk Hill (N.W.).	Obelisk Hill.
Tea (W.).	Stonebroken.
Pigeon (W.).	
'D' (W.).	South Tayanko.
Salt, [? Redoubt] (S.W.).	
Coast Batteries.	
White Wolf.	
No. 1.	
„ 2.	Tiger's Head.
„ 3.	
„ 4.	
„ 5. } On Tiger's Peninsula.	
„ 6.	} Chi-kuan-shan.
„ 7.	
„ 8.	Man-tzu-ying.
„ 9.	
„ 10.	
Lighthouse.	
No. 12 (S.).	
„ 13, Golden Hill (S.).	
„ 14 (S.).	
„ 15, Electric Cliff (S.).	
„ 16 (S.E.).	Six-inch Gun.
„ 17 (S.E.).	
„ 18 (S.E.).	
„ 19 (S.E.).	
„ 20 (S.E.).	
„ 21, Long Battery (S.E.).	
„ 22 (S.E.).	
Other Places.	
Kuen-san Hill (N.E.).	Ken-san Hill.
Sia-gu-shan (E.).	Shokozan; Hsiao-ku-shan.
Ta-ku-shan (E.).	Ta-ku-san.
High Hill (N.W.).	203 Metre Hill; Royusan.
Angle Hill (N.W.).	174 Metre Hill.
Long Hill (N.W.).	Namakoyama.
Divisional Hill (N.).	
Flat Hill (N.).	Akasakayama
Wolf's Hills (N.E.)	Feng-huang-shen.

CHRONOLOGICAL TABLE OF PRINCIPAL EVENTS

1904.

Feb.	8.	Japanese torpedo Russian Fleet.
,,	25.	Japanese attempt to 'block.'
Mar.	10.	Japanese bombard the harbour.
,,	17.	General Smirnoff arrives.
,,	22.	Japanese bombard the harbour.
,,	25.	Japanese attempt to 'block.'
April	13.	The *Petropalovsk* blown up by a mine.
,,	14.	The Viceroy, Admiral Alexeieff, arrives in Port Arthur.
May	2.	Japanese attempt to 'block.'
,,	4.	Japanese land at Petsiwo.
,,	5.	The Viceroy leaves Port Arthur.
,,	15.	The *Hatsuse* sunk by a Russian mine. The *Fuji* damaged.
,,	16.	Action at Shanshihlipu.
,,	20.	Japanese attack by sea.
,,	26.	Battle of Kinchou. Dalny evacuated.
June	18.	General Stössel receives a telegram of recall.
,,	19.	Sortie of Russian Fleet. *Sevastopol* damaged by a mine. Japanese attempt to torpedo Russian Fleet.
,,	26.} 27.}	The fight on Green Hills. Russians lose Kuen-san Hill.
July	3.} 4.} 5.}	Russian attempts to recapture Kuen-san fail.
,,	26.} 27.} 28.}	Russians driven from Green Hills position.

1904 (*continued*).

- July 29. Russians driven from Wolf's Hills position.
- " 30.
- " 31. } Investment commences.
- Aug. 8. Ta-ku-shan and Sia-gu-shan lost by Russians.
- " 9. First attempt to recapture Ta-ku-shan Hill fails.
- " 10. Sortie of the Russian Fleet.
- " 11. Second attempt to recapture Ta-ku-shan Hill fails.
- " 16. Japanese suggest surrender of Port Arthur.
- " 21.
- " 22.
- " 23. } Great Japanese assault. Nos. 1 and 2 Redoubts captured by Japanese.
- Sept. 19. Japanese capture Water-supply Redoubt.
- " 20. Japanese capture Temple Redoubt.
- Oct. 1. Japanese commence firing from 11-inch howitzers.
- " 29.
- " 30. } General assault by Japanese. No. 2 Open Caponier captured by them.
- Nov. 20-26. Japanese assaults.
- Dec. 5. 203 Metre Hill captured.
- " 6. Japanese commence to shell Russian ships.
- " 15. General Kondratenko killed.
- " 18. Chi-kuan-shan Fort captured.
- " 28. Erh-lung-shan Fort captured.
- " 31. Fortification No. 3 captured.

1905.

- Jan. 1. Eagle's Nest captured.
- " 2. Capitulation signed.

CONTENTS

CHAPTER		PAGE
I.	THE BOMB-SHELL	3
II.	SETTLING DOWN TO IT	8
III.	DEVELOPMENTS	17
IV.	SMIRNOFF ARRIVES	23
V.	STÖSSEL STAYS	27
VI.	THE WORK OF JAPANESE MINE-LAYERS	32
VII.	NEWS FROM THE NORTH	36
VIII.	MORE BLOCKERS	41
IX.	WHAT WE DID WHILE THE ENEMY WERE ADVANCING	44
X.	THE NAVY LOSE A CHANCE	50
XI.	PREPARATIONS ON THE KINCHOU POSITION	54
XII.	THE BATTLE OF KINCHOU COMMENCES	61
XIII.	THE BATTLE CONTINUES	67
XIV.	NANGALIN RAILWAY-STATION	75
XV.	THE LAST OF DALNY	80
XVI.	THE FATE OF THE FORTRESS	84
XVII.	THE LOSS OF KUEN-SAN HILL	91
XVIII.	THE JUNE SORTIE OF THE FLEET	96
XIX.	FORTIFYING OUR LINE	103
XX.	THE ATTACK ON GREEN HILLS	110
XXI.	THE BATTLE CONTINUES	120
XXII.	STÖSSEL HOIST BY HIS OWN PETARD	133
XXIII.	THE LOSS OF TA-KU-SHAN HILL	140
XXIV.	THE SORTIE OF THE FLEET ON AUGUST 10	150
XXV.	OUR SECOND ATTACK ON TA-KU-SHAN—A FLAG OF TRUCE	155
XXVI.	DEATH OF PRINCE MACHABELLY—ALL-ROUND FIGHTING	163

CONTENTS

CHAPTER		PAGE
XXVII.	STÖSSEL DISOBEYS—PROGRESS DURING AUGUST	173
XXVIII.	AWARDS—SOME PERSONAL NOTES	186
XXIX.	SEPTEMBER PASSES	191
XXX.	MOLE WARFARE	206
XXXI.	JAPANESE VIEWS—GENERAL FOCK'S MEMORANDUM ON FORTRESS DEFENCE	222
XXXII.	HINTS OF SURRENDER—MORE ASSAULTS	233
XXXIII.	THE FIGHT FOR 203 METRE HILL	243
XXXIV.	THE LOSS OF THE HILL	252
XXXV.	A RETROSPECT ON THE POSITION AT SEA	259
XXXVI.	A COUNCIL MEETING	265
XXXVII.	KONDRATENKO'S DEATH AND SOME RESULTS	274
XXXVIII.	THE LOSS OF FORT CHI-KUAN-SHAN	284
XXXIX.	THE SAPPERS—REWARDS	292
XL.	THE FALL OF ERH-LUNG-SHAN AND THE LAST COUNCIL	299
XLI.	THE FALL OF FORTIFICATION NO. 3.—THE FAILURE OF THE DEFENCE AND MEDICAL ORGANIZATIONS	310
XLII.	THE LAST DAY BUT ONE	322
XLIII.	THE END	330
	CONCLUSION	336
	APPENDIX I.	347
	APPENDIX II.	364
	APPENDIX III.	381
	APPENDIX IV.	385
	INDEX	389

LIST OF ILLUSTRATIONS

GENERAL SMIRNOFF	- FRONTISPIECE	
ADMIRAL LOSCHINSKY	TO FACE PAGE	20
COLONEL KHVOSTOFF	,,	23
ADMIRAL MAKHAROFF	,,	35
MAJOR-GENERAL TRETIAKOFF	,,	69
COLONEL LAPEROFF	,,	73
A WOMAN DRESSED AS A SOLDIER WHO WENT THROUGH SEVERAL FIGHTS	,,	87
A BOMBPROOF	,,	105
REAR-ADMIRAL GRIGOROVITCH	,,	151
INSIDE A TRENCH ON THE EASTERN FRONT	,,	166
GENERAL GORBATOVSKY	,,	171
ON THE ATTACKED FRONT	,,	174
THE ASSAULT REPULSED	,,	182
BURIAL-PARTIES AT WORK	,,	185
COLONEL RASCHEVSKY	,,	188
PANORAMA OF NORTH-EAST FRONT	,,	193
A CANET GUN MOUNTED ON FORT V., SEPTEMBER 22	,,	197
A COMPANY IN THE TRENCHES	,,	200
BOMBARDMENT: JAPANESE SHELLS BURSTING ON HILL	,,	208
RESULTS OF A BOMBARDMENT	,,	210
GENERAL SMIRNOFF FIRING THE CAMOUFLET	,,	217
KUROPATKIN LUNETTE AFTER THE ASSAULT IN OCTOBER	,,	221

LIST OF ILLUSTRATIONS

B BATTERY	TO FACE PAGE	231
RESERVES WAITING UNDER 203 METRE HILL	,,	246
GENERAL BIELY	,,	256
GENERAL KONDRATENKO	,,	276
NORTH FORT, CHI-KUAN-SHAN, SHOWING GREEN HILLS IN THE DISTANCE	,,	285
ADMIRAL WIREN	,,	330

THE
TRUTH ABOUT PORT ARTHUR

'Culpam pœna premit comes.'

PORT ARTHUR has fallen. . . .

The bare fact is now a matter of history; but at last the time has come to reckon up in detail all that happened during the blockade by land and sea. As late war correspondent in the theatre of operations in Kwantun, as a close witness of all that took place, and as one who voluntarily went through that terrible time, I look upon it as my sacred duty to narrate what this defence cost the garrison and inhabitants of the unhappy town—to tell the truth, the whole truth, and nothing but the truth.

All who went through that heartrending siege, and who reflected at all on what was passing before their eyes, became gradually aware of—and finally, I might almost say, resigned to—two great facts. First, that the Fortress Commandant, Lieutenant-General Smirnoff, had two enemies to fight—one inside the Fortress and one out; second, that it was the internal enemy which proved too strong. The immense efforts of General Smirnoff and of his immediate assistants—the late General Kondratenko, Admirals Grigorovitch, Loschinsky, and Wiren, and Generals Biely and Gorbatovsky—were in vain.

Why?

To this question the following pages will, I hope, supply the answer; but, before commencing my narrative, I should explain that I shall only recount facts either confirmed by documentary evidence or witnessed by myself.

CHAPTER I

THE BOMB-SHELL

WHEN, one hour before midnight on February 8, 1904, our warships began to belch fire from their many steel mouths, and the seaward batteries suddenly thundered forth their angry death-dealing tidings, no one dreamed that the noise was War, for no one had taken the constant rumours of the rupture of diplomatic relations and of approaching hostilities at all seriously. Those who heard the increasing cannonade buoyed themselves up with the vague hope that some surprise combined manœuvres were taking place between the fleet and the coast defences. When three rockets, however, snaked up into the inky night from Golden Hill and burst on high, they told their message, and finally when the gun-fire from Electric Cliff and the adjacent batteries changed to salvos, those who understood the message of the rockets doubted no longer.

Thus was all hope of a peaceful issue to the negotiations with Japan shattered. Our incapable, idle, and utterly short-sighted diplomacy, which had so long and so stupidly exhausted the patience of the Mikado's Government, was now at an end. It was to enjoy a dishonourable repose, whilst others reaped the harvest of its handiwork. The hour had struck for the cold, impartial judgment of history.

Although the sky in the East had for weeks been blood-red with the menace of immediate war, yet when it came the surprise was absolute, its horror intensified by our complete unreadiness.

Regiments hearing the alarm fell in. Officers, surprised in bed, at a ball, at the theatre, or in restaurants, hurried off to march their units to the alarm posts: hurried, but went without speed—for, alas! no one had hitherto taken the trouble to become acquainted with the geography of the Fortress, and the consequence was that most of the troops wandered about unknown roads and hill-tracks, in vain searching for the posts assigned to them. The confusion which ensued was incredible—a fitting prelude to the fall of Port Arthur. Finally, when the troops did arrive at their posts, to their amazement they found in them either no small-arm ammunition at all or else only the ordinary quantity for the guards. To the men it was at first a huge joke; they naturally thought they were only doing a 'sham fight.' But the jest wore off as they sat on through the night, and through the next day, hungry, and chilled to the bone by the pitiless icy wind which was howling down the hill-sides. It was possibly good training for the hardships to follow? It was not until the morning that it struck some bright staff-officer to send up ammunition. This reached the frozen detachments on the following evening, together with the means of cooking. Yes, certainly Luck did favour us sometimes in Port Arthur; she did that night, in that the Japanese did not press a land attack.

While this cheerful state of chaos reigned in the Fortress, on the sea the prologue to the war was already over. One Russian ship alone—the *Novik*—could be heard, hull down on the horizon, firing at Japanese destroyers. In the town itself a doleful rumour spread apace, that some of our ships had been blown up. It was not believed. We were afraid to believe what we did hear, but did not want to hear the truth, which we dreaded still more.

Next morning Port Arthur woke earlier than usual. Every one wanted to know what had actually happened during the night. Alas! the reports as to Japanese torpedo attacks were only too well founded, and the *Cesarevitch*, *Pallada*, and *Retvisan* were *hors de combat*. Despite the completeness of the night attack, and the calculating thoroughness with which the enemy had done their work —clearest proof that man could want of the outbreak of war—in the absence of any official communication from the Commandant, the population still hoped against hope. The more impressionable prepared to leave, but otherwise things went on much as usual. At the wharf a crowd collected to look at the *Retvisan* lying in the entrance to the harbour; from her appearance it was difficult to believe that she had sustained any damage, and the reports were pronounced untrue. The printing office of the *Novy Kry* was another centre of attraction, every one hustling round to buy a paper with some account of the night's work. But in the paper was no word of war.

Although outwardly the current of life in Port Arthur seemed to flow unruffled, this calm did not extend to those in authority. The staffs, which up to the preceding evening had been peacefully slumbering for six years, were now extraordinarily busy; their activity was proved by the utter confusion which reigned. The disorganization of the Fortress Staff particularly was almost ludicrous: officers hurried hither and thither, contradictory and impossible orders were being issued and countermanded, and above and through all this confusion resounded the ceaseless chattering of the telephone-bells. It was not a sight to inspire confidence. It seemed as if the staff momentarily anticipated some fatal and sudden blow, but did not know what to do in order to ward it off. Colonel Khvostoff, the Chief of the Fortress Staff, and his immediate assistants alone kept their heads. He knew that the time was approaching when every one would see the real state of things, and to what extent the 'stronghold'—Port Arthur —was impregnable. [Several alarmists had already been punished by the Commandant for spreading rumours that many of the batteries were gunless, and many of the guns without ammunition.] He and his predecessor, General Flug, had done all that was in their power, but they might as well have knocked their heads against a wall.

Meanwhile the Viceroy's staff wrote orders, which ended up in the Viceroy's own words: 'You must all keep calm, in order to be able to perform your duty in the most efficient manner possible, trusting to the help of God that every man will do his work, remembering that neither prayers to God nor service for the Tsar are in vain.'

In the outer harbour the Pacific Ocean squadron was lying, steam up and cleared for action, waiting the order to go out and engage the enemy. When, at 10 a.m., the *Boyarin*, having returned to harbour, signalled that the Japanese fleet was approaching in force, the Viceroy and General Stössel, escorted by a troop of Cossacks, and followed by a numerous suite, went up on to Golden Hill. It certainly was to be hoped that General Stössel, to whom the Emperor had entrusted the Fortress, and who had recently reported to him that it was ready, would 'keep calm' and do his duty 'in the most efficient manner'; but those who were privileged to see him on that historic morning saw no traces of calmness in his demeanour.

After about an hour the presence of the whole Japanese fleet on the horizon was signalled, but the majority of the people knew nothing, and all was quiet in the town. A little later and Port Arthur was paralysed with fear, for the very ground quivered with the shock as the guns of both fleets and of the coast batteries suddenly opened fire. The battle had begun, and the fleet of young Japan, a nation which had only begun to take lessons in

Western culture thirty-two years ago, was pitted against that of Russia—founded two hundred years ago by Peter the Great.

In twenty minutes' time 12-inch shells were detonating in the streets of the town, and the population began to flee in panic to the hills. The battle waxed, but there was curious silence on Liao-tieh-shan and Quail Hills—two peaks which commanded the ground all round Port Arthur. The first was armed with a lighthouse and the second with a fire observation-tower! In spite of the fire, but little damage was done on either side—the enemy could not hurt Electric Cliff and Golden Hill, and the bark of our shore batteries was worse than their bite, owing to the short range of their guns. Indeed, owing to lack of guns and ammunition, some of our batteries were actually firing blank, whilst others maintained a haughty silence. Though Russia did not then know of this, the Japanese did, but, with their natural cunning, held their tongues. The British knew of it, and chuckled whilst they kept silence for their allies.

Just before noon the bombardment ceased, and the Japanese fleet steamed off. The first wild panic subsided, and the little railway-station was soon crowded with fugitives, all anxious to depart.

What the Viceroy, Alexeieff, said to Stössel that day is hidden by a veil of obscurity, but that he decided to remove him from the post of General admits of not the slightest doubt, for Lieutenant-General Konstantine Nikolaevitch Smirnoff was chosen by the War Minister to supersede Stössel as Commandant, and left Warsaw for Port Arthur on February 25.

CHAPTER II

SETTLING DOWN TO IT

FROM that day onwards Port Arthur was, after dusk, plunged in complete darkness, the screened windows and deserted streets giving an ominous impression of desolation. The town became noticeably empty, though numerous families, anxious to share the fate of husbands and fathers, were still allowed to remain. In spite of the Viceroy's order (No. 49) that all families should be sent out of the besieged Fortress, General Stössel made no effort to enforce this. In vain it was pointed out that women—except nurses—and children are a most undesirable element in a fortress: he took no action.

About this time much valuable time and labour was wasted by Stössel on the construction of an inner wall* with a ditch round the Old Town. The futility of this as a defence would have struck a first year's cadet, for it ran all along the hollow in which the town was situated, and would therefore be absolutely useless should the Japanese seize the hills in rear of the line of forts. Whilst he thus squandered time, labour, and money on this 'folly,' Stössel delayed the work on the forts, and paid no attention to the fortification of that most important position—Kinchou.

Another curious point about the conduct of affairs was that officers were strictly forbidden to make themselves acquainted with the topography of the Fortress. In fact,

---

* The Central Wall.

the object seemed to be to handicap our forces as much as possible by ignorance of the ground, for practice manœuvres were only held once, and the troops which had taken part in these manœuvres and were the only ones that knew the ground—the 3rd Siberian Rifle Division—were sent away to the Yalu. Their places were taken by corps fresh from Siberia.

Though Russian officers were not allowed to learn their way about the Fortress, numbers of officers of the Japanese General Staff, disguised as washermen, coolies, etc., were permitted to move about the batteries without hindrance. No one watched them. Not only were they able to learn all they desired and to make maps, but they drew up accurate range-tables for the siege-guns which afterwards did such brilliant service. When Smirnoff arrived and organized a fortress gendarmerie this was put a stop to.

The supply question was another branch of the organization that was shockingly mismanaged. Slaughter cattle, etc., were largely requisitioned from the surrounding district, but, owing to the disgraceful system of accounts and to the fact that the civil authorities in charge of the work were much understaffed, only about one-half of what was available was obtained. In spite of the advice and protests of Colonel Vershinin, the Chief Commissary for the civil population, Stössel went his own way and quite serenely left the Fortress under-supplied. After the departure of the Viceroy to Mukden he assumed complete control of the commissariat, and, in addition to the failure of the system as far as supplies went, earned the resentment of all the civilians by the severity of his regulations. The Chinese naturally tried to drive away their cattle into Manchuria, as the requisitioning price was not a large one, and after a proclamation issued by Stössel on February 21, by which requisitioning was still more restricted, they were largely successful. Thus, with a close blockade looming in the near future, the district round the Fortress was being denuded of live-stock.

Stössel's influence was not confined to the question of slaughter cattle. As the armies in the north gradually concentrated, a horde of officers turned up in Port Arthur trying to purchase supplies of every sort, and whole vans of sugar, flour, salt, tinned milk, green foods, preserved fish and meat, etc., were actually allowed to be taken from this important fortress—a fortress separated by many thousands of miles from Russia, blockaded by sea, and expecting, according to the natural course of events, to be blockaded also by land. General Stössel, who wrote in his order No. 126, of February 27, that there could be no retirement, since the sea was on three sides and the enemy on the fourth, allowed—nay, encouraged—the export of articles of vital importance. There was, consequently, in October, November, and December a shortage, which brought on an epidemic of scurvy. To all protests he replied that Kuropatkin would never allow us to be cut off, and, if we were cut off, it would only be for a very brief period. When the protests were repeated he 'came the senior officer,' and said that, as Commandant of the besieged Fortress, he would stand no interference. The civil authorities, who were under him, watched with silent indifference the melting away of our reserves. Several of the shopkeepers, indeed, hearing that supplies of every kind were badly wanted by the army in the north, themselves began to despatch truckloads. The state of affairs was almost a burlesque. Port Arthur, instead of being a fortress preparing itself for a siege, might have been a sort of general market, a principal supply depôt for the main army, to which every one came to do business, or to gamble, and dissipate, for although Stössel allowed only three restaurants for general use and closed the gambling hells, rowdyism was rampant and money flowed like water.

Never in my life have I witnessed such orgies as I saw that February in Arthur before the arrival of General Smirnoff, and this in spite of the most severe efforts at prevention.

Whenever I passed by the fire-brigade station in the morning I heard the swish of whips and the heartrending shrieks of men being flogged for drunkenness, for permission had been given to the Chief of the Police to correct drunkards with some 'homely treatment.' The usual procedure was as follows: The men to be corrected—workmen, cab-drivers, Chinamen—were drawn up in the prison courtyard. The inspector presented the charge-sheet, and the police-officer stopped in front of each prisoner.

'What have you to say?'

'Sir, yesterday——'

'One hundred lashes, two weeks' cells. Next. What have you to say?'

'Yesterday, sir——'

'One hundred lashes, to-day and to-morrow.'

And so on to the end. And then these God's creatures, some of them future heroes who died for the honour and glory of Russia, were removed and flogged. Later, owing to the protests of the Chief of the Fire Brigade, the flogging was carried out in the prison-house, where it was still more cruel. I know that men are flogged in Russia, but there it is only after trial. With us in Arthur things were more simple, more patriarchal.

During that time laws did not exist in Arthur. Once when Colonel Vershinin, the Civil Commissary, remarked with regard to an order that it was illegal, a staff-officer replied: 'How can you have laws on service? General Stössel's orders are law for us.' And this was the state of affairs right up to the capitulation, more especially after Stössel's appointment as aide-de-camp to the Tsar.

After he had left the garrison and the sick and wounded

to their fate and departed to Russia, Japanese military law came into force. It was strict, but it did not prevent freedom.

On February 22 we perused the following order by the Commandant with fear and trembling:

'Colonel Petrusha will ride round the Old and New Towns and the New Chinese Town, and will make prisoners of all men who are drunk or disorderly, and anyone else whom he may consider it necessary to arrest.'

This was alarming. Colonel Petrusha authorized to arrest 'anyone'? Several people went to the military Procurator to find out what it meant. It would be dangerous to go out in the streets, for if Colonel Petrusha thought it 'necessary' he would arrest you. The following day you would be up under the cold grey eye of the Chief of the Police. He would ask, 'What have you to say?' and you would be flogged. The only advice that the Procurator could give us was to be careful and retiring.

As February passed guards were placed along the whole of the railway-line from Tashihchiao to Arthur, and guns were mounted near the longer bridges, for bands of Hunhuses were now on the prowl. Train-loads of soldiers from the reserve battalions arrived every day, and the confusion and lack of system shown in their distribution were hopeless. Though all concerned strove to appear busy, it was mainly in the direction of writing orders that their energy was expended.

The general mental attitude towards the enemy was at this time remarkable, for from Stössel down to the last-joined recruit all professed the greatest contempt for the Japanese. The whole nation was judged by the specimens seen in Port Arthur. 'A Japanese? Pooh! he's a mosquito. Why, I'll stick a pin through him and send him home in a letter,' was a favourite remark of the moment. The General commanding the 4th Rifle

Division, who led Stössel by the nose, absolutely, assured all and sundry that the Japanese were 'fools.' 'The Japanese are fools, because in their field regulations it is laid down, that in the attack, the firing-line should extend at wide intervals.' Sitting on his horse in front of the regiments under his command, he would explain this, and then say: 'Front rank, tell me why the Japanese are fools.' The soldiers would shout in chorus: 'Because, when attacking, their firing-line extends widely.' Is it to be wondered that our men thought the Japanese fools—till their first engagement, and that after systematically retiring before the 'fools' and suffering heavy losses they lost confidence in their General?

Having spent more than a year in Japan, I knew of the enemy's energetic preparations for war. But our people would neither pay attention to the serious articles in the newspapers nor to the warnings of their own keen officers who had been through the Chinese campaign. The majority, especially those who had recently come from European Russia, preferred to accept Fock's estimate, for, thanks to the inferiority of our professional military literature, the army had no idea of what modern Japan was like, and in particular of her military strength. This stupidity and ignorance was shameful and sad. Whose fault was it?

On the whole, the daily life in the town little resembled that in a besieged fortress, for there was a false sense of security, and people did not seem to realize the position. Because, since bombarding us on February 9, the enemy's fleet had disappeared and made no sign, people almost believed we were not at war, and things went on as before. The population, especially the garrison, believed that everything was 'all right,' and, together with their commanders, carelessly passed the time without worrying about the future.

'Why, if there was a chance of our being cut off, do you suppose for a minute that Stössel would let supplies be sent out? Do you really imagine that the Japanese can wage war on two fronts? They are concentrating against the main army on the Yalu, and Stössel says the more that land in Kwantun the better. He will take them all prisoners,' were remarks made. Nearly all talked similar nonsense, and, what's more, believed it, and beyond mining the shores, carried out by Admiral Loschinsky, no precautions were taken to prevent a landing.

A certain amount of activity was visible within the Fortress. We commenced laying a fortress telegraph, but the system was overhead. Both the telephone and telegraph systems worked very badly when they were installed, and their faults were intensified when falling shells cut the wires. It was usually quicker to send an orderly than to attempt to get a telephone message through the exchange. Not only was the system unreliable, it was also unsafe, for the private and military lines were all together, so that, owing to the induction, anyone could overhear the most secret military message. Such a state of affairs in a besieged fortress was a monstrosity. One might have thought that at a place like Port Arthur a proper telephone system would have been organized in peace-time. But no! A system had been worked out by a certain captain of artillery, and the money had been allotted; but when the time came this officer was sent to the north, and the scheme was not carried out. The question of what happened to this money would form an excellent subject for an inquiry.

In addition to his intense activity in writing profuse orders, Stössel developed a mania about 'signalling.' He was convinced that the enemy were being continually signalled to from the hills, and the strictest orders were issued to watch day and night for the culprits. The hills were always being patrolled, and 'signaller-catching' became a kind of amusement. Even the civilians joined in, although anyone who gave the matter a thought knew that the Japanese would not require to have messages sent them when they already knew every inch of the place; but owing to this practice many an innocent human being was wafted to a better world. An order on the subject—No. 120, of February 26—ran as follows:

'Athough twenty men were caught yesterday in the act of making some kind of signals, about 3 a.m. this morning some one was seen signalling with a lantern between my house and the commissariat depôt. It was impossible to catch him, as he ran off to the New Chinese Town. Pickets detailed for this work will in future fire on any men seen signalling, if they run.'

Though in the majority of cases, of course, the military procurator was unable to produce any proof of guilt against the Chinamen arrested, after this order they were shot like partridges.

Though many were lulled into a false security by the absence of any military operations by the enemy since their first attack, yet to every one the complete state of unpreparedness of the Fortress, as well as the chaos reigning in every corner of it, was patent. *In vino veritas*, and in the restaurants and clubs the strongest opinions were expressed about Stössel and his actions by those who had exceeded. So much of this criticism went on that a special order upon the subject was issued:

'It has come to my knowledge that in the garrison club officers busy themselves over matters which do not concern them, criticize the course of the military operations, and repeat various stupid stories, picked up from God knows where. An officer's duty is to think how best to carry out his orders, and not to judge the actions of his seniors. Those who cavil do much harm, and I, of course, will punish them to the utmost of my power.'

After this tongues ceased to wag, for it was known that the Commandant had wonderful ears. Officers even began to suspect each other of espionage and tale-bearing.

CHAPTER III

DEVELOPMENTS

AT 1 a.m. on February 25 some destroyers, which were covering the advance of a blocker* towards the narrows into the harbour, attempted to torpedo the *Retvisan*. The battleship sank one destroyer, while the blocker was set on fire, and ran on the rocks of Tiger Peninsula. Here she lay blazing close to the *Retvisan*, a source of extreme danger, as she might at any moment blow up. Later on the enemy's fleet appeared on the horizon. The *Bayan, Novik*, and *Askold*, lying in the outer Roads, at once moved out and engaged it. From the hill I was on, I watched that rare picture, a fight at sea; but it did not last long. In face of a force four times their own strength, our ships were finally forced to seek shelter under the guns of the Fortress. Just at the end of this fight one of two of our destroyers, returning from night reconnaissance, was forced by the enemy's cruisers to beach herself. This was entirely due to the unfortified state of Liao-tieh-shan.

On February 28 a remarkable order by Stössel was published in the *Novy Kry*. It was also telegraphed all over the whole world, and presumably redounded to the credit of its author:

* A blocker is a ship which is intentionally sunk so as to block up the entrance to a port or a channel.—E. D. S.

'The troops know well, and I now make known to the civilians, that there will be no retirement; in the first place, the Fortress must fight to the last, and I, as its Commandant, will never give the order to retreat; in the second, there is no place to which to retreat. . . .'

As a matter of fact, Stössel, *quâ* Commandant of the Fortress, never did give an order to retreat, because the question did not arise; but, as Officer Commanding the Kwantun District, which district he abandoned within two months, he surrendered the Fortress, despite the protests of the then Commandant, General Smirnoff, and the whole of the Council of Defence.

In spite of the extensive range of subjects touched upon in the literature issued in the shape of orders, it was astonishing how little was said about the defences proper of the Fortress, which were still in the most incomplete state, or of the Kinchou position, where practically nothing had been done. It was only in an order of March 7 that the works were mentioned for the first time, and then it was the Central Wall—already mentioned as a monumental folly—which called for attention! The cost of this folly in cash was £20,000; its cost in work left undone elsewhere cannot be estimated.

As we were not disturbed by the enemy from February 25 to March 10, we had time in Port Arthur to attend to home affairs. About March 4 Stössel received a wire from a certain General Bogdanovitch. In this the sender congratulated him on his victories, and expressed the hope that Arthur would give birth to new Nakhimoffs, Korniloffs, and Istomins. The telegram was quite genuine. It was thought that such a siege would certainly produce some heroes. Smirnoff and Kondratenko were not then known, and Bogdanovitch's kind wishes evidently referred to Stössel and his assistants, whose names had been well before the public since the Boxer campaign. Lieutenant Prince Karseladse of the 25th Regiment, who knew very well what was really going on, sent a reply wire to Bogdanovitch, to the effect that:

'There are no Nakhimoffs here; there is nothing but miserable incompetence.'

This wire was not despatched, but was handed over to Stössel. As a result, a District Order upon the subject of official telegrams was issued, and the sender of this message was placed under arrest and tried by court-martial. He was sentenced to some days' arrest. For reporting well on the prisoner, the report being made at the request of the court, Colonel Selinen, who commanded his regiment, was deprived of his command by Stössel, and immediately left for Russia.

One morning towards the end of February, I was informed by an aide-de-camp that Stössel wanted to see me. He received me very affably, but at once gave me to understand, not rudely, but in unmistakable terms, that he was General Stössel and I was only Nojine. On my asking to what extent the defences were ready, and in particular those stretching for miles on the land side, he said:

'I must tell you that I am a fighting infantry General, and don't understand anything about the Fortress or its surroundings. I am here temporarily. As you know, I have been appointed to command the 3rd Siberian Army Corps, which is on its way to the Yalu, and am only waiting for the new Commandant to arrive. He will soon put everything in order.'

'And under whom will Kinchou be?'

'Under him—under him. He is a most competent and clever officer. The papers say he has passed through almost ten academies. Why, he'll be a walking encyclopædia. My duty is to fight, and not to run a fortress. Lord! what a deuce of a lot of money has been spent on it! How can the Japanese, yellow-skinned little devils that they are, get into the place?' He then went on to threaten me with the awful things that would happen to journalists generally, and to me in particular, if we were not careful, and ended by saying that in the Fortress the Commandant was 'both God and the Tsar.' Only one thing comforted me as I left, and that was that Stössel was not long destined to be the Commandant of Port Arthur.

While we in the Fortress exhausted our energies on the useless Central Wall, Rear-Admiral Loschinsky, who had arrived on February 11, organized a mine defence of the Liaotun Peninsula, paying particular attention to Dalny, where the enemy might land. He then drew up a scheme for mining the Port Arthur waters, and every place which seemed suitable for a landing. Unfortunately, after the sad accident to the *Yenisei* and *Boyarin*, the officer commanding the fleet was very sceptical about the value of submarine mines, more especially as he believed that three months would see us again in command of the sea. On March 8 Vice-Admiral Makharoff, who had just been appointed to the command of the fleet, arrived, and great naval activity was at once noticeable; the dockyard literally hummed with work. After many attempts, the *Retvisan* was on the same day successfully floated off the shoal at Tiger's Tail, and taken to the western basin, a coincidence which made a great impression. The officer to command the balloon park also arrived; but there were neither balloons nor materials of which to make them, as when the *Manchuria* was captured in the beginning of the war they fell into the hands of the enemy, together with a large quantity of ammunition. We used later on to watch with great interest our own balloon float

ADMIRAL LOSCHINSKY.

To face page 20

up from behind Wolf's Hills. It spent much time in the air, but not for our amusement; for while it, our own balloon, was watching, our own shells were shrieking on their way towards us.

In the early hours of March 10 our destroyer division went out scouting. At dawn they were engaged by the enemy, and we lost the *Steresguschy*, which was sunk. At 8.18 the enemy's fleet appeared off Liao-tieh-shan. At 8.30 three battleships and two light cruisers separated from the rest and took up their position about a mile from that hill, whose cliffs ran at right angles to our shore front. None of our batteries could fire on them, and Liao-tieh-shan had on it, as already stated, instead of guns, a lighthouse. They were in 'dead water.' It was impossible for us to use high-angle fire, controlled from the highest point of that hill, against these ships, for the gun-mountings in the seaward batteries did not allow of enough elevation or of all-round fire. Telephone connexions to the observation-posts also were then only in the process of construction. This simple manœuvre of the enemy rendered us absolutely helpless.

At 8.45 a.m. an incessant roar commenced, followed by the detonation of 12-inch shells in the New Town. It was galling to see these shells falling and no action being taken on our part. The Fortress Staff every moment were receiving information of the damage being done to the New Town, but could do nothing to drive off the enemy's ships, which lay in three lines under shelter. The first line fired systematically and deliberately, evidently trying to hit our ships and the harbour, for several of the shells struck the port workshops, and fell into the western and eastern basins. At 11 the firing suddenly ceased, and our observation post reported that the first line was steaming off, their stations being taken by the battleships in the second line. At 11.25 they started again. This time all the shells fell in the inner harbour; some even struck the ships, but did not stop the work. About 1 p.m. the enemy steamed off in a south-easterly direction and disappeared. From 9.30 a.m. to 1 p.m. the Japanese had fired 208 12-inch shells, and none of us will ever forget our humiliation that we should have been shelled by a fleet which could come right up to our shores, but which we could not touch.

From March 10 all work on the armament of the place came to a standstill, save for guns being dragged up and mounted on Liao-tieh-shan. In the fleet and the port alone was work hurriedly pushed on, for the artificers from the Baltic yards began to arrive from St. Petersburg. These, under the immediate supervision and direction of that energetic and clever engineer Kuteynikoff, set to work to repair the ships, and things hustled.

While work was thus being feverishly carried on in the port, the military garrison, bored by the want of occupation, got out of hand, and soldiers took to highway robbery. This became so common that private persons feared to go out alone.

COLONEL KHVOSTOFF.

To face page 23.

CHAPTER IV

SMIRNOFF ARRIVES

At last!

It was on the footboard of a railway-carriage, lighted up by the glimmer of a railway-station lamp, that we first saw Smirnoff, for he arrived in Port Arthur at midnight on March 17. Though quite grey-headed, as he stepped out on to the platform in the uniform of an officer of the General Staff, he seemed the embodiment of energy. Casting on all around a keen glance, which expressed determination and capability, he gave utterance to a few polite sentences—for all the senior commanders were there to meet him—and drove off at once to his quarters with Lieutenant-Colonel Khvostoff, his Chief of the Staff. It is difficult for anyone who was not actually present to appreciate the pleasing impression he gave. No sooner had he arrived than he began to get a grip of affairs in Port Arthur, and accompanied by his trusted and indefatigable assistant, General Kondratenko, set to work to fortify and arm the Fortress. These two men spent days together going over the landward defences.

On March 17 Stössel issued a farewell order preparatory to departing to command the 3rd Siberian Army Corps. In it he said that 'Arthur is now an impregnable stronghold.' The *Novy Kry* objected to publish this order, as it was obviously inaccurate. It was all very well to tell those not in the know that Arthur was 'impregnable,' but why say so to us, who had gone through three bombardments, and especially that of March 10? Report it to St. Petersburg—yes: St. Petersburg was many miles away; but why stultify himself before the whole garrison?

Having inspected the line of forts, batteries, and earthworks on the landward, and part of those on the seaward side, General Smirnoff was horrified at what he found. The heavy semi-permanent works which it was proposed to construct in order to complete the girdle of fortifications as laid down by Imperial order, were either not begun or in a very embryonic condition; and it was the same with the laying of the armoured concrete for casemated buildings —work which required time. Scarcely anything was being done to the intermediate field-works. There, where menacing works sprang up afterwards within five months, were now naked rocks. Military roads had alone been made— many of them by the Chinese. The sites for Little and Big Eagle's Nests, Zaredoubt, Zaliterny, Tumulus, Cemetery Batteries, Obelisk Hill, and Fort No. 6, were then rock as bare as my hand; they had not been even traced out on the ground. The strengthening of Fort No. 5 had not been commenced. On the greater number of old fortifications to be strengthened, but which were not yet completed, guns had not even been mounted, or had been so badly mounted that the work would have to be done over again. Of a third line of defence no one had even thought. It was the same with 203 Metre Hill, Divisional Hill, Long Hill, Flat Hill, Angle Hill, Ta-ku-shan and Sia-gu-shan Hills, etc. In a word, a picture of absolute unpreparedness was unfolded before the new Commandant. This was alarmingly increased by the fact that the different advanced works were very badly sited, and badly designed for their sites at that. He decided to depart considerably from the proposed plan of the polygon of defences, and found it necessary to move several of the works forward, and to strengthen the above-mentioned hills, well knowing that once the Japanese got possession of Kinchou and a strict blockade commenced on land, the Fortress could not long hold out in the state in which he found it. With his arrival all the best men, headed by the late General Kondratenko, joined hands, and the work proceeded apace. Though the gangs of Chinamen employed on the earthworks day and night were large, they were not large enough, and a dearth of labour was at once felt. The Chinese would not agree to work for the fairly high wage offered to them, and began gradually to slink away to Chifu. The Japanese spread proclamations among them, of which the following—a typical one—was published:

'Port Arthur will soon be cut off, and then captured. No Chinaman who has in any way assisted the Russians to defend the place will be given quarter.'

All the labour of fortifying and arming the Fortress fell upon the 7th East Siberian Rifle Division, under General Kondratenko, and upon the reserve battalions. The work done by these simple, rough Russians was the work of Titans, and only those who watched them delving, shoving, and hauling on the slopes of those rocky hills for months can appreciate what the labour was.

General Stössel, hanging 'twixt heaven and earth, daily expecting orders to leave for the corps he commanded, now 'sat very tight.' All to whom Arthur and the honour and glory of Russia were dear were delighted, for they were convinced that in the hands of Smirnoff and Kondratenko the place would be transformed into a veritable inaccessible stronghold, if not too late. The Commandant held long and constant consultations with the officer in command of the fleet, at which combined operations were worked out, in case the enemy should land. Liao-tieh-shan was rapidly and energetically fortified. Canet guns were got into position, new telephone-lines were constructed, and the finishing touches were put to the mine defences. Arrangements were also made for high-angle fire over this hill, in case the Japanese fleet should attempt to repeat their tactics of March 10, and the guns in the coast batteries were mounted so as to allow of all-round traverse, and greater angle of elevation, and others were borrowed from the navy. The gunboats *Otvajny* and *Giliak* were stationed in the narrows as look-outs, and the cruisers issued at night by turns into the outer roads for the same purpose. Work went right merrily, confidence increased, and every one grew calmer.

CHAPTER V

STÖSSEL STAYS

EARLY on the morning of March 22 the enemy's fleet, in three divisions, consisting of six battleships, six armoured cruisers, and six second and third class cruisers, slowly approached us from different directions. At 7 a.m. our cruiser squadron, led by the *Askold*, flying the flag of the officer in command, slipped out into the outer Roads. In rear of them steamed the battleships. The enemy moved towards Liao-tieh-shan, and at 9.30 opened fire with their 12-inchers, which at measured intervals thundered forth one after another. First a bright yellow spurt of flame tinged with red, a little cloud of smoke, then the boom of a gun, followed by the horrid groan of the shell hurtling through the air, and the final crack of the burst.

From the top of Quail Hill the whole scene was clearly visible—the Fortress, the sea, and the ships. That day the Japs again fired 208 shells, the majority of which fell in the narrows, in the western basin, on Liao-tieh-shan, or in its vicinity; but their shooting was bad. We replied by indirect fire, and also enfilade fire from our ships, lying in the outer Roads. By 11 o'clock we got in several hits, and the enemy moved off, and, in spite of their superiority in numbers, did not attempt to prolong the battle. A good instance of the disregard shown by the army to these naval bombardments occurred that day. When the gun-fire ceased the rattle of musketry was heard from the direction of Pigeon Bay, and on the Commandant telephoning to ascertain what it was, it turned out that a company commander was merely putting his men through musketry.

The rest of that day we heard the names of Smirnoff and Makharoff on all sides, but never a word of Stössel.

As soon as General Smirnoff had inspected the position at Kinchou, he saw of what enormous strategical importance it was, and he gave orders for it to be fortified with the utmost rapidity, and in his order No. 228, of March 23, he authorized the Fortress Commanding Engineer to draw £1,000 for this purpose from the Defence Fund. As I have said before, the position was under the actual command of General Fock, commanding the 4th Rifle Division. What Fock accomplished between the beginning of hostilities up to May 26 the reader will see in the following pages.

After midnight on March 25 the sky cleared, and the moon lit up the sleeping town and harbour. In the inner roads the shapes of our ships and the closely-crowded destroyers looked black against the transparent blue of the quiet night. There was no sound in the Roads. The darkness increased, and seemed to be cut into by the rays of the searchlights. Suddenly a single shot rang out from the narrows, then another, then a cannonade commenced from the seaward batteries. The blockers at it again? It was, and despite the hail of shot, they continued at full speed straight for the boom. Three of them got right up close to the entrance, and then, suddenly turning to starboard, dashed at full speed on to the rocks under Golden Hill. The fourth first turned to port, then sank just out of the fairway, riddled with shell.

Every day after riding round the positions Smirnoff consulted with Generals Kondratenko* and Biely,† and Colonels Grigorenko‡ and Khvostoff.§ In conjunction with them, he settled the most important questions *re* future work. His labours cannot be judged from his written orders, for he had no time to write — questions were decided on the spot. He gave his verbal orders there and then, and they were at once carried out.

From day to day we expected to hear of Stössel's departure, but instead, officers of the 3rd Corps began coming in to him. It was rumoured that he would operate with his corps in the peninsula, and might never go to the Yalu. We were afraid to think that he might remain, and all who valued Arthur as the mainstay of Russia in the Far East hoped that such a trial might be spared us. But the blow fell, and dire was the shock when we read his Orders of March 27:

'. . . I have received the following telegram from the Viceroy:

'"It is the Imperial wish that you should assume temporary command of the land defences in the Kwantun district, the Commandant of the Fortress being under your orders. You will exercise the full powers of an officer in command of an independent corps, directly under the Officer Commanding the Manchurian Army. The Commandant of the Fortress will have the powers of an officer commanding a corps which is not independent. . . ."

' General Roznatovsky, Chief of the Staff of the 3rd Siberian Army Corps, is also appointed to be Chief

---

* O.C. the Fortress Division.
† O.C. Fortress Artillery.
‡ O.C. Fortress Engineers.
§ Chief of the Fortress Staff.

Staff Officer of the District, and the Commandant of the Fortress and the Officer Commanding the 4th Rifle Brigade will send all orders and information, etc., into the office of 3rd Siberian Army Corps.

'STÖSSEL, Lieutenant-General.'

This was the worst piece of news we heard during the whole siege.

The 29th of March was the sixth anniversary of our occupation of Port Arthur. For six years we had been spending millions on the fortifications, on building Dalny, and in constructing a railway from distant Russia. What was the result when war commenced? Does Russia realize the gigantic work done by Smirnoff and the garrison under him? No, not yet.

When it was reported to General Smirnoff that quantities of articles of the first importance were being exported from the Fortress, he at once issued an order forbidding it. He received several complaints, but adhered to his decision. The dissatisfied ones then went to the Officer Commanding the District to complain about the Commandant. Among them was a school friend of mine, Captain Radetsky, who was acting as a commissariat officer, and had come from the main army to buy what he could. He took away several waggon-loads.

In spite of the very strict orders about not exporting, Stössel wrote to Smirnoff that he considered exportation should be permitted, and he sanctioned the request made to him to take out supplies, and asked Smirnoff to rescind his orders. Smirnoff at once instructed the Chief of the Gendarmes to see that his orders were carried out to the letter, adding that any neglect would entail a court-martial. To the Officer Commanding the District he politely explained that he could not permit anything to be taken out of the Fortress which was entrusted to him, and which might any day be strictly blockaded. The confusion caused by this interference can be imagined.

Day followed day and Easter came and went, but work during the holiday stopped for one day only.

CHAPTER VI

THE WORK OF JAPANESE MINE-LAYERS.

AT 7 o'clock on the evening of April 12 our destroyer division of eight ships went out, in beautiful weather, to do a long reconnaissance. By 10 the weather had rapidly changed for the worse, and the sky was overcast. A thick sea mist covered the water and it was hailing. In such a night there was nothing to prevent the Japs getting within half a cable of the place without being discovered. Notwithstanding the little practice our men had had at sea in peace-time, they were not at all put out by the weather. Those who assert that Russians do not make good sailors, lie: all they want is good leaders. By midnight our destroyers drew near a group of islands, and here the fog and murk of the pouring rain were so thick that it was impossible for the vessels to distinguish one another. Around were solid darkness and deathly silence, broken only by the beat of the engines. Owing to the fog, the proximity of the islands, and the rocky nature of the coast, the division kept at low speed, being only able to get its bearings by the cries of the gulls roosting on the shore hard by. About midnight among the islands the *Strashny* lost touch with the rest. At 2 o'clock she made out some lights, and thinking them to belong to her division, steamed slowly towards them, only to be met as dawn broke by a sudden broadside. Instead of being with our ships, she was in the middle of six Japanese destroyers and two two-funnelled cruisers.

Returning the fire, the commander ordered 'full steam ahead' and made for Port Arthur; but it was too late. The enemy had everything in their favour — numbers, strength, and speed. The *Strashny* was overhauled and riddled. But though Captain Urasovsky, who was commanding, and all the crews of the bow guns were killed almost at once, and she was soon full of dead and dying men, the engines still worked. She had not been deprived of her life, her mobility—and she moved. Life was dear to every man aboard her, and they fought like devils. Lieutenant Malaeff, upon whom the command had now devolved, was everywhere—now forward, now aft—giving orders and encouragement. In him the desire to live beat strong, and a faint hope of assistance or of escape made him disregard the slaughter all around him, the enemy's increasing fire—all else but the main chance. Sub-Lieutenant Akinfieff fell wounded in the side; the crew were falling fast. The swish, crack, and whistle of shells was mingled with the groans, prayers, and shrieks of the wounded.

Choosing a favourable moment, Malaeff fired a torpedo from the stern tube at the nearest cruiser, and hit. She heeled over and stopped, and the other cruiser and two of the destroyers went to her aid. Things now looked better, as only four destroyers were left against the *Strashny*. Encouraged by what Malaeff had done, torpedo-man Cherepanoff dashed to the other torpedo-tube; but he had not got hold of the firing-lever when a shell struck the torpedo and exploded it, with awful results. Engineer-mechanic Dmitrieff was blown in half, and every man near was killed. The engines stopped. The Japs also stopped, and continued firing at a range of 80 yards. Akinfieff, who up till now had been still able to give orders, was struck by another shell. The last 47-millimetre gun was disabled; the vessel was penetrated below water-line, and must sink. Convinced that there was no chance, Malaeff raised the head of his dead comrade Dmitrieff, kissed him, then returned to the crew. 'Better die than surrender,' he said, and, going to the quick-firer, which had been taken off a blocker, he fired point-blank at the enemy.

The fire of this little gun brought down the bridge of one of the destroyers and the funnel of another. The Japanese, infuriated at such dogged resistance, mercilessly shelled the *Strashny*. Malaeff fell, wounded in the temple. The little vessel, her deck awash with blood and loaded with dead and dying men, began to settle. Suddenly the enemy ceased fire and were seen to be sheering off: the *Smiely* had put out from Liao-tieh-shan to the rescue. But it was too late, for the *Strashny* sank, leaving behind but a trail of crimson bubbles and some wounded struggling in the water. Of four officers and forty-eight men only five were saved, picked up under a heavy fire by the *Bayan*, which had come out.

The danger for the *Bayan* while rescuing the wounded increased every moment, for the fire of six big ships and a destroyer division, which had come up, was now concentrated upon her. But our fleet dashed upon the scene, the *Petropalovsk* leading, and the remainder in single column after her. Getting into battle formation, and being joined by the *Bayan*, the fleet steamed towards the enemy, and, opening fire, drove them off. In the distance, more than hull-down, could be seen the enemy's main fleet, consisting of eighteen ships: both of his divisions were moving towards Liao-tieh-shan to concentrate. Our fleet had turned and begun to change front under the protection of the guns of the Fortress, when suddenly a great column of water shot up by the stem of

ADMIRAL MAKHAROFF.

To face page 35.

the *Petropalovsk*, and there boomed forth the dull sound of a submarine explosion, followed immediately by a second and louder report. The whole of the centre of the huge battleship was enveloped in a sheet of flame and a cloud of yellow-brown smoke. Her stern rose high out of water and her screws glistened in the sun as they whizzed round, racing. In a minute and a half the *Petropalovsk* had ceased to exist: where she had been was cold, dirty water, flecked with foam.

The explosion was witnessed by many, and was signalled to the harbour from Golden Hill, so the town received the awful news almost at once; but no one knew any further details, nor wished to believe that Makharoff had perished with his ship, and I shall never forget the consternation in the harbour as reports were anxiously awaited. At last the Captain of an incoming destroyer shouted through his megaphone: 'The *Petropalovsk* has gone down, and with her the Admiral: they are searching for his body.'

And what was the cause of this catastrophe? On the preceding night the Admiral had been on the *Diana*, which was doing duty in the outer Roads. Some small ships were sighted from the cruiser behind Flat Cape. Makharoff thought they were our destroyers, and despite convincing proofs that they were not, he would not open fire. They were Japanese laying mines, one of which destroyed the *Petropalovsk* and injured the *Pobieda*.

And so perished the gallant Admiral whose command of the fleet had in an incredibly short time done wonders, and who, had he been spared, might have changed the whole course of after-events.

CHAPTER VII

NEWS FROM THE NORTH

THE Viceroy.* arrived in Arthur and assumed command of the fleet on April 14. Evidently anxious to ascertain what impression had been made by the death of Admiral Makharoff and the destruction of the *Petropalovsk*, the Japanese showed up again at 9 a.m. on the 15th, the approach of the fleet creating quite a flutter amongst the inhabitants. We all got nervous, and prepared for a fourth bombardment. Steaming towards Liao-tieh-shan, the fleet opened fire on the seaward defences, concentrating on the batteries on Tiger's Tail and the narrows. Our batteries and ships, which were lying in the inner Roads, replied energetically, and very luckily, with indirect fire. The bombardment continued at intervals till lunch-time, and was, from the Japanese point of view, fruitless. After this the Viceroy gave orders for the sea near Liao-tieh-shan to be at once mined. Admiral Loschinsky had, some time before, reported to the late Admiral Makharoff the necessity of mining Arthur and Petsiwo where a landing was possible, but the latter was exceedingly sceptical as to the value of mines, for the same reasons as his predecessor had been. It had only been after the bombardment of March 10 and 24 that Loschinsky was ordered to mine the southern shore of Liao-tieh-shan.

* Alexeieff.

We now got some news from the north, and heard that a disaster had occurred on the Yalu. We became convinced that Arthur would be cut off and that the enemy were preparing to transport troops for a landing. There were continual rumours also that they would make another desperate attempt to block the entrance to the harbour. Though great progress was made on the arming and fortifying of the Fortress itself, on the position at Kinchou, owing to the insufficiency of men, of building materials, and to the incomprehensible apathy of the Officers Commanding the District, little was done. Stössel sat in Port Arthur, writing orders and interfering with Smirnoff, and left the Kinchou position entirely to other hands.

The state of affairs there was incredible. Colonel Tretiakoff, commanding the 5th East Siberian Rifle Regiment, was appointed to command the position, but was given no power. Whenever he asked for guns and ammunition for the weakly armed position, for engineers, labour, and building materials to repair the unserviceable batteries, or pointed out the necessity for constructing bomb-proofs, and urged that new positions on the hills might be fortified, the General would fly into a passion and shout: 'Traitors! all traitors! Who says that Kinchou is badly fortified? The Japanese will never take it. I will destroy their whole army if they only dare to land. We all know they are fools, but they will never send a large force here, and so weaken their main army.' Being convinced of the futility of dealing with the General, Tretiakoff, himself a 'sapper,' together with another engineer officer, Schwartz, set to work with his regiment to try and get the place into order. Although he continued, at every convenient opportunity, to point out the unsatisfactory state of the position against which the first blow of the besieging army must fall, not only was he not given more labour, materials, or engineers, but those that he did have were taken away from him. This sounds impossible, but is literally true.

Amongst the large number of men now employed on the works there was naturally a proportion of undesirables and the Commandant being anxious lest the results of the work and the plans of the newly-created fortifications should be communicated to the Japanese, ordered a service of police gendarmes to be organized, under which were to be all the railway, town and gendarme police Captain Prince Mickeladsey was in charge. Strict watch was now kept over the Chinese, and the Japanese knew nothing of what was going on in the Fortress. On June 10, however, Prince Mickeladsey, with all his gendarmes, was sent by Stössel to the other side of Liao-tieh-shan, without the right of entering Arthur, and the Fortress being left without a gendarmerie, offered grand scope for spies. But more of this later.

After the sinking of the *Petropalovsk* the Japanese came almost every night into the outer Roads and laid mines Rarely a night passed without something happening: either destroyers or mine-layers always appeared, and the searchlights used to pick up these gallant craft, which were then shelled by the whole front. Later the enemy became more cunning, sending junks in front of the destroyers to draw fire, thus enabling the destroyers to lay mines with impunity. The navy had hard work from now, fishing for mines, and ships were told off daily for what could not but be a most dangerous duty. The continual night duty also was most harassing, and the gunners—officers and men—were becoming exhausted.

While the isolation of Arthur came closer and closer, little was being done by the Officer Commanding the District as regards providing the Fortress with the necessary reserve of war materials, supplies, and hospital appliances, and poor progress was being made in requisitioning slaughter cattle and horses, for Stössel paid no sort of attention to these points. This was perhaps, after all, logical, as he would not admit of the possibility of the isolation of the town. He informed the Commander-in-Chief that he wanted nothing — neither troops nor ammunition. Although 50,000 field troops at least were essential for a successful defence of the Fortress, and we had less than this number, men were actually sent from us to the north. As an instance of what happened, take this order, No. 328, of May 4:

'The following details, whose departure for Liao-yang has been reported, are struck off the strength of the garrison from this date: One officer and 134 men from the 3rd Reserve Battalion and 250 men of the 7th Reserve Battalion.'

In this case, curiously enough, the men never actually went. After the Battle of the Yalu, in which the 3rd Division suffered heavily, reserves were ordered to be sent from the Fortress to replace casualties. The Commandant obeyed the order, and despatched the required number of men within twenty-four hours. They were wanted for active service, and at once, and were sent off in 'serviceable'—not in 'first-year'—tunics. After their departure a telegram was received:

'Why have the reserve men not been supplied with first-year tunics? They have been sent back.'

And back came more than 300 men a distance of 200 miles! Why? For better coats! The Commandant sent for the Fortress Intendant, who explained that, according to the local military regulations, reserve men were not supplied with first-year tunics, and that none were in store for them. Tunics were, therefore, issued from the Fortress Artillery stores, refitted, and the men again sent off to the front, and this actually on the day before the communications were cut, when the Commandant had implored that every available waggon might be used to bring into the Fortress ammunition, guns, hospital appliances, medicines, etc. But though the men were actually in the train, they never reached their destination, for by then the line had been cut. 'It's an ill wind that blows nobody any good,' and we profited to the extent of a few hundred more defenders.

The supply problem also became more acute. As the reserve of live stock was so small, for reasons already given, preserved rations were issued; but not only was the reserve of the latter not kept up as issued, but tons of preserved stuff were still allowed to be exported by the merchants, who held large stocks. As regards the collection of live stock, the position was more hopeless than ever. The Civil Commissary pointed out that requisitioning for cattle should commence on the furthest point from Port Arthur—in the country bordering on Manchuria, and work inwards—so as to make it impossible for the Chinese to drive away their cattle in that direction. The Officer Commanding the District, however, decided that the requisitions were to be served first in the sections nearest Arthur. As might have been expected, the Chinese, who are no fools, at once began to drive their cattle northwards. The district officers, under-staffed as they were, could only stop this to a very small extent, for, besides driving them, the Chinese resorted to loading cattle on junks and taking them to Chifu.

And so May arrived.

CHAPTER VIII

MORE BLOCKERS

THE 2nd of May was a trying day, for there was a rumour about that we were again to be attacked. The day wore on until the sun slowly sank in the west on its way to hide behind Quail Hill, and its slanting rays gave a farewell glint of light upon the sea, the hills, and the town. Soon all was veiled by the cloak of night; everything behind the huge hills seemed to sleep. But the Fortress was not sleeping; it was only pretending, for now and then searchlights flashed from the dark mass, like the eyes of a monster, and their rays wheeled dazzlingly across the sea. Yet the monster had not eyes enough; there were only five all told. It was midnight, and the gentle moon above the hills lit up the whole scene. Suddenly, as if by word of command, the shore batteries opened fire. A minute passed—a second, a third, and everything was once more quiet; but though silence again reigned, the town was awake, and life was visible in the streets. The vibrating rattle of a machine-gun could be heard in the channel as it fired at an escaping rowing-boat, for one blocker had been sunk. A cutter put out from the *Sevastopol*; in it was the Viceroy, Alexeieff, going to the gunboat *Otvajny*, which flew the flag of Rear-Admiral Loschinsky, and which was lying right in the narrows by Tiger's Tail; further forward near the boom itself lay the *Giliak*. Again the awful whirlwind of metal thundered, whistled, and roared, seemingly destroying everything that came in its way; the condition of the narrows beggars all description; the water literally boiled with falling shells. On the forebridge of the *Otvajny*, in the very centre of the narrows, stood the Viceroy, personally directing the defences, inspiring every one by his calmness under the hail of small shell from the quick-firing guns of the blockers and destroyers. Loschinsky, in the conning-tower of the *Giliak*, was methodically directing the repulse of one of the most gallant attacks ever attempted in this world, made by unarmoured steamers against the whole front of a powerful naval fortress. The cannonade increased till individual shots could not be distinguished, but were blended in the thundering echoes.

Two rockets shot up from the *Giliak*, and there was silence for twenty minutes, after which fire recommenced and continued almost without ceasing for two hours. Three rockets shot up from Golden Hill, lighting up the narrows and the Roads close by. The batteries again ceased fire. In the blinding glare of the bursting rockets a dreadful picture was revealed: against the dark background of the waters, almost in the narrows, lay the sunken vessels, masts and funnels clustered with men. It was only a lull before a fresh storm—a boding silence—for in the distance more blockers were seen to be tearing in. The whole Fortress slumbered for a moment, then woke up and turned all its force to beyond the narrows, towards which the doomed vessels, brilliantly lit up in the rays of the searchlights, were dashing at full speed. The enemy's fleet stood afar off on the dark horizon, as if frightened.

But the attempt was all in vain; the narrows were quite clear. Out of twelve blockers, ten had ceased to exist—had been absolutely destroyed—and with them two destroyers, and many a Japanese hero had been hurled into his cold grave. With morning the fight ended.

This incredible attempt to block the entrance to the harbour in the face of the whole front of the Fortress—incredible by reason of its magnificent daring—had failed, thanks to the vigilance of the guard-ships and the skilfully organized mine defences. I venture to assert that the whole honour of repulsing the blockers, and, in consequence, of preserving all our ships from dishonourable inactivity when the enemy were preparing to land, is due almost entirely to the ships of the mining defence and to Rear-Admiral Loschinsky. Of nine of the blockers, two were blown up by engineer mines, two by mines laid by steam pinnaces, one by a Whitehead torpedo fired from one of the blockers which had been sunk on March 27; three never reached the narrows, but anchored outside and blew up, all on board being killed, and one ran aground at Electric Cliff.

After dinner on the evening of the 4th I was sitting in the ward-room of the *Otvajny*, where several of the officers were relating their experiences of the previous night. Conversation had gradually turned to the doings of the army in the north and the connexion between the desperate attempts to block the entrance and the probable landing of troops in the north, when about eight o'clock an orderly came in and told Captain Pekarsky that they had called him up on the telephone from Golden Hill. After a few minutes he returned.

'Gentlemen, I've just got a message to say that the enemy have begun landing at Petsiwo. The Viceroy, in accordance with Imperial orders, leaves for Mukden to-morrow.'

For a minute we sat silent, for, although it could hardly be called unexpected, the news was depressing.

We were cut off!

CHAPTER IX

WHAT WE DID WHILE THE ENEMY WERE ADVANCING

On the 5th the Viceroy left for Mukden, having handed over the command of the fleet to Rear-Admiral Witgeft. A worse choice could not have been made. That Witgeft expiated his shortcomings as a fleet commander by his gallant death in the execution of his duty does not alter the fact that it was wrong to appoint a shore admiral to the command of a fleet before which lay such a tremendous task. The main duty of the fleet in Port Arthur was to co-operate with the army and to prevent a landing on the peninsula. This was entirely appreciated by Smirnoff and Makharoff, who worked together and settled many questions in regard to future combined operations. Fate, however, decided against their execution, for Smirnoff became subordinate to Stössel, and Makharoff was struck off the roll of the living.

The enemy, who had landed at Petsiwo without opposition, attacked on the 6th our weak advanced posts of Frontier Guards and compelled them to retire, after cutting the railway near the station of Pulienten. Telegram after telegram came in urging energetic measures. Even the station-master at Kinchou made a report as to the landing, but was reprimanded, and ordered not to talk nonsense, for Stössel saw no urgency. The only opposition to the enemy's disembarkation was made by about fifty scouts of the Frontier Guard, under the command of Lieutenant Sirotko, who, after making an obstinate resistance, were obliged to withdraw before the enemy's advanced troops, which were nearly twenty times as strong. Although everything was ready at the station of Nangalin for the despatch of a train full of reserves, it was not sent, and the Frontier Guards were not reinforced.

On May 8 the last train, loaded with ammunition, came in from the north. She brought the news that north of Pulienten the telegraph had been destroyed and the railway damaged by the Frontier Guards retiring to Wafangtien. What some had known must happen, but of which others had doubted the possibility, did happen—Port Arthur was actually cut off, and henceforth upon its garrison lay the serious task of attracting and retaining a whole army, and so decreasing the enemy's concentration against our forces in the north.

The evacuation of Dalny is a good example of the ill-informed and over-centralized control of our General Officer Commanding the District. The peaceful inhabitants of this town were first disturbed on the 3rd and 5th of May by the news of the enemy's landing at Petsiwo. They began to flee, but only a few got away. On the 6th the railway was cut, and steps were taken to repair it; but Stössel's order, No. 168, of May 8—

'The inhabitants of Dalny and Talienwan are to remain quietly in their houses, as they are not in the least in danger from the enemy'—

somehow did not produce the expected feeling of security. Afterwards, on the 11th, when the rail had been again cut, a train full of civilians was, by Stössel's permission, sent off. It was met by the enemy, fired on, and sent back to Dalny.

Now that we were isolated, the blockade by sea became

stricter, while to the north the disembarkation of the besieging army was permitted to take place without opposition. The second phase of the military operations in the Kwantun Peninsula had commenced, for we were now absolutely dependent on our own resources. This is my excuse for again referring to the vital question of supply. What had been done on the whole? From February 8 till May 8 Port Arthur had been connected by rail with Siberia, and only blockaded by sea in a half-hearted manner, and during that time all necessaries could have been poured into the town. Nevertheless, now that we were cut off, we found ourselves very badly off for provisions. It had evidently been forgotten that, for a successful defence of a fortress one of the chief essentials, in addition to troops, guns, and ammunition, is an ample supply of food and a rational organization of the sanitary department. It is necessary to emphasize these points in order to show up all the factors which led to Port Arthur's fall. By the orders published, which I do not quote, it is clear that even in May some anxiety was felt by the authorities, especially the Commandant, as to the food-supply. From the beginning of that month the troops were put on short rations. When one considers the exceptional conditions of service and the continued arduous work carried on at high pressure in the Fortress and district, it appears that, to last out, the men should rather have had increased rations. But it could not be done, and they had to carry on for eight months on insufficient food. Yet, though the rail had not been used as it might have been to bring in food, that mountain of packing-cases near the station showed that it had not been idle. This mound, which served as a landmark—a sort of a triumphal arch by the entrance to the Old Town—was composed entirely of—vodka! We might lack food in Arthur, but never drink. Can a more hopeless state of things be imagined? For of all places in the world where drink can do harm, a fortress full of half-nourished men is the worst. Stössel's efforts to repress drunkenness were beyond praise, but what could he do? The sale of spirituous liquor was forbidden in all shops, stores, or public-houses; but it could always be got for money, and all drank what they wanted to. It was there.

All we knew of the enemy was that they continued to advance undisturbed along the Mandarin road towards Kinchou. On the Kinchou position everything was quiet. Work was being carried on by Colonel Tretiakoff alone with the regiment under his command. General Fock occasionally paid the place a visit, went round the works, joked with the soldiers, gossiped with the officers, and went off to Dalny. The one point he insisted on was the arming of the right flank and the construction of a battery on Lime Hill. General Stössel sat in Port Arthur, and kept all in a continual state of astonishment by his orders. In the Fortress we had, up to now, placed a good deal of confidence in the Kinchou position, for General Stössel had told every one that the Japanese would never be allowed to come beyond it, and few except the Japanese knew what was going to happen. On May 10 we read the following order:

'On account of the possible arrival (from Kinchou) of the whole of the 4th East Siberian Rifle Division, the Commandant will make arrangements for the building of field-ovens.'

Our Commander, without even having seen the enemy, was already looking behind him! To many it was now evident that the stronghold at Kinchou was not particularly to be relied on, and alarming rumours began to be circulated about it. Every one at once declared that as a position it was beneath contempt, but the Officer Commanding the

District paid no regard to such things, and continued to publish weighty orders, such as that of May 12:

'I am always meeting private soldiers, particularly those of the 7th Reserve Battalion, wearing felt boots. This is irregular, and it would be better that skins should be bought at the butchers' and cured.'

As a detail, the men wore felt boots because during the whole siege they had nothing else, because for six years the Fortress had never been supplied with a sufficient quantity of leather boots.

Up to the present no serious steps had been taken at Kinchou; only a few weak battalions had been thrown forward in advance of the position. That was the real state of affairs, though other information was invented for the inhabitants. At this time men who knew the ground and could scout well, like some of the Frontier Guards, were invaluable, and yet they were scarcely ever employed. For some reason they did not find favour in the eyes of the Generals. Every one knew the splendid qualities of these Frontier Guards, but they were ignored till they came under the command of Kondratenko. Even when the enemy advanced and seized the position near Shanshihlipu we did nothing. In Dalny Fock did the 'dictator'; in Arthur we continued to write orders. For instance, No. 187:

'To-day, near the church, I met two officers with a lady; she was wearing an officer's rifle forage-cap. It appears that one of the officers was Lieutenant Erben, and the lady his wife. I do not think that I need dwell upon how out of place it seems for one of the female sex to wear a military cap with a cockade, when even retired officers and reserves are not allowed by regulation to wear them.'

In Dalny there were numerous buildings, docks, and the most splendid breakwaters running out into the sea for a distance of one and a half miles, but nothing had so far been done to destroy them in the event of the town being abandoned. It was only by an order of May 14 that a committee was appointed to settle which of the larger buildings should be destroyed. The result was that the Japanese eventually found the docks and quays untouched, and of the greatest service to them when they used that place as a base. On the 14th also the fact that the enemy had landed in force at Petsiwo was first mentioned in Orders. This news was twice repeated in the paper—once as an official *communiqué* upon the doings of Fock's troops, and again as a true account of the reconnaissance. As a matter of fact, they had by this time occupied the village of Shanshihlipu, but of this the staffs of both Generals Stössel and Fock were in complete ignorance till the fight of May 16. That they did not know of it is proved by the fact that the 3rd Battery of the 4th East Siberian Rifle Artillery Brigade, on occupying the southern heights at Shanshihlipu, was almost blown out of existence by the enemy's artillery, which had already, somewhat earlier, taken up a position on the northern hills opposite. On my asking the Colonel how this had happened, he said:

'Everything was in such a muddle that it is a wonder any of us are alive to tell the tale. Stössel gave one order and Fock another—every hour brought fresh instructions.'

Fock, who had always declared that Kinchou was quite unassailable, seeing that the enemy had landed and were advancing in earnest to the attack, stated publicly that to give battle at Kinchou would be a crime, that a division there would be merely destroyed. The 15th and 16th East Siberian Rifle Regiments were hurriedly entrained, and moved backwards and forwards, first to Dalny and then back to Port Arthur. The confusion boded ill.

CHAPTER X

THE NAVY LOSE A CHANCE

WHEN describing the repulse of the blockers on the night of May 2, I essayed to bring forward the importance of the work done by the guard-ships, and now a word as to the destruction of the Japanese battleship *Hatsuse*. From the beginning of the blockade Admiral Loschinsky and the Captain of the *Amur* had studied the usual course of the enemy's ships, with a view to laying mines along it. This was impossible for some time, owing to the fog and the number of ships, especially destroyers, cruising about. At last, on May 14, during a council held at Admiral Witgeft's, at which Loschinsky was present, the Captain of the *Amur* asked permission to set to work. Loschinsky turned to Witgeft, as his senior, and asked permission to start this important but risky work. 'As you like; it is entirely your business and you are responsible,' was the reply. Loschinsky then turned to the Captain of the *Amur*. 'The enemy is not visible; there is scarcely any fog, and what there is will only help us. Go, and God be with you! Lay not less than fifty mines, and none nearer than ten miles.' The Admiral himself did not go on this trip, as the meeting had only just begun and was a very important one. The *Amur* left at three and returned after five, no one at all suspecting what an invaluable service to the besieged place she had done that day. At eleven o'clock next morning, in sight of the whole Fortress, the Japanese battleship *Hatsuse* struck a mine and perished even more quickly than the *Petropalovsk*; the *Fuji* also was badly damaged. Thus did the *Amur* avenge the *Petropalovsk*.

Loschinsky and several others were at the moment with the naval Commander-in-Chief. As the tide was at the flood, those who were present advised Witgeft to take advantage of the favourable conditions, and at once to send out three battleships, all five cruisers, and the destroyers to capture the damaged battleship and its escort of three. 'Everything will be done in its own good time,' was the answer. Even when Balashoff, the Master of the Hunt,* hurried up to point out with great earnestness the necessity for the fleet putting out in order to make an end of the Japanese on the sea, Witgeft repeated: 'Wait; everything will be done in its own good time.' Only at 12.30 were orders given to the cruiser division and the destroyers to get up steam. The former could not put out at all, for, being a holiday, their crews were ashore, and it was two o'clock before the destroyers got under way. The *Novik*, which happened by chance to be under steam, joined them. Out they went at full speed, and, regardless of danger, tried to approach the wounded battleship in broad daylight—but the psychological moment had passed: the enemy had carried out repairs, and opened such a fire that it was impossible to get near, for every destroyer was valuable, and there was no object in throwing them away. They returned.

The garrison and inhabitants were disgusted. The navy had again made a mess of it. Had Witgeft been a man of decision, had he kept his fleet ready for battle, the picture would have been different. For had the fleet

---

* A Court title.—A. B. L.

gone out at once, the *Fuji* and the battleship and two cruisers with her would undoubtedly have been destroyed. This would have so weakened the enemy's fleet that the fight on July 11 would have had another result. All the same, the destruction of the *Hatsuse* greatly influenced the defence afterwards, in particular during the strict blockade. From the moment she was destroyed not a single big ship except the *Nisshin* and *Kasuga*, which stood at long range, and threw some 10-inch shells on to Cross Hill, ventured near Port Arthur. The Fortress was thus ensured from the dreadful prospect of being bombarded from the sea, and therefore all the big guns on the sea-front, from the 6-inch up to the 11-inch howitzers, were turned towards the land, and gave invaluable help in the land defence to the end.

After the blowing up of the *Hatsuse*, the sweeping, blocking, and defence of the Roads was made over to the officer in command of the cruiser division, and the hunt for mines went on day and night. The cruisers went out by turns at night into the outer Roads. This almost invariably called forth an attack by the enemy's destroyers, which, covered by the confusion of the fight, laid mines. Our destroyers were ordered by Witgeft to lie in pairs in Takhe and White Wolf's Bays. Despite Loschinsky's energetic protests that it was the duty of the fortress artillery and guard-ships to wage war against mine-layers, and not the work of the destroyers, which ran great risk of being blown up, Witgeft was immovable. But the wisdom of Loschinsky's advice was proved later, for on one dark, foggy night the *Lieutenant Burakoff* and the *Boevoy* were rendered *hors de combat* by Japanese torpedo-boats, which crept up to them unawares in Takhe Bay. In the middle of May Witgeft gave orders that mines should be laid by junks near Inchenzy and Melankhe, which was done. When the *Amur* was laying mines west of Liao-tieh-shan she ran on to the mast of a sunken blocker, and damaged herself badly. It was impossible to dock her, as the only dock was occupied, and we had to make use of the *Bogatir* and afterwards the *Reshitelny* for this work.

CHAPTER XI

PREPARATIONS ON THE KINCHOU POSITION

AFTER much hesitation, opposition, many quarrels, alterations, and frequent fresh orders, a column consisting of two regiments and three batteries was formed on May 15, on which evening it moved out of Nangalin station to take the field. The advance-guard, under the general command of Lieutenant-Colonel Laperoff, was composed of the battalions of the 13th Regiment and the 3rd Battery of the 4th East Siberian Rifle Artillery Brigade. At daybreak on the 16th the column got near the Shanshihlipu heights, where, as soon as it was light, the advance-guard heard firing in front. This altogether puzzled Laperoff, or he knew that none of our guns were ahead of him. It turned out that, owing to ignorance of the country, the main body had lost its way, got in front of its advance-guard, and had attempted to occupy these heights, without having reconnoitred them or even despatched scouts in advance. Fock, commanding the 4th Division, had trusted to luck, and we paid the price, especially the 3rd Battery, under Romanovsky, for the enemy had occupied the position before us, and opened a heavy fire on this battery as it came up, almost destroying it.

This battery was admirably supported by, and only got away out of action with the assistance of, the 'bullock battery,' under Lieutenant Sadikoff. On the initiative of this young officer, whom our gunners afterwards dubbed the 'Guardian Angel,' some old Chinese guns had been collected and formed into a battery drawn by bullocks. Laperoff did not know what to do with his advance-guard under the peculiar circumstances, for it was no longer in advance, he received no orders, and the fire was getting hotter. Briefly, the result was that our force had, after heavy casualties, to retire to Nangalin without effecting anything. As soon as the withdrawal began General Fock, who had hitherto been with the rear guard, suddenly turned up. When Laperoff reported the mistake and its disastrous result, he began to excuse himself, saying that he had never given the orders, and complained of the inactivity and idleness of his Chief of the Staff. 'Traitors! they are all traitors! They never obey my verbal orders; they only obey written ones.'

This fight showed the superiority of the enemy in artillery preparation, in fire control, and in knowledge of how to use the ground. After taking Shanshihlipu they were able to mask their guns perfectly, but we, not understanding the value of ground, exposed ourselves needlessly, and suffered much. While they, after a tedious sea-voyage, victoriously advanced, we, on our own ground, with every chance of selecting and fortifying the best positions beforehand, only tried to occupy them after the enemy had already done it. So, after the first brush, we withdrew rapidly and with much loss to the celebrated but worthless position at Kinchou.

After carefully watching everything that happened throughout the whole campaign, and thus getting to know and appreciate the Russian soldier under service conditions, I have come to the conclusion that he was not only a hero, but a Titan, and I must say I had never dreamed that he would exhibit the moral and physical strength that he always did. Possessing such qualities, had he only received proper training, and been well led by the more senior of his officers, we would never have witnessed that pitiable slaughter—for which General Fock, with the approval of the Officer Commanding the District—at Kinchou was responsible. The first fight at Shanshihlipu, its failure, and the rapid retreat had a disastrous effect on the *moral* of the men. They lost that confidence which counts for so much in war.

From the moment of the withdrawal from Shanshihlipu up till May 26 the ground lying in front of Kinchou was never properly reconnoitred. I would lay particular stress on this absence of any regular and well-organized intelligence work, because, operating as we did with our eyes shut, we always allowed the enemy, who was energetic, insistent, and cunning, to take us unawares.

And now to the Kinchou position. The fortification of it was still being carried on solely by the labour of the 5th Regiment, which gallant corps did not belong to General Fock's division, and so was not spared. As has been already mentioned, Colonel Tretiakoff, commanding the regiment and nominally in command of the position, knew well that it was anything but ready even for a temporary defence. As before, so now, especially after Shanshihlipu, he recognized the absolute necessity of masking the guns, which were standing exposed on the highest points, without any attempt at concealment. He fully realized that durable splinter-proofs, and not mere 'hen-coops,' were necessary, that the infantry trenches should be made deeper, and that all the communications should be greatly improved; but his representations still met with little success. Though Fock continued to talk much, he no longer said that he would destroy the whole Japanese army here. On the contrary, he turned round and declared, in self-contradiction, that to attempt to hold the place long would be a crime.

The navy had given us two long-range Canet guns, which had been got into position on the left flank, under the idea that the attack would develop there, which, as a matter of fact, it did. A great deal of labour and time had been expended on doing this, and the guns were splendidly masked. But a few days before the battle General Fock insisted on their being dismounted, taken down, and dragged off to a position on the right. He was told that this flank on Lime Hill was not important, and that the enemy would never attempt to advance that side (which was justified by the event); but he would not reconsider his order. The guns were taken down; there was no time to remount them again, and so they fell, unused and uninjured, with two waggon-loads of ammunition, into the enemy's hands.

The batteries on this most important position, called in the highest military circles the 'key to Arthur,' were commanded by Lieutenants and Sub-Lieutenants, and the command of the artillery was given to a very young officer, one Captain Visokikh. He continually reported that he had not enough ammunition, asked for projectors to light up the Kinchou Valley, and begged for sand-bags, sleepers, rails, beams, etc., for thickening the cover and making the buildings splinter-proof, but without result. I know for a fact that his brother, commanding the 7th Sector in Port Arthur, so well appreciated his helpless position that he, quite illegally, upon his own authority, sent ammunition to him. Tretiakoff, finding that even Stössel would do nothing to assist him, at last went direct to Smirnoff, and telling him everything, asked his help. The latter did everything that he was able so as to delay the fall of Kinchou, if only for a few days; but what he could do was little, for his powers did not extend beyond the Fortress glacis. When some of the necessary materials did arrive, the men worked like slaves to improve the defences, the Fortress artillerymen assisting the men of the 5th Regiment, under the supervision of Colonel Tretiakoff and Captain Schwartz. But it was too late.

Now, shortly before the battle the state of affairs in the district was, to put it mildly, slightly mixed. If the staff issued an order, the General, instead of at once carrying it out, wrote long-winded memoranda and proceeded to do the opposite. Trains stood in the stations ready to start day and night, and, as can be seen from the orders, the wretched 15th Regiment spent its time entraining and detraining, being taken out one day and brought back the next. The authorities seemed to have lost their heads, and orders were only issued to be at once cancelled. The day before the battle was a nightmare of confusion: no one knew what was being done or why it was done. Men were worn out by being 'messed about' uselessly from one place to another, and were never long enough in any place to get to know it. The work on the position which had for a short time been proceeding again had to cease for want of materials. For instance, the frontal battery on Lime Hill, under the command of Lieutenant Solomonoff, to a certain degree important as being able to fire on the approaches to the right flank, was armed with four old Chinese guns. It had no traverses, and no bullet-proof shelter for the gunners or ammunition, and was not connected by telephone with the Commandant.

This was the state of the Kinchou position.

In Port Arthur, after the Viceroy's departure and the assumption of command of the fleet by Witgeft, there was a lull in naval operations; but rapid progress was being made with the repairing of the lame ducks. The battleships and cruisers—too precious to use—lay motionless in the inner Roads, the destroyers, gunboats, and the *Novik* were alone active. The latter were kept with steam up, and were always cruising about, protecting the mine-trawlers, laying mines, or doing short or long reconnaissances, which were called by the men 'adventures'— a very suitable name. Complete ignorance of the coast generally, pointless tasks, lack of speed, bad engines, absence of well-thought-out plans, a numerous, keen, and powerful enemy, who always operated systematically and cleverly, rendered these expeditions abortive of any result except fatigue, waste of coal, and loss of vessels.

Having served all his time ashore, Witgeft naturally could not give an example of useful activity; moreover, the very weak line he took with junior officers undoubtedly greatly undermined his own authority and naval discipline generally. The attitude of the younger officers towards him and other seniors was deplorable, and noticeable even to outsiders; the juniors not only saw the defects, and the incompetence of their seniors, but they publicly criticized them. At the same time, a great gulf grew between army and navy, and scarcely a day passed without a conflict between the officers of the two services; they insulted each other in the streets. And the position of the sailors was a difficult one, because they themselves were not to blame: it was not their fault that they did little cruising and were generally in port in peace-time; that they had not been taught how to shoot and know their ships; that the only thing required of them was spittle and polish. Like the infantry, the naval officers were not trained for war.

General Stössel, instead of endeavouring to get the two services to pull together, made matters worse, and in his effort to gain personal popularity amongst the younger army officers did not even refrain from making fun of the

Officer Commanding the Fleet. However, later on, when soldiers and sailors fought together and were struck down side by side in the trenches, all differences vanished—men recognized men.

On May 20 we had another sea attack, carried out by seven ships and two destroyers. It lasted from shortly after midnight to 2 a.m. The result was immaterial.

CHAPTER XII

THE BATTLE OF KINCHOU COMMENCES*

THE days passed monotonously. Wherever one looked one saw men—our rough peasants in the guise of soldiers—digging and delving, not in their native heath in the hope of a fruitful harvest, but in the stony, sandy soil of the inhospitable peninsula. It was depressing to watch them, sleepless and hungry, and I often wondered how many would ever again see their fields. The monotony, however, was sometimes broken by General Stössel's orders. On May 23 he wrote:

'Before May 28 all cattle must be removed from the country round the town of Kinchou—*i.e.*, north of the position of that name.'

Remove the cattle from country already in the possession of the enemy? Was it a joke?

On May 24 I went to Kinchou. In the same train was the 15th East Siberian Rifle Regiment, which had only arrived in Arthur on the 20th, but was now on its way back to Nangalin. Lieutenant-Colonel Yolshin, commanding the military communications, was in the officials' carriage, and with him were Captain O., the officers of the 15th Regiment, the railway engineers, and myself. Sitting at the common table in the saloon, con-

* Also known as the battle of *Nan-shan*.

versation turned on coming events. Colonel Yolshin, looking out of the window, said: 'I wonder how long all this will be ours? Can we hold out at Kinchou? Do we know how to? The enemy is advancing in considerable force: scouts report that they have brought with them a quantity of artillery.'

'Can you tell us, Colonel,' said an officer of the regiment, why we are being continually taken into Arthur and then back again? The men can't have a square meal and never get any sleep, and we are losing a lot of forage. To-day we have again been sent off suddenly, and the men had to snatch dinner at the station. Why is it all done?'

'There you are. There is the man who knows,' replied Yolshin, pointing to Captain O.

'Yes, I can tell you. I have been made Chief of the Staff of the Rear-Guard, of which your regiment is to form part,' said the newly fledged staff-officer in a smug tone. He then relapsed into the mysterious silence beloved of the staff-officer. He evidently wanted to see what impression he had made on those present, and especially on those junior to himself, and looked at me none too kindly, for it behoved him to be careful of what he said in the presence of a mere civilian, even though an official war correspondent.

I detrained at Tafashin, the head-quarters of the 4th Division, near the Kinchou position, where I attached myself to some Frontier Guards, and with them made a night reconnaissance towards Mount Samson, in front of the position. This was to me exciting and novel, but the main feature of general interest was that, though one of our objects was to investigate Mount Samson if possible, we were suddenly recalled before we reached our objective, as the reconnaissance had been countermanded. We thus nearly lost the advance patrols we had sent on ahead of us, and returned without finding out if there were many enemy on Mount Samson or none at all. I got back to our starting-point at dawn and slept soundly, tired out by the varied and unusual impressions of the night. In my dreams I seemed to hear noises, which got louder and louder, till suddenly I woke. Every one was throwing on his clothes and the alarm was sounding.

'What's up?' I asked, half dazed, for the whole building was trembling from the noise of firing.

'It's nothing; the enemy are bombarding us with the Lord knows how many guns!'

Shrapnel were bursting over the position, and the hills seemed to be smoking from the bursting shells.

Our patrols of the Frontier Guards only returned in the middle of the day, and they reported that the enemy had occupied Mount Samson in considerable force. They had seen their bivouac, guns, and horses, and had heard the noise of work and the ringing of telephones.

At 5 a.m. horses were brought us, and Lieutenant Sirotko suggested that we should go on to the position together. The fire increased, the heaviest falling on the guns under the command of Egoroff. All the batteries on the position kept up a hot fire; but the enemy rained shell after shell on Egoroff's unit, literally plastering it with lead. At times as many as ten shells appeared to be bursting above the battery at once, and it seemed as if it must be swept away. The Japanese field-batteries were a long way off, firing at their longest range. At 6 a.m. the enemy opened fire from some concealed howitzers on the left; we judged them to be of large calibre by the noise of the bursts and the powerful effect of the explosions.

It was difficult to range on the enemy's guns, thanks to the use they made of the ground; we were shooting by guess-work at unseen targets. In addition to this, their fire was extraordinarily accurate and concentrated by turns on each battery. At 6.45 a.m. the fire slacked off, and at 7.45 there was a lull all along the position.

I was struck by the calmness and endurance of the gunners during the whole time of this, their first artillery battle; whence did they get it? No exhibition of fear for their lives was at all visible. It was not that they did not realize the danger, and had not yet seen any wounded, because up to the end of the siege they behaved in the same way—like men. If we bow before the heroes of the late war, we must first bow before the gallant defenders of Port Arthur.

While our leaders were still playing, writing endless letters, long orders, reports, etc., the enemy made the most of the valuable time; while we were thinking about making reconnaissances, issuing orders for them, and then countermanding them, they came right up to Kinchou; while our General was delaying on the Kinchou position they occupied Mount Samson, whence they could see all we did distinctly; they had concentrated the previous night and were getting their guns into position right under our very noses. And we? The majority of the gunners told me that the fire suddenly opened on the position came as a complete surprise, for at 5 a.m., when it commenced, everyone was peacefully asleep.

After this morning's artillery duel silence again reigned. It was only at 3 p.m. that a few guns began to fire on separate bodies of the enemy, which showed up in the valley of Kinchou and near Mount Samson. Lieutenant Solomonoff opened from his battery, but he did not know what was happening, for he was not connected by telephone to the position. He sent off a mounted orderly for information, but the man had to go two miles. At last it was plain, for dense columns could be seen at the foot of Mount Samson, between the nearest peak and the old Chinese houses. The enemy, extended in thick lines and endless ribbons, commenced to advance against our right flank, under cover of the houses, without firing a single shot; but it was only a demonstration. They wanted to attract our attention to, and make us concentrate our reserve on, that flank.

The whole area was not more than two square miles, and everything could be seen distinctly. The history of warfare throughout the whole world cannot produce another instance where such a big fight, and one with such vital consequences to a war generally, has been waged in such a confined arena. We could not make a single move without the enemy seeing it, for from Mount Samson, which we had presented to them, the Japanese saw everything.

At sunset Solomonoff's battery ceased fire, and orders were received that when night came on the companies were to occupy the trenches on the right flank, and 'be particularly vigilant.' Solomonoff declared that if the position were stormed his battery must at once be destroyed. 'We have no bomb-proofs; instead we have tents, which, though pleasant in summer, are not effective in action. I have nowhere to give shelter to the wounded or to protect the ammunition.' By 9 p.m. every one was ready, and the companies fell in. Saying good-bye to Colonel Radetsky (when I next saw him he was lying naked in a cart, dead), we started for the trenches, and in an hour we were in them. Here thousands of men were waiting for the foe; thousands of eyes were trying to penetrate the darkness. In front of us were the enemy, who were close, and clearly about to attack very soon. We waited anxiously, wondering when and where the blow would be delivered. The narrow neck of land joining the Kwantun Peninsula with the mainland gradually became enveloped in a light fog. The movement of the machine-guns could alone be heard, as troops continued noiselessly to occupy the first and second lines of trenches. The men were very silent, peering ahead over the parapet. Towards the centre of the position were heard occasional shots, rockets flashed out, and the beam of a small searchlight swept the front: the large projector had come up too late to be mounted, and was lying in a ravine. Away down in the valley the advance on the town of Kinchou had commenced, and fighting was going on between the enemy and three sections of the 10th Company of the 5th Regiment.

The sky became more and more overcast, and a strong south-east wind blowing in fitful gusts brought up clouds of dust. It was midnight, and it grew darker. Having said good-bye to the Frontier Guards in the trenches, I went on towards the guns on Lime Hill. The Commanding Officer was lying down in his tent, fully dressed. We went on to the battery, and found everything quiet and the sentries by the guns. The air seemed oppressive and charged with electricity, and in the distance we heard the growl of thunder. There was a blinding flash of lightning, then another, and the rattle of thunder shook the earth: we ran to the tent. The rain poured down as if out of a bucket. By 3 a.m. it had stopped and all was silent; the darkness of night was giving place to the rosy light of the approaching day, and a blanket of haze lay over the valley towards Mount Samson.

CHAPTER XIII

THE BATTLE CONTINUES

SERENE and calm dawned May 26, but by five o'clock we were aroused by the relentless sputter of machine-guns and the sound of bursting shrapnel—our réveillé—and all peace was gone. During the night the enemy had deployed their batteries along the heights between Kinchou Bay and Khinoeze Bay,* and were now concentrating their fire on us, taking our works in front and flank, while from Kinchou Bay some of their gunboats were pounding our left with 10-inch guns. This bombardment, now commenced, did not cease the whole day. The panorama from Lime Battery before the sun was well up was remarkable. In the dim light the flashes of the enemy's artillery showed up against the dark mass of gigantic Mount Samson like long threads of fire, like golden chains swaying up and down, rocking to and fro. As the sun crept higher the gold gradually faded into silvery white, and the chains seemed to turn into little bunches of fleecy clouds. Higher and higher rose the sun; not a single cloud flecked the delicate turquoise of the heavens. From the ground rose clouds of dirty grey smoke, each followed by a dull roar: the enemy were firing *rafales*, half of the guns being loaded with shrapnel, fuzed to burst in the air, and half with common shell with percussion fuzes, which, bursting on impact, raised

* Hand Bay.—E. D. S.

a pillar of dust and suffocating smoke. At present the fighting was limited to an artillery duel, but our position presented an awful sight, for now, under the concentrated fire of more than 150 guns, it was smoking like a crater. Every minute the intensity of this fire increased, the guns being systematically directed on to each of our batteries in turn; it was hellish. Lieutenant Solomonoff, who was coolly directing the fire of his battery, came up to me, and glancing towards our centre batteries, remarked:

'I expected all sorts of things, but nothing quite like this. It is almost incredible. I doubt if any of them will get out alive. They are still shooting hard, but their fire is all over the place, for they can no more see the enemy's batteries than I can; we are firing into the valleys more or less by guess-work. By Jove! how well the enemy mask their guns! And we——'

At that moment a shell burst by a gun on the right. 'Take the wounded to the rear. Steady there, steady! This is nothing.'

'They are ranging on us, sir, and will open on us in a moment,' said the sergeant-major.

'Keep cool. They haven't touched us so far.'

'There's another.'

It was now after nine, and the attack gradually developed. The enemy had indeed got the range to a nicety, and soon began to plaster us—a repetition of what had happened to the centre batteries. A field battery came into action on our right, but being instantly smothered by a murderous fire, the detachments were compelled to move down in rear of the hill under cover. Lieutenant-Colonel Laperoff, commanding the 2nd Battery of the 4th East Siberian Rifle Artillery Brigade, took his unit over to the left flank to a well-concealed bit of ground on the Tafashin Heights, whence he was able to open a useful fire on the gunboats. At this moment the gunboat *Bobr*

MAJOR-GENERAL TRETIAKOFF.

To face page 69.

appeared in Khinoeze Bay, and crumpled up the enemy's left flank with enfilade fire. Its arrival and its comparatively successful fire had a wonderful effect just then upon us, for it awakened a feeble hope of a successful issue to the battle. We were at the centre of a circle, of which the enemy's guns composed the arc. While they were able, from their distributed position, to concentrate on to us, as a focus, we had to distribute our fire over a great distance in directions diverging like the sticks of a fan. The air-lines of the telephones were destroyed early in the battle, and all fire control or direction was impossible: each battery, under a storm of projectiles, replied spasmodically as it could. They fired because they felt obliged to, but the result was never visible, and so aim could not be corrected. Colonel Tretiakoff, who remained in No. 13 Battery, was helpless: he could not telephone, and most of the orderlies sent off by him never reached their destination: this battery was subjected to such an intense fire that it was impossible to work the guns until the *Bobr* diverted the attention of the opposing artillery about 10 a.m., by which time all our batteries had suffered sorely.

The infantry attack was now launched, and in spite of our steady rifle and machine-gun fire, the attacking columns fearlessly came on. At times they could be seen to halt and lie down, only, however, to rise again and creep to closer range. Meanwhile, another column was seen to be advancing through the shallow water in Kinchou Bay, in order to turn our left flank; but Lieutenant-Colonel Laperoff was able from the Tafashin Hill to get their range and to hurl them back.

When the attack was at its height, when our batteries were being gradually silenced, when hundreds of men had laid down their lives, and others were in their death-agony, Major-General Nadein, commanding the troops, received from somewhere a report to the effect that the Japanese had been repulsed and were on the run! The news of a victory was instantly telegraphed to General Stössel in Port Arthur, and was at once circulated all over the town. In Stössel's quarters a convivial company gathered to drink champagne.

It is curious to picture the Officer Commanding the District sitting in Arthur, sixty-seven miles off, drinking champagne and babbling of victory, while the first decisive battle of the war was being waged—a battle upon the issue of which depended the future course of events, not least among them the fate of Port Arthur.

The enemy's artillery fire supporting their attacking columns now became unendurable, and the whole of our position was enveloped in black-brown smoke. From Lime Hill I sadly watched our batteries being silenced in rotation. By 10.30 all the ammunition of those of our guns which still possessed gunners was expended, and by midday our artillery position was silent. The whole strength of the enemy's fire was then directed on the infantry trenches held by the 5th Regiment, who were pouring a rifle and machine-gun fire on the attacking columns. The mangled remnants of our artillery began to move off behind the Tafashin Hills, from which fire was opened at times by the field batteries. The Japanese were most skilfully directing their gun-fire and the movements of the attacking columns from Hill 75 and Mount Samson. It was now evident that our position, having lost its guns, could be held no longer unless the 5th Regiment received strong reinforcements.

One hour later General Fock at last arrived on the field of battle by special train. At 1.30 the fire intensified, and the attack was renewed with greater fury. Colonel Tretiakoff sent message after message, begging for two battalions from the reserves; but Fock refused.

While at Kinchou the 5th Regiment literally melted away, defending the ground entrusted to it, the four regiments of the 4th Division — 16,000 bayonets — were kept behind the Tafashin Heights, doing nothing, passive spectators of the formal slaughter of their comrades!

Fock arrived on the ground when the fight was practically over, and meeting gunners retiring along the roads to the rear, worn out with ten hours' fighting, said to them, 'Get back to the trenches, cowards! Take rifles and shoot!' The men crawled back utterly exhausted both morally and physically, and, rifle in hand, returned to die under the hail of shells in the trenches. These poor worn-out fellows, quite unfit for any work, were sent back, while 16,000 fresh men were, so to speak, round the corner doing nothing; for the General would not risk his division: it was wanted to defend the district and the Fortress!

At four o'clock there was a lull. The Japanese were evidently preparing for a fresh attack. Every gun on the position was silenced, while the fire of those on the Tafashin Heights was ineffective. The position was still held only by the 5th Regiment, and two companies of the 13th Regiment which had arrived during the night. About twenty companies of the enemy with guns could be seen between Mount Samson and Hill 75, quietly and slowly extending against our right flank. Their advance was quite uninterrupted: they were beyond the range of our infantry, and our guns were silent. After an hour their guns again started to shoot and the attack was renewed. It was plain that the object was to capture the centre from the left, and therefore all the weight of metal was directed against that flank. Tretiakoff saw it was useless to reinforce the left, and he wanted to keep his reserve, although small, in hand. He continued to ask Fock for fresh troops, but in vain. Line after line of the enemy now advanced against the trenches on the left flank. Heavy musketry fire began; rifles got hot; the trenches were full of killed and wounded, whom it was impossible to carry away, for of seventy-two stretcher-bearers only twenty-eight remained. All along the line of trenches the parapets were battered into a shapeless mass, heaped up with dead. It was six o'clock, and it was impossible to hold longer on to the left flank without reinforcements. The companies, reduced in strength, began to withdraw, to hold the second line of trenches. The gun-fire slackened and the fury of the infantry assault increased. Tretiakoff continued to ask for reinforcements. None were sent him.

The Japanese made a desperate advance along the whole line, and the enfeebled regiment was unable to hold them back. Ammunition ran short: it was impossible to replenish the supply. The companies in the centre of the position were in danger of being cut off from the left flank, which was giving way before the enemy's determined advance. Communication between several of the redoubts and lunettes was interrupted, and Tretiakoff felt the position to be desperate. But while daylight lasted a general retirement was impossible, and orders were given to hold on at all costs. Seeing that some of the companies were falling back, he despatched his last orderlies to the rear to explain that a general retirement was out of the question till dusk, and to implore that even one battalion might be sent to enable him to hold the position till nightfall, and so prevent the utter annihilation of his regiment; but he was not reinforced by even a section.

While light remained the Japanese refrained from actually charging to close quarters, and contented themselves with pouring a heavy rifle and a gradually slacken-

COLONEL LAPEROFF.

To face page 73.

ing artillery fire on the position. The sun was almost setting. At about seven o'clock the 5th and 7th Companies slowly gave way, and no sooner had Stempnevsty's company abandoned its position on the extreme left than it was occupied by the enemy. From that moment the position of the company entrenched in the centre was very critical, as it was taken in a cross fire. The 2nd Infantry scout detachment was surrounded; both its officers were instantly killed, and of 115 rank and file, but eighteen escaped. Having occupied the central batteries, the Japanese opened a steady reverse fire upon our trenches. But the sun was now sinking behind Mount Samson, and under cover of the rapidly increasing darkness, the retirement was carried out. The companies which had held the left flank retreated along the road leading to the Tafashin Heights, and thus covered the retirement of the centre and right. But though the Japanese were now in possession of our batteries, and though their artillery had advanced to a position between Nos. 2 and 3, for some reason or other, they did not press the pursuit, and contented themselves with shooting into our retreating columns.

Lieutenant-Colonel Laperoff, who had all along kept up a fire from his battery on Tafashin, noticed as darkness came on that the Kinchou position was crowded with troops. His guns were excellently placed, and he could have poured a crushing point-blank fire into these masses in the open. But he had no orders, no information as to what was taking place, and though he and his officers strained their eyes endeavouring to make out who these crowds might be, it was impossible to ascertain whether they were friend or foe. That a general retirement had taken place, and that the Japanese had occupied our main position, none of the staff had considered it necessary to inform him. He finally found

Fock at the railway-station, and was peremptorily ordered to withdraw his guns.

Darkness came. The day had passed, and with it hundreds of lives — the usual price of every military triumph, on this occasion the price paid for the glory and honour of the 5th East Siberian Rifle Regiment.

CHAPTER XIV

NANGALIN RAILWAY-STATION

ALONG the roads and paths and across the fields the remnant of the 5th Regiment dribbled towards the Tafashin Heights. Behind these hills confusion was worse confounded. The whole 4th Division streamed away past this wonderful natural position, the strength of which can be seen at once, even from a map; but no one seemed to have noticed its tactical importance before, and nothing was now done to take advantage of it to resist the invaders further. Back, back streamed all. When it was quite dark, when the men of the different units were thoroughly mixed up in the disorderly retreat, so that control was impossible, some one shouted that the Japanese cavalry were coming. What then happened it is difficult to say, but the infantry opened fire on their own men, there was a lot of miscellaneous shooting, and a convoy of wounded from under Tafashin was taken for the enemy and fired on. Batteries hearing the firing and having no infantry escort hurried off to Nangalin. Colonel Laperoff's battery, marching ahead in good order, was almost swept away by the other batteries galloping on top of it in the dark; all was blind panic till daylight. It was indeed lucky for us that the Japanese did not pursue: the results of such a pursuit are painful to think of, and the enemy might have got into Port Arthur on the heels of the 4th Division.

Nangalin Railway-station presented a scene of dreadful chaos. Trains loaded with wounded were leaving for Arthur. Owing to the suddenness of the retirement and the disorganization, no arrangements for food had been made, and men of all branches of the service, badly wounded and exhausted by the long battle, lay tortured with hunger, thirst, and cold. The dim forms of the gunners of Kinchou could be seen prowling about the platform as they searched for food; others were lying huddled together, sleeping. The first and second class refreshment-rooms were filled with officers, whose numbers were being momentarily increased by fresh arrivals by train, on horseback, on bicycles, and on foot. Nobody knew anything or what to do; every one waited for orders which did not come, for none of the commanders were there. The majority of the senior officers, having eaten, were lying on the floor.

A long train filled with wounded was standing at the platform ready to start; it had been there for some time. The medical officers were performing acrobatic feats in their efforts to pass along from one goods waggon to another, and were doing their best by the dim light of the lamps to alleviate the terrible suffering.

'Tell them to get us some water; the men want something to drink, and we have only got distilled water required for doing the dressings,' said one of the doctors to a railway official.

'There isn't any. We never expected this rush, and what we had has been used. There is only dirty water.'

'But the men are dying of thirst, to say nothing of hunger. How much longer is the train going to stop here? It is torture to the wounded.'

'Captain —— won't allow us to start.'

Opposite the station buildings I saw a group of men

gesticulating and heard angry voices. I went towards them, hoping to find out what the delay was.

'... I ask, I demand that the train be started at once. In the name of humanity all haste must be made to get the wounded into a hospital as soon as possible. Every moment with some of them means life or death. It is utterly absurd to talk of *issuing rifles* to them, and it would take hours.' It was the senior doctor of the hospital train speaking.

Taking advantage of his authority as a staff-officer of the district, Captain —— insisted that the rifles piled up on the platform should be issued to the wounded men. Both men got angry, and the staff-officer, annoyed that a doctor should attempt to question his arrangements, assumed a haughty and peremptory tone.

'Don't torture the wounded. The train is a long one, full of awful cases, and they are lying all on top of one another. There's no room for rifles,' implored the doctor.

The captain was furious, and striding to the telephone, returned after a few minutes to insist on his orders being obeyed; but the medical officer, losing patience at what seemed to him pigheaded cruelty, flatly declined to allow the wounded to be disturbed, and insisted on the immediate despatch of the train.

'Even the regulations of the Peace Conference lay down that wounded sent by hospital trains must be disarmed,' he shouted.

'I care nothing for the Peace Conference, or any other damned conference. I must send these rifles into Port Arthur, to prevent them falling into the enemy's hands,' was the reply.

Boiling with indignation, I could remain no longer a spectator of this disgraceful scene, and walked off along the train. It was an unusually long one. Wrapped in my thoughts, I strolled some way from the station.

Suddenly I heard a noise—neither groans nor screams, but more like lowing. Where I was and what had happened suddenly came back to be. It was a very dark night, and close to me were standing some waggons, from which were proceeding these noises. Have you ever, when travelling by rail, stopped in a station or at some siding at night alongside a cattle train, and heard the noise of the cattle? If you have, I need not attempt a further description of the sound of the hospital train at Nangalin station that night. I walked slowly along it. In the unlighted goods-waggons crowds of men were lying about, some on straw and some on the bare floor. One heard choking sighs, groans, sobs, prayers, curses, and calls for help, combined with the howling of men in unbearable physical agony.

'Drink, drink! something to drink—I'm burning!' was jerked out at me in a hoarse voice from an open door. With difficulty I clambered up, and then almost fainted at what I came upon. In the dimly-lighted waggon lay a shapeless heap of men, coats, boots, canteens, greatcoats, heads, arms, and the place reeked of blood.

'Sir, a drink—a drink, for God's sake!' The cry stabbed me. From the indistinguishable pile of flesh and —other things—I saw at my feet a blood-stained head, a sheet-white face lit up by two burning eyes, and an arm stretched towards me. I gave it—this thing—my water-bottle. The wounded man seized it with both hands, but after a second let them fall helplessly, his head lolling back on someone's enormous and blood-smeared boots.

'Ach! cold. Cover me.' He was in an ague.

It was sickening, revolting, horrible. I tried to slip out, but involuntarily my eyes were caught by the sight of a grinning face on which danced the expiring light of the flickering wall-lamp. A smile? and amid such surroundings? Stepping carefully across the wounded men, I went up to it. No! it was not grinning: 'twas the play of light and shadow on the face of another cold corpse. The rows of teeth, the half-opened lips, and the fixed, glazed, staring eyes—a ghastly grin indeed.

Alongside, with his face turned towards and almost touching this—this grin—lay another mangled man, groaning piteously and breathing fast. Every now and then he opened his eyes, but apparently did not know where he was. What would have been his feelings, I wonder, if on the way to Arthur he had come to himself? Throwing my handkerchief across the dead face, I jumped out of the waggon and hurried to the station, to find the wrangle still continuing. I was boiling with fierce indignation. I kept hearing the animal noises and groans of hundreds of suffering men imprisoned in this train, which till a few hours before had been, as was amply evident, filled with cattle.

I left this inferno and went off and joined the artillery. We soon started, and marched through the moonlight night, along with troops, transport, and herds of cattle, all hurrying, scurrying towards Port Arthur, passing many Chinese villages, seemingly quite deserted. Once we heard a shout, 'The Japanese cavalry are on us!' By dawn on the 27th, having again gone more than thirty miles, we arrived at the station of Inchenzy. Worn out and hungry, and finding no food at the station, we lay down on the platform. At six o'clock some hot food was provided for the men. The officers were asked to have some refreshment in a saloon carriage, the very one in which, three days ago—little expecting what was in front of us—I had gone to Kinchou. At seven I left for Port Arthur in one of the trains of wounded coming from Nangalin, and at nine o'clock I reached the Fortress, The town was stupefied.

CHAPTER XV

THE LAST OF DALNY

When Dalny heard the heavy fire from the direction of Kinchou early in the morning, little did the people think how that day would end for them. Afraid of what would happen, they had some weeks before asked permission to leave for Port Arthur; but Stössel had strictly refused, and had even sent back one or two families which had started: he had told the Mayor that there was nothing to be alarmed about, that he would send word directly there was any need for them to move. The sound of firing increased, but the town remained quiet—life moved along the usual track. Even if some felt doubtful as to the result of the battle, there was no idea that the 26th would be the last day for them in Dalny. Midday came; the distant firing slackened off, then increased, and the curious collected on the church tower to see what was happening, for no information had been received from the staff of the district. [Stössel was about that time celebrating his 'victory,' not thinking of Dalny.] The sun sank in the west and evening came on; still no news, and complete ignorance as to what was happening at Kinchou. Evening changed to night; the electric lights blazed up in the streets, and Dalny went to bed.

At ten o'clock the last train but one departed from the station. At eleven the empty waggons returned from Nangalin, and brought news of what had happened at

Kinchou. Almost at the same time two telegrams were received. One, to the Mayor from Colonel Yolshin, ran as follows:

'The Officer Commanding the District has sanctioned the departure of the inhabitants from Dalny, but not by rail.'

The other telegram was from the District Staff to the same effect, saying that as the trains were required for troops, they could not be used to move civilians. The sleeping town woke up; the police began to arouse the inhabitants, who, greatly alarmed, ran into the streets half dressed, to know what had happened. The news soon spread that our troops had hurriedly retired to Arthur, and that the Japanese cavalry might at any moment enter the town.

Then began an awful and indescribable panic, for the seeds sown by imagination on the soil of fear are prolific. A massacre by the Japanese or Hunhuses was expected. Men, women, and children wandered helplessly and aimlessly about the town, not knowing what to do. Many rushed to the station, only to be told that the railway would not take them. There were practically no horses in the place.

By midnight the majority of the residents had collected on the Upravlensk Square, where the Mayor, having told them of the telegram received from Stössel, proposed that they should abandon the town; he said that he would not be responsible for any that remained. Then the unfortunate inhabitants, leaving all their property to its fate, set out along the shore front towards Shaopingtao. Some were able to hire rickshaws, but the majority went on foot. Those who happened to see the unfortunate women, half dressed, bareheaded and barefooted, with crying children in their arms, will never forget the awful picture; and it might have all been avoided if General Stössel had listened to the constant representations made by the Mayor with regard to a timely departure. All those 470 men, 92 women, and 57 children who hurriedly left Dalny on the night of May 26 owe their misery to General Stössel.

As the flight commenced the Mayor received this last and most noteworthy telegram:

'General Stössel desires you immediately to blow up all the waggons and trucks remaining in Dalny.'

Staff-Captain Zedgenidsey was ordered to Dalny to demolish all the buildings which might be valuable to the Japanese, as, for instance, the breakwaters, docks, cranes, floating material, railway, etc.; but, owing to want of time, nothing, except a few of the railway bridges, was blown up, and all fell into the enemy's hands in complete order. They also got more than 250 waggons and 300 trucks, all full. Besides the numerous town, harbour, and railway buildings, there was an immense amount of private house property, as well as large warehouses stocked with food and stores of all sorts, both public and private. The enemy got possession of them all undamaged, just as they were. After the capture of Arthur the Japanese confessed that by not destroying Dalny we had assisted them enormously in their difficult task of disembarking their siege-train, and that the railway had enabled them easily to get it into position in the investing lines. Russia had spent over £200,000 in breakwaters for the Japanese to land 11-inch howitzers!

The electric lights now shone down on empty streets, for Dalny was deserted. At two o'clock in the morning the last train, a long one of forty-seven waggons, left the station for Nangalin, and early on the morning of the 28th, after more than twenty-four hours' march, the tired and hungry refugees began to straggle into Arthur. Those Arthurites who happened to see this sorrowful procession arrive opened a subscription list to assist these wretched people, who in one night had lost their homes and everything they possessed.

We have often talked over and discussed the result of Stössel's reign, and what he did or did not do during February, March, April, and May, and there is little doubt that he might, by taking reasonable precautions and by wise and timely action as to the choice and fortification of positions, have delayed the fall of the Fortress at least till June 1, 1905.

CHAPTER XVI

THE FATE OF THE FORTRESS

WITH the fall of Kinchou and the retreat of Fock's entire division towards Arthur, all glances were directed to Lieutenant-General Smirnoff. Those who had believed absolutely in the impregnability of the former position now lost heart, and began as fast as possible to clear out of the place, going in Chinese junks to Chifu. When the battered remnants of the 5th Regiment—the regiment which by its gallant defence of Kinchou had covered itself with everlasting glory, and which had lost more than half its men and two-thirds of its officers—marched into Arthur, it was given a most unexpected, not to say unique, welcome.

'You are a wretched, undisciplined corps of traitors, cowards, and blackguards. I will try the lot of you by court-martial. How did you dare leave Kinchou? Don't dare to show yourselves in Arthur, lest by your presence you infect the whole garrison with your cowardice,' was Stössel's greeting.

The regiment had no divisional commander, and no one dared to take its part. Discipline prevented the officer commanding from replying to Stössel, and he and his officers had to bear these totally undeserved insults. One General put the whole blame of the defeat on the regiment, and assured Stössel (it was not hard to convince him, as he was not at Kinchou) that the abandonment of the position was solely and entirely the fault of the 5th Regiment, and the senseless way in which it had fortified the place.

This cruel and shameful injustice to this gallant regiment was soon known by all the others, and it had a very bad moral effect on the whole garrison.

After the Kinchou *débâcle*, the Commandant drew up an order as to the distribution of the different units in the Fortress, and on June 1 took it to Stössel for official approval. The latter rudely cut him short, and, without either reading the order or looking at the scheme, said that it was inopportune.

'The publication of any such orders with regard to the distribution of the troops might,' he said, 'become known to the Japanese through their spies. [He had himself, on May 29, issued an order detailing troops to various positions on the hills.] The district under my command has almost entirely passed into the hands of the enemy. Arthur alone remains, I shall take upon myself the defence of the Fortress. Its present staff will be broken up, for it is a useless body. My staff will be sufficient. I will send Colonel Khvostoff to command a battalion. You will be on my staff. It is impossible for two equal commanders to be in one place.'

This was on June 1: we actually held on to the district outside the Fortress for two months after this date.

The Commandant was in an awkward position. Stössel defied him, and the Fortress, which, thanks to his own efforts and skill, was being gradually got into a state of readiness, was to be taken from him and to be commanded by a man who would wreck all. That moment settled the relationship between these two. It was the first act of the tragedy, which ended on January 1. Quietly, and with perfect politeness, Smirnoff answered:

'I was appointed Commandant of this Fortress by the Tsar; the Fortress Staff is the organ of the Commandant, appointed by Imperial orders. I have no intention whatever of resigning either the rights entrusted to me by the Tsar or the duties consequent on them. You, sir, as my commanding officer, can give me general orders relating to the defence of the Fortress, but I remain its master until the Tsar himself deprives me of it. If my removal from the duties of Commandant admits of no delay, you have it in your power to publish an order to that effect.'

During this scene those present anxiously awaited the result, for in those few minutes the fate of Arthur was decided. In an angry voice Stössel replied:

'I do not mean to remove you from duty. You will remain Commandant, but I shall run the Fortress. Whether legal or not is my affair; I will answer for that.'

What could Smirnoff say?

There was a knock at the door; an orderly entered to announce some officers, and the episode was over. But as every wall has ears, this incident was soon known to the whole garrison, and indignation knew no bounds. We were all afraid for the fate of Arthur, and made conjectures as to the action Smirnoff would take. Some declared he would leave on a destroyer; others, in indignation, said that Stössel should be invalided and forced into hospital; others swore that the day and hour had been settled when Smirnoff would surround Stössel's house with a whole regiment and arrest him, as well as Fock and others. The moment would have been an appropriate one, for the discontent in the garrison was very great, and the hatred of Fock and Stössel had much increased since Kinchou. Everything depended on Smirnoff's

A WOMAN DRESSED AS A SOLDIER, WHO WENT
THROUGH SEVERAL FIGHTS.

decision; but to adopt such violent measures was risky—a dangerous precedent for the discipline of the troops. Stössel also had St. Petersburg at his back. Even the Viceroy could not interfere with his recent appointment as Officer Commanding the District, though much against it. Who could say that Stössel's arrest would not have results quite opposite to those wished for? It was most likely that St. Petersburg—that hotbed of the most revolting scandals and intrigues—would represent Stössel's arrest to the Tsar in such a light as to cause an immediate order for his release. Was it not all possible?

Finally, Smirnoff, in spite of the many suggestions and proposals, decided to settle the matter as peacefully as possible. He accordingly sent for General Kondratenko and Colonel Reuss, and told them that he recognized the necessity for a division of authority, and so was quite prepared to give up all his powers, save only the actual defence of the Fortress, for which he intended to remain responsible. Reuss expressed regret for all that had happened, and promised to use his power to keep evil influences from getting at Stössel.

Next day Order 285 was issued by the Officer Commanding the District, and clearly showed that Stössel was not inclined to conciliation:

'As the enemy has appeared in the area of the Fortress, and the 4th East Siberian Rifle Division, with its artillery, has joined the troops in it, I now assume supreme command of the defence, and, in order to centralize authority, the Chief of my District Staff will in future be present at the Council of Defence established under the presidency of the Commandant. All resolutions, etc., of the Council will be given to him to report to me for my confirmation.'

Why did he publish the order? Its only result was to take the control of the Fortress from the hands of the real chief, who, according to all regulations, should have been in supreme command. Then, when Fock's entire Division arrived on Wolf's Hills, a council was summoned, at which the question of what further steps were to be taken was brought up—whether the outer positions on Green Hills were to be held, or whether the defence of the advanced fortified positions of the Fortress was now to begin. The Commandant protested against the latter, energetically insisting that the Green Hills must be held, because the Fortress itself was not quite ready, and, what was more important, because Wolf's Hills and Ta-ku-shan and Sia-gu-shan Hills were not fortified, and were most important strategic points. Fock asserted that it was unsound to attempt to hold the enemy on field positions; that it would be a mere waste of men and ammunition, which might be so essential for the defence of the Fortress itself, to which a withdrawal must sooner or later be made. It would be wiser to neglect Wolf's Hills and retire at once into Port Arthur, and so commence its defence with the maximum number of men. Stössel agreed with Fock. Then the Commandant explained his scheme in detail, and pointed out that as soon as the blockade became strict the Japanese would get possession of Wolf's and Sia-gu-shan and Ta-ku-shan Hills; that, in that case, the inner and outer harbours would be impossible for ships, as the waters could be reached by indirect fire, and that none of our works could be successfully held.

Smirnoff's brilliant and lucid statement carried the council, which, by a majority of votes (including Stössel's), decided that Fock's Division should be sent back to occupy the best of the outer positions still in our possession. It is interesting to note that as the country had not even up till now been thoroughly reconnoitred by the District Staff, they were unable to say at the meeting which were the best remaining positions! Of the splendid positions on the heights at Nangalin no one had given a thought. According to the reports of our scouts and reliable

Chinese, these were already occupied by the Japanese. Next day some of General Stössel's staff rode out to choose positions. They stopped on the chain of hills named Upilazy, which border on Inchenzy Bay and Green Hills, stretching along the Lunwantun Valley to the little bay of the same name. The hills on the line of these positions, stretching for more than seventeen miles, were commanded by Kuen-san Hill. The positions on the Upilazy chain of hills (ten miles) were held by mixed companies of the four reserve battalions and the 7th Division with two companies of the Frontier Guards. To these were added eight field batteries and one howitzer battery. Fock took up his quarters at the seventh mile (the railway now only ran for twelve miles), and kept on repeating what he had said at the council—that it was only wasting men and ammunition to hold these positions—and was apparently quite ready to retire. Smirnoff, however, insisted on their being held. Engineers were sent to the flanks (there was only one sapper company of 800 men in the Fortress), and the fortification of the seventeen-mile-long positions was commenced. Fock would not hold the right, because he said the enemy would attack his left, and, as the position was too big for one division, Smirnoff sent the mixed companies above mentioned from the Fortress troops to hold the right. Owing to this the left was strongly fortified, but the right hardly at all.

The enemy having now taken complete possession of Dalny, at once used it as their base. There, quietly and comfortably, without any interference from us, they carried out the landing of troops for the investment. Ten transports would arrive daily, bringing everything necessary for the concentrating army. The railway from Dalny and all the rolling-stock was in perfect order, and by it troops, guns, ammunition, provisions, etc., were transported to the front. Everything smiled on them:

our fleet did not hinder them in any way; they had command of both sea and the land.

During all this time our intelligence services were very badly run, our only source of information being the Chinese, who, working both for us and the enemy, naturally favoured the latter, as the District Staff paid a starvation wage.

CHAPTER XVII

THE LOSS OF KUEN-SAN HILL

As the sea blockade was at this time very slack, communication with Chifu was easy, and Chinamen could always be found to make the trip. In addition, steamers with provisions often ran into Pigeon Bay. Stössel received inquiries from head-quarters, through Shanghai, as to what he wanted, and was informed that what he required would be sent. But he refused all proffers of assistance, saying we required nothing, and this in the face of Smirnoff's protests that big gun ammunition, preserved meat, vegetables, hospital appliances, etc., were urgently needed. We could at that time have obtained anything we wanted, for merchants and others were offering to run the blockade—at a price. One day a steamer owned by a private Frenchman ran into Pigeon Bay with supplies, among which was a large stock of tinned milk. It was with the greatest difficulty Stössel could be got to take this, yet milk was one of the first things to run out, and he warned the captain not to come again. It was almost impossible to send private letters out of Arthur, for all of them were censored by Stössel's staff, those hinting of the true state of things being destroyed and the writers punished. I myself had experience of this.

With the occupation of Green Hills, Smirnoff set to work to fortify the ground in front of Angle Hill, Wolf's

Hills, Ta-ku-shan and Sia-gu-shan Hills. The latter were of immense importance, as they were quite inaccessible, and protected the whole of the western front of the Fortress, but only so long as Wolf's Hills were in our possession. As far as intelligence was concerned everything went on in the old sweet way. The scouting was bad, the information gained was nil, and we remained ignorant of the enemy's position or movements. One good step taken at this time, however, was the formation of a town guard from all the citizens capable of bearing arms.

On June 23 the enemy, having concentrated, began to advance from Siabintao on the extreme right flank along the hills on the seashore. To oppose them two companies of Frontier Guards from Waitselazui, and three companies from Khuankhe-Chjuan were sent. A short engagement ensued; our men held their ground, and the enemy retired. This movement of the Japs was merely a demonstration with the object of finding out the weakness of our right flank. They had excellent information regarding the left from their spies and patrols, and knew well that considerable bodies of infantry and artillery were collected on that side, and that fairly strong fortifications were in course of construction. The weakness of our right was continually pointed out to Fock, but he did not send a single company there, even after this fight on the 23rd. At 5 a.m. on the 26th they opened a heavy gun fire, chiefly on the right, and made a general advance all along the line. At midday they pressed the attack on the centre and right more vigorously, and continued massing against those points till evening. Next day, at daybreak, they hurled all their might against the right. The fighting was obstinate, and the enemy, though considerably stronger than we, were obliged to fall back; we, however, owing to reinforcements not being received in time, were obliged to abandon Kuen-san.

This peak, which was really the key to our positions, for it commanded the whole line, was held by only one company of the 14th Regiment, commanded by Captain Lopatin. Realizing its great tactical importance, and naturally thinking that we did the same and would doggedly hold on to it, the Japanese attacked, after artillery preparation, with almost an entire regiment. But the General did not appreciate its value. Even when the Japs began to press its little garrison, he sent no reinforcements. The company only began to withdraw when it had lost three-fourths of its strength, and when, in spite of the several messages despatched asking for help, no support was given. At the subsequent inquiry upon this affair, Fock so represented the matter to Stössel that he had Lopatin tried by court-martial for abandoning the position prematurely, and without orders. Fock himself escaped blame. Before the sentence could be confirmed by the Tsar, poor Lopatin died of heart failure; but he had been sentenced to the loss of all his rights, and to serve with the prison companies for two years.

By the evening of the 27th the fighting ceased with the capture of Kuen-san and Green Hills. The troops holding the right fell back into the valley of Lunwantun, and occupied the heights in rear; but the loss of the two former made our position critical, as from Kuen-san the Japs could renew the attack, and force us back. There was nothing for it but to attack and at all costs regain possession of those hills. The District Staff accordingly issued, with the greatest precaution, secret orders to that effect. On July 1 I met a young officer in the street.

'Would you care to come with me to Green Hills?' he said casually. 'A night attack has been fixed for to-night on Kuen-san; but it is a great secret.'

As I also heard the move discussed by Chinese shop-assistants, I went at once to the District Staff and told the senior aide-de-camp, for, as the whole town seemed to know this 'secret,' it must, of course, be known now to the enemy.

'Yes, the General let it out, so we have telephoned to cancel the move. In any case it wouldn't have succeeded, as the General was dead against it. The attack will take place another day, and Kondratenko is going to command the right flank. Fock will now only nominally be the senior.'

This reply was only too true, for the General was jealous of Kondratenko, and would not co-operate in any way.

Early in the morning of July 3 our destroyer and gunboat division steamed towards Shaopingtao and opened fire on Green Hills; at the same time our troops advanced from the right flank against them, Kondratenko being in command. The ships did little actual harm, owing to lack of facilities for fire observation and correction. The fight raged all day, our main objective being Kuen-san. On the 4th it was renewed, but though we again got possession of Green Hills, we were unable to capture Kuen-san. The 13th Regiment took two-thirds of it, but could not advance further, as the Japanese threw in heavy reinforcements, and brought up a number of machine-guns. On the night of the 5th we had to withdraw, and abandoned further attempts to retake the position, as one attack alone had cost us 500 men. Green Hills were again ours, but the key to the position, from which all our roads, dispositions, and actions could be seen, and an enemy's artillery fire and infantry advance directed, remained in the hands of the Japanese. On the 7th everything was quiet, and from then onwards for three weeks the enemy did not fire a shot in reply to our occasional bombardments, for they were establishing themselves and fortifying the ground actually won. Smirnoff insisted on the positions recaptured by us being strongly fortified, and sent his best engineer officer, Raschevsky, to supervise, so good progress was made. At midnight of the 8th, in torrents of rain, they made a sudden attack on our centre, but were noticed in time and repulsed. On the 13th our howitzers bombarded the enemy's works for some hours, but drew no reply. On the 14th we made a reconnaissance of the Japanese position under Smirnoff, with like result. Twice only from the 8th to the 26th July did the enemy attack, and then only in small numbers.

CHAPTER XVIII

THE JUNE SORTIE OF THE FLEET

MEANWHILE the navy had not been altogether idle, though the result of its activity was not great. By the middle of June the *Pallada*, in dry dock, was ready to go to sea, and the battleships *Cesarevitch* and *Retvisan*—the pride of the Pacific Ocean Fleet—were ready to throw the bandages off their now healed wounds. We were all greatly excited, for if only the fleet could put out at full strength and get the command of the sea, the transport of troops to Dalny, now being carried on daily right under our very noses, would be stopped, and then what might not happen? Important meetings were frequently held at Admiral Witgeft's; but though the ships were ready, the council, attended by all flag officers and captains of ships, was divided into two parties—one for going to sea, the other against it. At the meeting on June 18 a telegram from the Viceroy was communicated, in which the fleet was ordered to steam out and engage the enemy, choosing the most favourable conditions, and taking every precaution. The time chosen for the start was the turn of the tide—daybreak—on June 24; but when the hour came the *Pobieda* was not ready, and her Captain was ill, so it was put off till dawn the following morning. There were great efforts made to keep this secret, as, owing to the removal of the gendarmerie to Liao-tieh-shan by Stössel, the place swarmed with spies.

At three o'clock, after the twinkling of many lights, a signal was hoisted, and the fleet came to life. At 4.21 the *Novik* slipped quietly out into the outer Roads, and after her the other ships in turn, the *Pallada* being the last to pass through the narrows; but the fleet was short of the following guns: one 12-inch, twenty-six 6-inch, and thirty 3-inch, and four of the ships had captains who had not commanded them at sea before. From the highest point of Golden Hill the whole squadron could be distinctly seen in the clear morning air. The channels in its course had been swept for mines, some of which, while being drawn in, had exploded quite close to the ships lying at anchor. Seven mines were found near the *Cesarevitch* alone! Notwithstanding all our efforts at clearance, the roads were always more or less full of them, and every officer and man going out to sea, though the enemy were miles away, was gambling for his life. This is mentioned because what our sailors had to go through and their great services at Port Arthur are now forgotten in Russia. Russia has forgotten in the whirlwind of the movement for political freedom that for eleven weary months her loyal sons in Arthur tried to save the waning greatness of their native land.

As the *Bayan* slowly passed out far below, the bitter words I had once heard about the state of the Russian navy, uttered by one of its officers, recurred to me: 'So long as our fleet is purely for parades and peaceful political demonstrations; so long as its Admirals do not serve and work hard in peace-time, doing active duty, and not merely writing orders; so long as the officers are promoted for anything but their capabilities and services; so long as they do not know their ships as the five fingers of their hands; so long as the whole complement of the navy does not like the sea; so long as the Naval Department does not cease trying to economize in what is the essence of a fleet (shooting and cruising); so long as it hesitates to rid the administration of the fleet of venerable, bent old men and "shore admirals"; so long as the Naval College does not turn out men fond of the sea and the navy, we and the senior officers can do nothing, and our fleet will glide down the facile descent of deterioration. I say this from bitter personal experience: I say that we are absolutely unprepared. We will do what we can; we are ready to die—and we must die in the unequal struggle.' As these words came back to my mind, suggested by the *Bayan* gliding slowly past down below, I looked up from her to the horizon where, far away, could be seen the Japanese ships waiting for ours. Of course they knew we were coming out, and were ready. What did they not know? Probably the opinion just quoted would be no news to them. By one o'clock our ships had moved out into the open sea, where Togo with his whole fleet was awaiting them. The destroyers out ahead, supported by the *Novik* and *Askold*, at once engaged the enemy's scouts, which drew off towards their main body. By 6 p.m. the squadron had gone down below the horizon, and could not be seen from the highest points in Arthur, but the booming in the far-away distance sounded like peals of thunder. We were all greatly excited to know how the fight would end.

About nine o'clock the quiet of evening was broken by the growing noise of heavy firing at sea. The fleet, attacked by a cloud of torpedo-boats, and firing with every gun, was retiring rapidly to Arthur. It was not yet visible, but the booming of the 12-inchers, the ceaseless cracking of the smaller guns, sounded louder and louder. We saw the reflection of the searchlights, and then some time later dim specks gradually loomed up, and the squadron itself appeared; the destroyers and *Novik* formed a rear-guard, covering the retirement with their fire.

The fleet steamed in and anchored, let down its torpedo-nets, and with its searchlights wove a regular net of light to seaward. On the way back to port it had been twice attacked by destroyers, but had beaten them off, and had made the outer roads comparatively without mishap. The *Sevastopol* alone distinguished herself. Getting out of column, she struck a mine and was injured, but was able to reach White Wolf's Bay and anchor. There was not enough water for her to go into the inner harbour, for no one had thought in peace-time of dredging the entrance.

Night soon came down very dark, and all seemed peaceful; but the calm did not last long, for that night the enemy made a madly gallant attempt to torpedo our vessels as they lay in the outer harbour, and hell was let loose. All night long Admiral Togo launched his destroyers to the attack in pairs. Though our whole fleet was one blaze of light, and though the shore searchlights perched up on high lit up the waters to a great distance, the heroic enemy did not desist. On, on they came, fired at from the whole front as the shore lights showed them up afar off; diving one moment into darkness, the next again into the glare, they dashed onwards. The fire of the ships became furious; the ceaseless flash of the guns made them look like torches, but, however brave, however fanatical the enemy, they could not withstand the hail of steel poured on them by the fleet. The destroyers came in very close before they fired their torpedoes, but still it was at ineffective range. Having fired the first torpedo, they turned to starboard, firing a second on the turn, and then at full speed steamed out to sea. The lucky ones got away; others sank in view of the whole Fortress. I sat through the night and watched these attacks till they ceased at dawn.

Next morning, on the flood-tide, our fleet came in to

the inner harbour. It had returned, the only result of its sortie being the injuries to the *Sevastopol*, the expenditure of thousands of shell, and a number of Whitehead torpedoes floating about in the outer Roads. Arthur was disappointed. The following order, issued by the Commander of the fleet before it went to sea, which appeared in the *Novy Kry* of the 24th, was depressing reading:

'As the ships which were damaged by our treacherous enemy before the outbreak of war have been repaired, the Viceroy has given orders for the fleet to put to sea, so as to assist our comrades on land to defend Arthur. By the help of God and St. Nicholas, the sailor's patron saint, we will endeavour to do our duty, be true to our oath to the Tsar and defeat the enemy, weakened by the destruction of some of his ships on our mines. The *Bobr* has given us an example of what can be done. May God be with us!

'WITGEFT, Rear-Admiral.'

The fleet was there again in its usual place in the western and eastern basins; but what was to be done? Who was to blame because it had returned without having brought on a decisive action? Some of the officers declared that a battle ought to have been brought on, that all the chances were in our favour; others said the opposite, asserting that a heavy engagement would have been the end of the whole fleet. Arthur was divided into two camps: one against the navy, the other in defence of it. I remember those heated quarrels about our naval officers, and the abuse poured upon men who were in no way to blame. The majority of those who spoke so bitterly of the fleet's return ignored the fact that it went to sea very weakly armed. It had met the Japanese fleet of four battleships, six armoured cruisers, six light cruisers, and a number of destroyers and other vessels, about twelve miles out. The fleets got within fifty or sixty cables of each other, and when our ships increased speed so as to shorten the range and bring on an action, the Japanese steamed off. Togo evidently wanted to entice our fleet on and make a torpedo attack during the night, and having thus weakened it, to bring on a decisive engagement in the morning. It was depressing to see our ships driven in again like this, and disheartening to give up all hope of obtaining command of the sea. A strict blockade of the Fortress must come in the future. How long it would last no one could say, but that men, guns, and war material were already scarce with us—more than scarce—we well knew. Still, the hatred shown towards the fleet was not sensible or just. Disappointed with our many misfortunes, people were searching for a scapegoat—for some one on whom they could vent their indignation. They became jumpy, and therefore in no condition to look at things calmly: they were glad to find some one to blame. From what I felt, heard, and saw on all sides —and my opportunities for judging were great, as I moved about in every grade of society in Port Arthur—I came to the conclusion, after the return of the fleet, that its rôle on the sea was over.

During the gradual development of the military situation in the district—when the most prominent features had been the extraordinary errors on the part of General Fock — General Stössel was acting the dictator in Arthur, where, in addition to his main task of interfering at every step with the useful work of General Smirnoff, he lost no opportunity of sowing dissension between the fleet and the army, especially after the squadron's unlucky sortie. Everywhere on shore—in the streets, in the restaurants—there was nothing but abuse and curses for the naval officers, from highest to lowest. Every one accused the sailors of not wishing to put to sea. One result of this was the production of a scurrilous allegory by two anonymous authors. The first described a dream, which he pretended to have had, and in which the enemy, in the shape of a bull, was eventually killed by Russian soldiers. The second narrated another dream, a sequel to the first, in which the navy were represented as hares which bolted and left the soldiers to fight the enemy alone. I happened to read this effusion when I was on board one of the ships, for some one had had it lithographed, and sent a copy to each of the ward-rooms in the fleet, including a copy to Admiral Witgeft. This kind act naturally did not tend to smooth matters between the services. Though the sailors endeavoured to ignore it, at heart they felt the undeserved insult deeply.

CHAPTER XIX

FORTIFYING OUR LINE

THE 4th of July showed the Japanese the power and energy of our troops. It illustrated their capabilities not only in defence, but of successfully delivering an attack; for it should be noted that the minimum number of troops on the advanced positions took part in the engagement of that day. Having retaken Big Ridge, Green Hills, and the foot hills of Kuen-san, still holding the defile—the second key to the advanced positions—and having made some progress with the fortifying of all the defensive line, we completely stopped the enemy's forward movement towards the outer forts, on which work was now being pressed on. At this time our mobile shore defences (a division of gunboats) were able to shell the enemy's positions, his rear communications, and his bivouacs, with great success. Thanks to the result of the battle of the 4th, the enemy felt that they were liable to attack themselves; the desperate and well-planned attack of our right flank, under the command of General Kondratenko, on that day had come as a nasty surprise. After Kinchou they had advanced victoriously—as they liked. The battle of June 26, with our abandonment of Kuen-san, confirmed them in the belief that Russians were incapable of taking advantage of and of holding good positions; but the actions of July 3 and 4 made them more careful, and not quite so ready to believe blindly in their lucky star. They now assumed the defensive, and began to construct field fortifications, to build wire entanglements, and to lay mines all along their defence line and captured heights. They became still more careful when our outpost line moved forward, and, attacking their outposts, occupied with our pickets the hills in front of Green Hills, from the foot of Kuen-san to the sea. If only that hill had been still in our hands, our position would have been splendid: under the energetic Kondratenko, we would have very soon turned it into quite a formidable fort, which would have been able to shell the enemy at every point, for all the roads leading from their position to Dalny would have been distinctly visible. But what could we now do? Fock had, knowingly or unknowingly, spoilt everything, and in the face of common sense given up the hill. I repeat, Kuen-san was never properly fortified, and so the Japanese had been able to capture it with small loss. Had it been fortified, they would have paid a long and heavy price for it.

One day when Butusoff, commanding the section on the right flank of Green Hills, was lying on his face on his favourite little hill, and looking intently at the top of Kuen-san through his glasses, I asked him what he thought of it. He had intended for some time to send some scouts there, and so he used to study all the approaches to the top by day.

'Oh, I think a lot of it! So long as Kuen-san belongs to the Japanese, we can do no good here. Remember that they can clearly see everything that we do. Now, look at the top; look up there,' he said, pointing. 'Not there—more to the right; up above that first point.'

'I see!'

'Look! You can see those little poles running all the way down? Those are for telephone-wires. From the top of that hill they will be able to correct the fire of the

A BOMBPROOF.

whole of their batteries, just as they did on Mount Samson. Do you remember? Well, all their batteries are being connected up with telephone to that peak. I stay here by the hour, and I have seen how they have connected up by telephone from one peak to another.'

Thanks to the fairly successful operations under General Kondratenko, people in the Fortress were now somewhat less nervous, and they began, with their usual optimism, at once to believe that the enemy would be checked for a long time on the advanced works. True, Kondratenko had taken the place of Fock, but the real state of affairs was not understood. Few knew that we might expect a decisive advance any day, and that it was impossible to hold the enemy long on our most absurd line of positions, stretching for seventeen miles, with such forces as were allotted by the District Staff. But however much it was hoped that we would succeed in checking the enemy for a longer or shorter time, every one quite understood that if we were not reinforced from the north the Japanese must sooner or later close up to the Fortress and begin to bombard it.

In view of this, the leading people, especially those with families, began to build for themselves bomb-proofs; but, owing to the lack of the necessary material, labour, and knowledge, most of these were made in a primitive fashion, and would have given absolutely no protection against shells, nor even against splinters; but, ostrich-like, the builders obtained a sense of security from the concealment afforded. Stössel, with his extraordinary ideas on everything, took a different view; in every unofficial way he showed his disapproval of these buildings and made fun of them. However, this did not prevent him having one built for himself in his own courtyard, and also one for the staff-officers of the district. In this the latter took refuge during the bombardment.

They might have built ten bomb-proofs each for themselves if they had liked, but why should they interfere with others, especially with those who had wives and children? It was absurd, barbarous. The building of bomb-proofs should have been encouraged. Kinchou had shown what damage could be done by small shells, and what might we not expect from siege-guns? The whole of Arthur should have been turned into a catacomb, for besides the healthy, there were all the sick and wounded to be protected; but, when no proper bomb-proofs had been constructed during six years in the batteries, it is not surprising that none had been built for the hospitals.

While Stössel harried those building bomb-proofs and created general annoyance by his extraordinary sallies and orders, things were elsewhere progressing. The work on Temple and Water-Supply Redoubts, which were destined, after Ta-ku-shan, to play so brilliant a part in the defence, and on which the waves of the August storm were to be broken, were pushed on. General Smirnoff, anticipating the course of operations, decided to fortify, as I have said, beside the main line of defences, the forts which at this time were almost ready—203 Metre Hill, the hills lying in front of Angle, Divisional, Long, and Orphan Hills. It must be remembered that at the time of his arrival in the Fortress there was only one advanced work; this was Temple Redoubt, with capacity for a company.

Much was done to improve this work, and after the destruction of Siushuing village, close by, and the construction of two lunettes, it really had some defensive value.

One interesting point was that Stössel and Fock insisted on the fortification of Angle Hill, which was of minor importance, in preference to strengthening 203 Metre Hill, which was of the greatest tactical value. This action was against Smirnoff's opinion, and necessitated the occupation of Pan-lun-shan and the forward slopes of Angle Hill. Work on these could only be useless, but, to avoid unpleasantness, General Smirnoff gave orders that they should be fortified, and he himself, together with Kondratenko, made a thorough examination of the ground, though no one realized better than he the waste of time, men, material, and guns, all of which were so urgently wanted in other parts. In the event Smirnoff's opinion proved correct. Angle Hill had to be abandoned, with its guns, on the first day of the August attack; but 203 Metre Hill held out for long, and it was only after its capture, on December 5, that the Japanese were first able to shell the harbour and shipping.

While we worked hard at the fortifications and swept the Roads for mines, everything went on quietly on the advanced positions now established along Green Hills. The enemy showed no activity, and did not disturb us with a single shot, but, like us, worked hard, getting troops into position and bringing up guns and ammunition to the front lines. Fock especially insisted on Upilazy Ridge being fortified, anticipating that the main attack would be against that flank, and, as he was complete master on that side and was supported by Stössel, he concentrated the greater part of the material, engineers, and sappers there. The right flank, to which he paid no attention, was left to itself. Heaven knows what would have happened on July 26 if Smirnoff had not discovered this in time, and, as already stated, sent Kondratenko there. From July 4 he, with the assistance of some engineer officers, began to get the position on Green Hills into some order; but General Fock was very displeased with his activity, and interfered wherever he could. Had Smirnoff and Kondratenko given way, the results of the fighting on July 26 would have been disastrous, and I am sure that such a rout would have taken place among our men that the enemy would have driven us right into Arthur. (The retirement on Fock's flank was almost a rout.)

In the middle of July Stössel inspected the advanced positions we were holding—at least, he visited the left flank, commanded by Fock. This was only natural, for the mere fact of Smirnoff and Kondratenko evincing interest on the right would have been enough to make him ignore it. I assisted at this visit, and was personally assured by Stössel that the attack would certainly fall on the left, while the enemy would merely demonstrate on the right. This inspection was indeed a farce, for all knew that, had Stössel given any orders, which he did not, they would not have been carried out.

We went along the Shininsky Ridge, and at 2 p.m. reached the howitzer battery. It consisted of two howitzers on wooden platforms. On one side was pitched a tent for the men, on the other one for the officer. The heat was unbearable, and not a breath of wind fanned the air. Kuen-san stood just above us, and with glasses we could see what was being done by the enemy. After a few words with his Chief of the Staff, Kondratenko came up to Stössel and, pointing out the desirability of delaying the enemy's work on that side, suggested that a few shells should occasionally be dropped on to them. Stössel agreed and gave the order accordingly; but no sooner had the men begun to load than the General came up, and rudely telling Kondratenko that he was in command there, persuaded Stössel to cancel the order. The incident was enlightening. We moved on, Stössel remarking on more than one occasion that bomb-proofs were necessary, and receiving the invariable reply that they were being made. None, however, were visible, nor had the fire trenches any sort of overhead cover.

Gradually we made our way homewards, back to the railway, and then by train to Port Arthur, to resume again our daily life, and to read the instructive orders in which Stössel gave us the benefit of his experience at the front!

CHAPTER XX

THE ATTACK ON GREEN HILLS

ON the morning of July 24 it was rumoured in the town that our best destroyer, the *Lieutenant Burakoff*, and another, the *Boevoy*, had been torpedoed during the night. The destruction of the former was particularly disheartening, as she had made several dashes to Yinchow and back, and been of the greatest service, and might have done much more for us still in the hands of her commander, Lieutenant Borodatoff, a most brilliant officer and the pride of the fleet, for she was the best and fastest of her type. The employment of destroyers for night duty was quite useless, and resulted in nothing except the fatigue of the men and the loss of the boats, for on foggy nights the enemy lay in wait for them.

Our patrols on the land-front used now to find proclamations lying about on the ground. These proclamations, written in bad Russian, were left by the Japanese outposts for our consumption, and were deliberate attempts to work on the *moral* of the men, by enumerating our defeats in Manchuria and reverting to political events in Russia.

On July 25 we on the staff of Colonel Semenoff, who was in command of the right section of the advanced defences, were visited by General Kondratenko. After tea conversation turned on the prospects for the following day. The General, with his elbows on the table, and stirring his tea with a spoon, smiled, and his small expressive eyes lit up. He looked at the speakers and said in his quiet way:

'The 26th is always a fatal date for us in Arthur. On May 26 we abandoned Kinchou; on June 26 we lost Kuensan; and apparently to-morrow will not be uninteresting. We mustn't forget that it is a great Japanese holiday—the "Chrysanthemum." They are sure to want to do something to please the Mikado.'

'Well, sir, what can be worse than having to remain on the defensive? We ought to attack; with the attacker lies the initiative. And you sit and wait, trying to guess when they will attack. It is an awful state of affairs,' said the keen, impulsive Semenoff.

'Yes; the rôle of the defender is none of the easiest or most advantageous—especially in conditions like ours. Many great errors have been committed, and there is heavy work ahead. To-morrow there will be a decisive and desperate battle, and we must hold our ground. By the way, Semenoff, have you given orders for the outposts to be strengthened, and warned all officers to expect an attack to-morrow?'

'Yes, sir.'

'The reserve will arrive to-night. The Commandant has consented to give us some companies from the reserve battalion, and they must bivouac here in the valley. To-morrow the general reserve will be under your orders. We have very few men, and so you must be particularly careful and economical with it. We must shell Kuensan well to-day: we don't yet know if the enemy's guns have got into position or not; but in any case it has a telephone and will be their chief observing station, and the battle will be directed from there. Perhaps they'll reply to our shells, and so unmask the position of their guns.'

When he left I accompanied him, while Semenoff, after conducting us to the Lunwantun Valley, went on to the outpost line. We finally arrived at the foot of Rocky Ridge, on which was the howitzer section. Kondratenko was evidently anxious, and was astounded on reaching this place to find that the howitzers had been run down below. 'Why is this? I sent orders that I would shell Kuen-san to-day. Who has altered them?' he asked angrily.

It seemed that Fock had had the howitzers run down. Kondratenko gave instructions for them to be brought back immediately; but while they were being dragged up the very steep ascent it began to get dark, and a cloud settled on the top of Kuen-san. By the time they had been got into position again half of the hill was in cloud, which concealed the enemy's works. It was now useless to attempt to fire. Kondratenko was furious, but did not show it in the presence of the various officers, and as it was now rapidly getting dark, we started to return. On the way back I for the first time saw him angry, and he used no measured language with regard to General Fock's interference. After giving his final instructions to Semenoff, he went back to Port Arthur. Semenoff then expressed his opinion that the idea of not holding on as long as possible to the advanced positions was absurd, though it was common.

He was quite right. For some time before the battle of July 26 I often heard the opinion expressed by officers that a dogged defence of the advanced positions would be detrimental to the ultimate defence of the Fortress. It seemed more and more as if the general inclination was to sit tight in the permanent works as being the easiest course. Having little knowledge as to the state of our bomb-proofs or of their durability, people drew a most rosy picture of the defence of the actual Fortress under a strict blockade. They thought that the bomb-proofs would save them. They compared the defence with that of Sevastopol, but unfortunately forgot that guns and shells are now somewhat different. They forgot that Sevastopol was in direct and unbroken communication with Russia, where the sick could be sent and whence reinforcements could come, and they forgot that, even under these favourable conditions, Sevastopol eventually fell into the enemy's hands. Port Arthur, completely isolated from the world, with a minimum reserve of provisions, ammunition, and men, and with incompleted works, was a trap for the army and fleet. People did not realize that the longer we held the enemy on the advanced positions, the longer time we should have to do in Arthur itself what we had left undone.

Next morning, just as a few men were moving about amongst the horse lines and the camp was beginning to wake up, a distant boom was heard in the direction of Oytselaza Hill. I looked at my watch: it was past half-past six. After a few moments we heard a second report, somewhat nearer, then a third and a fourth, each louder and nearer, and shells hurtled through the air and burst quite close to our tents. In a very short time the bivouacs had disappeared, for the majority of us had lain down without undressing, and the cannonade started all along the line. The day and the fight of the 26th had begun. The fire of the enemy's bigger guns, the shells of which were loaded with mélinite, was chiefly concentrated on the batteries under Prince Chkheydsey and Skridloff, and covered the tops of our hills with smoke, while the field and mountain guns kept up a hot shrapnel fire on the infantry trenches, preparing the way for an attack. Our own batteries, which were well concealed, replied steadily. At eight o'clock dense columns of Japanese were seen opposite the right wing of Green Hills, and, supported by the fire of their ships, they advanced in the direction of Big Ridge, just as speedily and in as orderly a manner as if at manœuvres. In front, all along the line of Green Hills, crackled incessant and rapidly increasing musketry fire. The infantry attack began. Thinking that our reserves were massed in Lunwantun Valley the enemy endeavoured to shell it and the approaches to it with shrapnel. By nine o'clock the fight grew hotter, and it rained hard. The fire of rifles and guns was at times so mingled that nothing except the rhythmic rat-tat-tat of the machine-guns could be picked out. From all directions down into the valley came orderlies to Colonel Semenoff, who was now at the mouth of the Litangon Valley.

'Ah! They have begun; they all want support at the same time. Look! there are men coming from the right as well as from the left.'

An orderly galloped up with a note; a second, a third, and then a fourth.

'They all ask for reinforcements. Surely, things are not as bad as all this. Here, Zagorovsky, you go off to the left; and Senkevitch, you go to the right. Go off as quickly as you can and find out what has happened.'

Kondratenko now arrived on the scene, and riding up to Semenoff, was, after a short consultation, soon acquainted with the position. Having given general instructions, he went on to the hill in front, into the zone of fire, in order to see for himself the state of affairs. It was now 10 a.m. Suddenly, in the distance, we noticed men in disorder running down from the right peak of Green Hills.

'What are they up to? Surely they are not retiring? Naumenko, do you see them?'

The latter looked through his glasses.

'Yes, sir; they are bolting down the slope of the hill as hard as they can.'

Kondratenko, without answering, put spurs to his horse, and we galloped along the valley; the General was in front, and in his white uniform on his black horse was very conspicuous. We could now clearly see a number of infantry-men against the background of the hill; they were running below in all directions. Kondratenko held up his hand.

'Halt, halt! where are you going to? Where's your officer? What's happened?'

And then up ran an officer, quite blown and scarcely able to speak. On his face were depicted terror and fatigue; he was red from running. His cap was all awry and his hand was shaking.

'Sir, it is awful there—awful. It is impossible to hold on. We have done everything—everything that it is possible, but it is a perfect hell.'

'Where were you?'

'There, sir, there,' he said, pointing.

Meanwhile the men were still bolting down, some helping the wounded, others going by themselves and the bullets were whistling thick over our heads. Big Ridge had been abandoned; High Hill, the extreme point on our right, was, owing to this premature retreat, cut off, but was held by Butusoff with two companies. A portion had been taken by the Japs; they might force their way through the line. The position was critical; in fact, the issue of the fight was in the balance, and the retirement must be stopped immediately. It was only the presence of mind of the General and his personal bravery which saved everything.

'What are you doing? Are you mad? Why, reinforcements are already on their way to help you. Company, follow me!' The men stopped and collected in a group. 'Follow me!'

The men quickly turned back, and those in rear called

out to those still further off to return, and they began to double back.

Having collected another company which had just come up, we led them, all puffing and blowing, up the hill. The enemy began firing on us. The General, standing at his full height, and half turning to the enemy, said:

'Men, it is better to die than disgrace yourselves by retreating. Remember that the Tsar and Russia rely upon us. There must be no retirement; we must all die if must be. And now God be with you—advance!'

The men extended, threw themselves down behind the rocks, and opened fire. Just then twenty or so men came dragging along our big clumsy machine-guns, and began to throw up cover for them. The companies who were extended advanced slowly and with great difficulty.

By midday the fight had somewhat abated, and the rattle of musketry was less frequent. The Japanese having seized Big Ridge and a point just opposite us, kept up a broken fire; High Hill was still almost cut off, but Butusoff was obstinately holding his ground with his two Frontier Guard companies. The presence under fire of the General of the Division, his striking coolness and pluck, inspired all with confidence, and improved the spirit of the troops, fatigued by long and constant outpost service. Sitting on one of the spurs behind the hill, sheltered from the bullets, the General was now quietly giving his orders, while Naumenko, on one knee, was writing them down.

'Tell Colonel Semenoff again that he must at once reinforce Butusoff.'

'Very good, sir,' and he wrote it down.

'Sir, Colonel Semenoff sends me to say that he has twice reinforced Colonel Butusoff: the reserves are almost expended,' said Zagorovsky, who had just come up.

'Thank you.'

'Zagorovsky, tell Semenoff to send a section of Petrenko's battery here immediately, at a quick trot. It will be an unpleasant surprise for the enemy on the ridge, and will relieve Butusoff.'

Before the General had finished his orders a mounted scout rode up from the right.

'Sir, Colonel Butusoff orders me to report that he is only holding his own with immense difficulty; the Japanese are climbing up in great strength and firing point-blank.'

'These Frontier Guardsmen are splendid fellows. I know that Butusoff would die rather than retire without orders. Ah, there's the officer commanding the section.'

Semenoff, slightly limping, came up.

'My reserves, sir, are practically finished; we must do a little shuffling, and take the troops from the points where the attack is not being pressed home.'

'Good; I think so too. How well those Frontier Guards are doing!'

'Yes, sir. Butusoff will never retire without orders.'

The guns now galloped along the valley and over the bridge.

'At last. Splendid! now everything will be all right. We will put the fear of God into them on that hill and relieve Butusoff.'

The guns were soon hauled up, and before a quarter of an hour had passed one shot rang out after another. 'Sir,' said the Chief of the Staff, 'you must get behind the hill; the enemy will be opening fire on this at once.' He was right, for in a minute or two shells began to whistle through the air, bursting high up and covering the hill with bullets.

'Things are all right here now; let's go and see what's being done on the left. I want to see General Fock.'

We went down into the valley, mounted our horses and

moved off. The road turned sharply to the right, and we came on to Naumoff's battery, which was covering the defile. The enemy's shells were falling all round it. Naumoff had beaten the enemy off during the whole morning, and they were determined, apparently, to destroy his battery; but they found it none too easy, as he had hidden the guns in a fold in the hill. Their shrapnel did not make the slightest impression, and their high explosive shells sang over into the Lunwantun Valley. At last we reached the village of Kodamin, where we found the General in a small Chinese house. The pomp surrounding him—for he had a staff of about fifteen officers and a whole section of orderlies—was a great contrast to the simplicity of the other.

After a frigid greeting and a few formal words Fock went away. We had some food, then rode on to the village of Khodziatun, where Kondratenko had been summoned to attend a Council of War under Stössel. The Generals sat down; Kondratenko stood, a smile on his lips. A quarter of an hour passed, and they were still sitting, and without sign of any conclusion having been reached; apparently Stössel and Fock were determined to get through what they had already decided to do. I looked on the picture with the greatest interest. At last there was a movement; they were going to disperse, and some of them seemed anything but pleased. Coldly saying good-bye, Stössel, with his numerous suite, moved off to the right towards Seven-mile Station, and by four o'clock we were back at the temporary head quarters of Colonel Semenoff. We found his staff very indignant.

'Our fleet is behaving disgracefully. We have very few guns, and if only our ships had opened a well-directed fire from the sea on the attacking columns, it would have helped us enormously; the Japanese would never take Green Hills.' And so the conversation went on.

As a matter of fact the gunboat division did make an effort to co-operate with the army. It steamed out towards Lunwantun, but was driven back by a superior force; our error lay in our not supporting the gunboats with the guns of our coast batteries. One Japanese cruiser struck a mine and had to be towed away, and one of their gunboats caught fire.

At five o'clock the Japanese gun-fire on Chkheydsey's and Skridloff's batteries became heavier, as did their rifle-fire, and as twilight came on endless columns advanced to the attack. Their gallant infantry came nearer and nearer, but were driven back with appalling losses. They got to within 600 to 800 yards, but were unable to get closer for a decisive assault. Besides our rifle and machine-gun fire from the ridge of Green Hills, the storming columns were under close-range gun-fire from the above-mentioned batteries, the fire of whose guns tore great lines through them, and strewed the valleys and slopes with dead bodies. At 7 p.m. a report came in that High Hill was once more in our possession, but that part of the position was still in the enemy's hands.

'We owe this to Butusoff. If he had retired in the morning we should not have been able to retake the hill. How well his men have behaved! We must relieve them. Send two companies from the reserve at once,' was Kondratenko's comment.

I was sure that the enemy would not repeat the attack that day. Having got to within 600 paces, they spent the night in entrenching and bringing up reserves, so as to be ready for a fresh effort in the morning.

CHAPTER XXI

THE BATTLE CONTINUES

At six o'clock on the 27th, as soon as the morning haze began to lift, the battle was renewed, and the artillery duel commenced. The enemy's fire was concentrated, as on the day before, principally on Prince Chkheydsey's and Skridloff's batteries, which suffered heavily. The morning was bright and sunny, and the light-green hill-slopes, tinted golden by the rays of the early sun, looked anything but a suitable background for the bloody events to come. Our infantry, sitting in their trenches, which, having no head-cover of any sort, were scarcely worthy of the name, awaited the commencement of the assault under a heavy shell-fire. After being directed on to the valley behind us, evidently to search out our reserves, the enemy's gun-fire slackened and rifle-fire commenced; their infantry advanced. But the nearer they came the more they suffered from our two batteries above-mentioned, and they were forced to lie down and entrench. Meanwhile, some of our ships had come out to assist us, but no sooner had they commenced to shell the enemy's lines than, as on the day before, a superior force of the enemy, appearing from behind Kepp Island, compelled them to withdraw to Port Arthur. One result was that the *Bayan* struck a mine, and was so seriously damaged that she had to be towed into the eastern basin for considerable repairs. At four in the afternoon the enemy's guns again got to work, and at 5 p.m. the fourth attack began. When the sun sank down below the hills, Green Hills still remained in our possession, High Hill and Semaphore Hill were lost; but the Japanese were nearer, and entrenched, ready for further efforts on the following day. So close were they in some places that we could hear their conversation. The day was ours, for we still held Green Hills; but how about the morrow? It was impossible to hold the seven miles length of the right flank with so few guns and men. Our reserves were reduced to one company of sailors and half a company of infantry, and Port Arthur sent no help.

A little later on the Japanese dashed forward and broke through the line—through the very place where Kondratenko had stopped the retirement yesterday. The last of the reserve was immediately sent up, and after some desperate fighting drove the enemy back. But now the reserve was used up, and what were we to do? Naumenko telephoned to Seven-mile Station to say that, to enable us to hold our position to-morrow, more troops must be sent to us; but the reply was vague and unsatisfactory. Through the night the enemy continued to seize and entrench advantageous points, while our men, utterly exhausted from the two days' battle and weakened by heavy losses, were in a bad way.

It seemed, under the circumstances, as if it would be impossible to hold on next day, and therefore best that the rear-guard action we should have to fight should be planned out at once and the successive positions selected. Kondratenko, who with Semenoff was moving about all night from one point to another, recognized this; but no definite reply could be got through the telephone, and he did not like to give orders for a retirement on his own account. At last, within a couple of hours of dawn, Kondratenko had to decide, and he decided that a withdrawal was the only thing to be done. Accordingly, orders were sent to Butusoff to retire, and the route to be followed was told him. These he received only just in time. I had gone to the staff to find out how soon the withdrawal would commence, and found Naúmenko still at the telephone, cursing at the impossibility of getting either orders or anything definite. Having other things to see after, he handed me the receiver, saying: 'Tell them we have begun to retire.' I rang and rang, and at last, after about ten minutes, got through:

'General Kondratenko directs me to ask you to tell General Fock that the withdrawal of the right flank has commenced.'

At four o'clock Kondratenko looked at his watch, and calculating that by now ordering the general retirement from Green Hills, Butusoff would have been given time to withdraw from High Hill and occupy a fresh position in rear, he decided to proceed. Just as he was giving the actual order to retire, a note was received from Fock: 'I am withdrawing; you can do as you like.' This masterpiece of military co-operation has been carefully preserved, and is now in Colonel Semenoff's possession.

Under cover of the morning haze, the first and the most difficult part of the retirement was carried out in perfect order and with inconsiderable loss, and our troops took up the new line from the village of Khodziatun to the seashore, along the heights running down into the Lunwantun Valley. The sun then came out and dissipated the mist. Instead of the panic on our part which the enemy expected, they ran up against our infantry holding new positions, and knew that our guns also would open on them from fresh points. During our abandonment of Green Hills they had got into difficulties on our left, for they had tumbled on to our mines. One caused immense loss, blowing a whole crowd of them to pieces, and this, with one or two smaller explosions, put such fear into them that we were able to get our machine-guns away at leisure.

The moment it was light the enemy shelled the positions which yesterday had been occupied by our batteries, but which were now empty. To discover our new gun positions was not so easy; for experience had now taught us how to take advantage of the ground and how to mask our artillery. At 7 a.m. the fresh companies, so urgently asked for during the night, began to arrive from Arthur to cover the further retirement. Bands were playing, and the enemy could not make out whether we were still retiring or were moving to the attack. With us everything was in perfect order; camp kitchens were smoking, and backwards and forwards along the road carts, rickshaws, and stretchers were moving. This was not what the enemy expected after a two-day battle; they thought Kinchou would be repeated.

The further retirement towards Arthur began punctually at 11 a.m., when, covered by a heavy gun and rifle fire, the companies gradually withdrew in perfect order. The enemy pressed our rear-guard hard, but could effect nothing, and by noon we were in sight of the forts. Some of the troops marched direct towards the fortress; others took up the last advanced position on the right flank on the hills of Ta-ku-shan to Sia-gu-shan. Behind Ta-ku-shan commenced the fortress rayon, and the position on it was the last advanced defensive point, and, in connexion with the positions on Wolf's Hills, was of great importance for the further defence of Arthur. Thus did the right flank, under Kondratenko, fight on the 26th and 27th, and retire on July 28. Let us see how General Fock's command—the left flank—fared during these days.

It was noticed on the evening of the 25th that the enemy, in considerable force, was moving across out of

Dalny towards this flank. Night passed quietly. Early next morning the Japanese began to press our outposts, which were forced in from the villages of Khumuchino and Khukhaia. The hills all round were enveloped in mist, and from the main position nothing was visible. By 5 a.m. it began to clear, and from Hill 113 it could be seen that the enemy was massing at the village of Sakaiza. Tents were struck and the trenches quickly manned, the cold morning air refreshing the men, tired out with continued outpost work. The mist lifted, and above the horizon of the Pacific Ocean appeared the copper-red segment of the rising sun. The enemy's artillery fire began to develop about 5.30 a.m., and the day's fighting commenced upon Hills 94 and 125, the former being seized by the enemy. We allowed them to mass there, and then swept them off again by our fire from Hill 125. At seven o'clock fifteen companies could be seen advancing in columns in the valley near the village of Khukhaia, close to Upilazy. They were moving towards Hill 125, and as soon as they came under fire they could be seen to extend in successive lines, one battalion remaining in reserve. Having extended, they steadily and quickly advanced to the attack in eleven lines. The distance between their firing-line and Hill 125 quickly decreased. Our men calmly watched them advancing.

'Don't fire without the order,' said the officer in command.

'Wait for the word of command,' repeated the section commanders.

'Twelve hundred!'

'Twelve hundred!' again echoed the section leaders.

The men were dying to fire, but waited quietly, though the shrapnel was screaming over them.

'Section, present—fire!'

'Section, present—fire!'

Volley followed volley, and the machine-guns vomited bullets. The enemy's firing-line could be seen to falter; then the second line melted into it. On they came. Our volleys rang out more frequently, but did not stop the advance; the third line melted into the remnants of the first two. Over our heads shots were screaming and on all sides wounded men were groaning; but the others paid no attention: they heard nothing but

'Section, present—fire!'

The Japanese were now close. As a line began to waver, it was reinforced and carried forward by the next in rear, and so it went on, fresh lines after lines appearing as if there was no end to them. Their firing-line now began to crawl up the hill from all sides. Volleys gave way to 'independent'—crack, crack, crack all round, and the deafening rat-tat-tat of the machine-gun. Now the range was point-blank, the crew of our machine-gun were all down—but—the enemy were repulsed. While they gathered down below for a fresh effort, their guns poured a hail of high-explosive shell on to our trenches, and did their work so well that our trenches were thick with wounded. Their infantry rallied, and again came on in swarms. At noon, though we had only 40 men left out of 150, our men gallantly held their ground. The foe crawled up on all sides; they showed up on the ridge, and dashed in with the bayonet. One of them, mad with fanaticism, got on to the top, shouting: 'How are you, Russkys?'

'Good-bye, Japanese,' was the answer given, as a bayonet was driven through his body, and he was hurled —a flabby mass—over the edge. But now the hill was surrounded on all sides, and it was impossible to hold out much longer. Burnevitch sent for reinforcements, and the men, expecting that they would come every moment, held out for another hour. Notwithstanding their numbers, the enemy could not gain the hill. At last an order was received from Colonel Savitsky 'to retire' on to Height 113. The withdrawal was effected, and then the men worked right through the night to make cover, having during the day learnt the value of good bomb-proofs —if they would not give protection from high-explosive shells, they would at least save them from the splinters.

As soon as it began to get light the outpost line, which had been thrown out the evening before round Hill 113, was called in, and, in expectation of a repetition of the previous day's artillery slaughter, the men were told to take cover in the bomb-proofs. Those destroyed by yesterday's fire had been repaired during the night, for it was recognised that this Hill 113 was the key to the Suantsegan position. At 5 a.m. on the 27th the first shot was fired by a Japanese battery in action behind Inchenzy Station, and the second day's battle had begun. Thinking that we had abandoned the hill, the enemy's infantry advanced to take it, but being hurled back by volleys at close range, they retired to a distance and their guns got to work, and so the bombardment continued till 1 p.m., their gunboats assisting.

The battle for possession of these hills was severe, and the coolness of our men was remarkable. If any of them ran away or if any panic set in, it was the fault of the officers, for any officer whom the men respect and love in peace-time can rely on their steadiness in war. How many Russian officers know and care for their men? For some reason or other they rarely mix among them and know nothing of them or their habits, and bitter are the fruits they reap in war.

In two hours not a vestige of trench remained. The bomb-proofs had kept out the field-gun shells, but were useless against the high explosive. At last an order was received that the little force on Hill 113 was to retire, and taking their dead and wounded, they made their way back under a heavy shrapnel fire. So it went on—the enemy pressing—gradual retirements by us from hill to hill. At night, when the fighting ceased, we were holding the line of Hills 139, 127 and Upilazy. Star after star came out and twinkled in the darkening sky, looking down on the awful shambles, while General Stössel, intoxicated with the 'success' of the two-day battle, congratulated everyone, ordered the bands to play and the troops to cheer, and himself left Seven-mile Station for Arthur to rest.

At a council of war in the evening it was decided to accept battle on the third day. But not a *single unit* was sent up to the front, the condition of the line on the right on which the real weight of the fighting had fallen was not ascertained. There was no co-ordination as regards command. Each acted independently—Fock on his own account, Kondratenko on his. The only cohesion was expressed in Stössel's categorical order 'to hold on.' That all the 'big wigs' expected us to hold on next day is clear from the fact that when Stössel left after supper that night for Arthur, he made his favourite Savitsky promise to come into Arthur next day to celebrate his 'name's day.' With the departure of the Officer Commanding the District, the staff rested on its laurels and did not worry about arranging for a retirement. The officers commanding independent units and sections of the line had no idea what to do in the event of the unexpected happening, and as our line was spread out for twelve miles in hill country, the unexpected was, to be paradoxical, to be expected. The troops themselves never dreamed that the morning would see a retirement: they were full of confidence and, forgiving him his mistake at Kinchou, still believed in Fock.

Their confidence was entirely misplaced, however, for though the General had agreed at the Council of War to continue fighting on the third day, he did not do so. He suddenly retired.

Kondratenko had been ordered to hold on to the right flank, which, had he been reinforced, he would have done. This sudden retreat of the left therefore might have left him entirely unsupported, and have resulted in the annihilation of his force which would have been taken in flank.

Daybreak came; the telephone rang, and orderlies rode up with the order to retire! This order and the suddenness with which it was delivered stunned the force on the left flank, who so little expected it. Confidence turned to fear, fear to disorder—so much so that the withdrawal turned into a panic-stricken rush to the rear, similar to the retreat to Nangalin.

How different from Kondratenko's orderly retirement!

All round for many miles was now a scene of complete disorder. Units, not having received any orders, retreated as each of their commanding officers thought best. It was a case of every one for himself; and to do full justice to the younger commanders and to the men, I should say that the fact that this retirement did not in all cases turn into a shameful and panic-stricken flight was largely due to them: that things were not worse was also greatly due to the indecision shown by the enemy. Had they energetically pursued, as they did on the right flank, individual commanding officers could not in the surrounding chaos have prevented a panic, and the troops, with Fock at their head, would have passed by Wolf's Hills and have appeared in Arthur that evening. Despite his extreme dislike for the Wolf's Hills position, the enemy's indecision compelled Fock to occupy it, but only temporarily.

When the force reached these hills and saw the trenches, they found a fresh surprise in store for them. They had been previously dug without any care, not on the slopes of the hills which it was necessary to hold, but at their foot: there was no communication between them, and the flat ground in front was densely covered with kiaoling the height of a man. As none of the crop had been cut, large numbers would be able to creep through it unseen, right up to our trenches, and hurling themselves upon us, might drive us out of them. Any retirement, also, would have to be made up the slopes and would be quite exposed. However, there was no time to dig elsewhere when the enemy's attack was expected at any moment. The men were more tired from the disorganization than from fighting or from privations, and on this particular evening the General's depressing influence on his division was more than ever noticeable. Officers and men looked with confidence only towards the Fortress and its forts; they felt that this chaos would end there. The Division knew that it was commanded by a man who was not equal to the task, and who would spoil everything.

By evening all the positions were occupied, and if the divisional staff had happened to mix amongst the bivouacs, and to hear what was being said in the trenches, they would have learned much to their advantage. The orders of the Officer Commanding the District for the night of July 28 were interesting, as showing his absolute ignorance of the situation.

Our troops, now occupying these trenches, such as they were, expected every moment to be attacked, and passed an anxious night. From the Japanese lines we heard nothing, for, true to their usual tactics, the enemy, having thrown out outposts, were resting in calmness and confidence. Their victory on our left flank had been quickly and easily obtained: their leaders were competent and trusted. Indeed, from the time of their landing in the peninsula things had gone without a hitch. At dawn on the 29th they commenced a forward movement. In front of us, taller than a man's height, grew the dense kiaoling: it was so high that it was only by the wavy movement of its surface that it was possible to tell if the enemy were there. All we could do was to fire volleys into it; but whenever we thought we must have done much damage—there was the movement again. In one place they got up so close that it was only by the great gallantry of our infantry that our guns escaped capture.

On July 29 we had the following order:

'Colonel Grigorenko and the officers under him will be good enough to arrange for the immediate construction of durable bomb-proofs on Wolf's Hills. Even though they work twenty-four hours in the day, this must be done, as it is vitally important.
'(Signed by order).
'REUSS, Colonel,
'Chief of the Staff.'

No head cover had been provided along the line of improvised trenches, and but few paths had been made on the slopes. The enemy were concentrating steadily, at any minute the artillery preparation might commence, and then the assault would follow. Everything pointed to an immediate attack, and yet here was our staff, in their usual short-sighted manner, writing of bomb-proofs—bomb-proofs whose construction required much labour and time. This order made many think that the authorities had decided to hold the positions for good [especially as a long line of two-wheeled carts left Arthur with wood, rails, and iron-sheeting], and the men set to work to carry it out, but they had no time. At 2 a.m. on the 30th the

Japanese, taking advantage of the natural cover afforded by the crops, attacked in force, and before it was properly light the assault was in full swing. The assaulting columns hid in the kiaoling, and our men in the trenches at the foot of the hills could see nothing but the sea of grain in front of them until the waving stalks parted and the enemy suddenly dashed out.

Blinded and shut in as they were, subject to heavy shrapnel and high-explosive shell-fire, and with an unseen enemy at close quarters, would it have been surprising if our men had fled in panic? Talking afterwards to prisoners, the Japanese officers said openly that if they themselves had been entrusted with the organization of the defence of these hills, and told to make it as easy as possible for the attackers, they could not have done it better than we Russians had done it for them. As soon as the assault began Colonel Laperoff poured a hot fire into the assaulting columns from his guns above, which caused the Japanese heavy losses, in spite of their invisibility. But they came on irresistibly, and by midday our retirement had begun. They forced in particular that portion of the line held by the 13th East Siberian Rifle Regiment. In the afternoon, when the assault was pressed with greater fury, our troops began to quit the position so hurriedly that the guns were left without infantry escort, and nearly fell into the enemy's hands. This all happened in sight of the permanent forts of Port Arthur. As Wolf's Hills were so close to the rayon of the Fortress, we might have been protected by its heavy guns, which could have shelled the enemy in front of this position and more or less have paralysed his advance by enfilade fire from the north-east front. But, thanks to the plan of retirement not having been communicated to Smirnoff, the batteries and forts of Port Arthur did not co-operate in the action.

Having seized Wolf's Hills, the enemy did not pursue further. This caution was quite comprehensible, as directly in rear of these were a number of exposed depressions, where they would have come under the fire of the Fortress guns.

With the loss of this position began the close investment of Port Arthur.

CHAPTER XXII

STÖSSEL HOIST BY HIS OWN PETARD

THE following order (No. 439) was published on the 29th by General Stössel:

'To-day the enemy attacked the position held by the 13th East Siberian Rifle Regiment and 4th Reserve Battalion in force, and crept up on to Wolf's Hills, but were hurled back by our guns. Nevertheless, it was impossible for us to hold the position longer, owing to the lack of frontal communications and the number of ravines, which made the enemy's advance easier, and another position has been taken up from Pan-lun-shan, through Temple and Water-Supply Redoubts.'

From this order it might be imagined that the enemy had been defeated, and that we had evacuated Wolf's Hills of our own accord, merely to occupy a new and more advantageous line. That we had retired, badly pressed by the enemy and in complete disorder, does not admit of the slightest doubt.

Had Stössel only conceived what was really in store for Port Arthur, instead of being so firmly convinced that speedy relief was coming from the north, he would by now have been with the 3rd Siberian Corps awaiting him up there. He had received a telegram from Kuropatkin, dated June 18, in which he was ordered immediately to hand over the command to Smirnoff, and to leave Port Arthur in a cruiser. Had he obeyed this order, it would have meant disgrace; on the other hand, if he stayed, even in defiance of orders, there was reason to suspect that one victory over the enemy would have reinstated him. He stayed. It was certain that some of the assaults before the relief would be repulsed, and for this he wished to obtain the credit; by that time Kuropatkin would arrive—a month earlier or later would not matter—and would relieve the besieged town. Once that happened, Stössel would be the saviour of Port Arthur. He would have succeeded in defending the Fortress, and no blame of his actions would get a hearing. Nothing succeeds like success.

On the 31st Stössel issued two interesting orders:

'The enemy is landing considerable numbers of troops from ten ships hidden in Louisa Bay, whence they are marching through the water to Pigeon Bay. Apparently they mean to attack the western front. From a letter found on a dead Japanese officer, it is evident that they intend, if possible, to take Port Arthur by August 10. I presume they will attempt an assault. I am convinced that the gallantry of the brave men under my command will repulse the enemy.'

In this order it will be noticed that a more humble tone was adopted. Stössel was convinced that the assault would be on the western front of Angle Hills and Liao-tieh-shan, and he set to work to build Fort No. 6, at enormous cost.

The second order (No. 441) read:

'Commanding Officers and Officers! we are now standing in front of the Fortress, on the last of the previously fortified advanced positions. . . .'

He and General Fock always thought that Angle Hill was not an advanced position of the Fortress, but was quite outside of it. With the original impracticable polygon of the Fortress—not in the least corresponding to the conditions of the ground—the fortification of Angle Hill, as a position of the enceinte, was a necessity. A glance at the map will at once show that 203 Metre Hill, and then Angle Hill, literally cry aloud to be fortified carefully and with permanent works. On the latter should have been a permanent fort, on the former fortifications of strong profile.

As a matter of fact, on Angle Hill we only succeeded in tracing out fortifications for a weak armament, while on to 203 Metre Hill a road was made, and materials and guns were taken up. It should be remembered that it was Velichko himself, one of the most noted military engineers in Russia, who drew out plans for the original polygon. To return to the order:

'... Remember what this means. It means that you must at all costs check the enemy, and not let him reach the forts of the Fortress. I have reason to believe that they will attack over the open in order to gain time, which for them, is all-important. The assault must be repulsed. It will fall on the advanced positions, and you, gentlemen, on these positions must not for a moment dream of letting them break through, though the assault be, as is probable, at night. You must remain at your posts alive or dead. You must hold the enemy till dawn; if they do not retire then the Fortress will finish them. Remember that you are glorious Russian soldiers.'

General Stössel was of opinion that his troops had not yet come within the confines of the Fortress, and were holding the last positions outside it. This order was, therefore, a District Order. As a matter of fact, with the loss of Wolf's Hills the investment of the Fortress proper had begun, and by the Regulations for the Guidance of Commanders of Fortresses the *Commandant of the Fortress* was now in supreme command. Accordingly, Stössel, having given up his district, and retired with his force within the enceinte of Port Arthur, should have been subordinate to the Commandant. The Commandant of the Fortress, Smirnoff, imagining that, from the moment the troops entered into the Fortress he was in sole command, issued an order on July 31, which, in conjunction with what General Stössel had written, gave the impression that we had two commanders in the one fortress. It was a bad omen. Stössel considered that he was still operating in the district; Smirnoff, considering that Angle Hill, Ta-ku-shan, and Sia-gu-shan were the advanced positions of the Fortress proper, assumed that the blockade had begun, and therefore that all the troops were subordinate to him. On reading the order issued by Stössel, Smirnoff protested, but not very forcibly. Why? Because he had not the smallest idea that a telegram (that of June 18) from the Commander-in-Chief had been hidden from him, or that Stössel had been ordered to leave Arthur and hand over the command to him.

Stössel was now in rather a quandary. He still hoped, of course, that Kuropatkin would listen to and grant his petition,* or at least give consent by silence; but at the same time he knew that, in the event of Kuropatkin's original order being confirmed, there was an end to his dream of glory, for he would have to leave Port Arthur in disgrace. If a grand attack, however, should occur while he retained command, and be repulsed, he would be saved. So, characteristically, he now after this protest began to 'hedge' and make friends with Smirnoff. He visited the latter, and said openly: 'Well, my duty is over now. It is for you to act, and I won't interfere with you in any way. The whole defence is absolutely in your hands.'

Smirnoff, in ignorance of the hidden telegram, had every reason to believe in Stössel's sincerity. It never,

* See p. 174.

of course, entered his head that the other was playing a waiting game. Every one was convinced that when the news of the rapid loss of the district which had been entrusted to Stössel reached the Commander-in-Chief and St. Petersburg, he would be shorn of all authority, and everything would be given into General Smirnoff's hands. Every one was also certain that, once the 'District' ceased to exist and its troops came into the Fortress, they came under the direct orders of the Commandant, and therefore Stössel, having neither district nor troops, had no power. Besides the simple logical issue, there was another and more material reason for supposing that Smirnoff, with the cessation of operations in the district, would assume complete control: this was based on an article in the military regulations, in which it is laid down that the Commandant of a besieged fortress must not subordinate himself to the Commander-in-Chief of the field army, but must act as he thinks best—as the person most conversant with the defence of the fortress. Unluckily in our particular case, thanks to the complicated circumstances, to this paragraph was added a rider— an Imperial order, which clearly defined that the Commandant of Port Arthur was subordinate to the Officer Commanding the District; but, of course, when this was written it was only intended to mean *before* the commencement of military operations. Stössel and his Chief of the Staff were unable to justify any part for themselves to play in the Fortress once the district had ceased to exist: they appeared in it as stars, and, as there was already a Commandant and a Staff existing, they did not know what to do. They well knew that they were not competent to conduct its defence. While waiting for the Commander-in-Chief's answer, they busied themselves with writing the most voluminous orders, which, if things went right for them, would be conclusive evidence of the minute care with which they had gone into every detail of the defence.

At last, with the close investment, the time had come when General Smirnoff could speak with the authority of the commandant of a besieged fortress; the moment had come when he should free himself for ever from Stössel's encroachment and attempts to usurp his authority, Though he knew nothing of the concealed telegram, yet, as the absolute master of the Fortress, being well aware of the work done by the 'band of heroes,' and therefore of the demoralizing and harmful influence exercised by the Generals in the defence, he ought to have stated categorically in Orders that, in accordance with the regulations, he had assumed sole command, and that any harmful interference in the sphere of his duties or authority, or any encroachment on them, would be tried according to military law in the field, and reported to the Commander-in-Chief. General Smirnoff did not do this. Notwithstanding his great strength of will and firmness, he was a true Slav. With all his brilliant qualities as a strategist, tactician, and administrator, he had not sufficient decision to run counter to an Imperial order—the order which had placed him subordinate to Stössel. Though he never lost his head in the most difficult crisis, and impressed every one by his coolness and presence of mind, yet he could not decide to take this all-important step — a step which would have spared Russia the shame of the premature capitulation. He let the present opportunity slip, and subsequent events, which unexpectedly developed, tied his hands. Later he was powerless to control Stössel; then the only thing left was to arrest him and Fock just before the surrender. He failed at the critical moment to play his cards properly, and for his lack of decision paid bitterly.

And so Wolf's Hills had passed into the possession of

the enemy. With glasses numbers of them could be seen constructing batteries. Ta-ku-shan and Sia-gu-shan could not long hold out, being liable to be shelled from front and flank from Wolf's Hills. The operations on the advanced positions were over, and the enemy had reached the forts.

CHAPTER XXIII

THE LOSS OF TA-KU-SHAN HILL

AND so the strict blockade of the Fortress, which we had dreaded, had now commenced in grim reality. No sooner had we abandoned Wolf's Hills than the civil population, who felt sure that the fall of the Fortress itself could not now be long postponed, were seized with fresh panic. They had lost confidence in our power of resistance, and those who could afford it, at once took steps to charter Chinese junks for their conveyance to Chifu. The District Staff, being incapable of dealing with the situation, said, in reply to all inquiries, that they had nothing to do with the civil population, who should go to the Commandant. Every one, accordingly, hurried to the Fortress Staff Office, where those who had the right to go away were at once given permission to leave, and we, accordingly, soon saw a long line of carriages stretching along the road to Pigeon Bay. The majority of these, however, returned after a few days, as the Japanese would allow no junks to leave. A few did succeed in evading the enemy's guard-ships and got away to sea; the others were stopped and had to make for land.

Meanwhile there was no news from the north.

On August 4 we had the usual church parade and march past, and the usual martial speech to the troops from General Stössel. The sun was shining, and to see this collection of gaily-dressed ladies and glittering uniforms, one would not have said that an enemy was crouching below the hills within view of the heedless crowd. Its indifference was curious. Was it submission to fate, trust in luck, or stupidity?

The first bombardment from the land side began suddenly on August 7. It was a glorious day, and the churches were filled with crowds attending a service to pray for the safety of Port Arthur, when the booming of guns and shriek of shells commenced. Alarm was at once visible among the kneeling congregation, who got up, then again knelt down. The priest in a trembling voice brought the service to an abrupt end, and every one dispersed in search of safety. The bombardment continued all day, though doing little material damage.

Next morning, from 2 to 5 a.m., we heard heavy musketry fire from the direction of Ta-ku-shan: the enemy, leaving the town and the main defences in peace, were turning their attention to it. This hill corresponded in the east to 203 Metre Hill in the west, and was equally important and equally unfortified. It and Sia-gu-shan, the natural forts of Arthur on the eastern front, had a bad time. In the first place, they had not been made the most of, for in the original plan of defence of Port Arthur they had not been thought to be important points, and so had been neither fortified nor armed as their position with regard to the Fortress warranted, and Smirnoff had only recently succeeded in arming them to a small extent. In the second place, they became, after the abandonment of Wolf's Hills, open to flanking fire, and therefore untenable. The companies of the 13th East Siberian Rifle Regiment sent there went literally to their death, but, together with the gunners, they held on as long as possible. As Ta-ku-shan was not a fort or even a semi-permanent work, but only an artillery position, without casemates or splinter-proofs in which the defenders could get protection during the artillery preparation, it can be easily imagined what the place was like when the enemy turned on to it the fire of both big and small guns. At eight in the evening the last small force on the right flank retired behind the main line of works after a desperate fight. The Japanese attacked fiercely in dense masses, and also pounded the whole of the eastern front, as well as some of the shore batteries. When they at length did succeed in getting possession of Ta-ku-shan and Sia-gu-shan, after heavy loss, we in our turn concentrated such a heavy gun-fire on those hills that they were unable to effect their object of building batteries.

Later in the evening I climbed up on to Golden Hill Battery to see what was to be seen. During supper a telephone message was received instructing us to open fire at once on Ta-ku-shan, firing at intervals of five minutes. Captain Zeitz, who was in command, immediately set to work at the chart and got out the range. Above, men began moving about the guns, while we remained below, sitting in the concrete casemate, which, in spite of its solidity, had been penetrated by a 12-inch shell during the sea bombardment. When after five minutes the battery opened fire with its 11-inch monsters the lamps in the casemate were at once extinguished, and several of the table utensils were smashed by the blast through the open hatch. Hatches and doors were then shut, but to little purpose, for almost every discharge put out the lights and the noise was deafening. I went up on to the battery, and found it quite dark, though the howitzers, their muzzles cocked up, showed clearly against the white masonry. The howitzer crews were moving about with lanterns.

'Number 1!' A streak of flame, a stunning roar, and away sped the steel messenger with its ever-lessening scream up into the air.

Down below in the casemate the telephone rang.

'Short, sir. Please shell the slopes *towards* the enemy,' was the message.

'Number 2!' Again the roar and shock.

One could scarcely distinguish the shots being fired from the neighbouring sea batteries. Uncle Moshinsky had opened fire, and, further off, Cape Flat and Cross Hill also; in fact, the whole front was rumbling with noise.

'Sir, that shell fell on the saddle of Ta-ku-shan. You are requested to shell the slopes *towards the enemy*,' again came on the telephone. Captain Zeitz ran down below into the casemate. After consulting the outspread map, he dashed up again and altered the sighting.

'Number 3!' Every five minutes a shot boomed out.

Going to the edge of the glacis, I looked over the steep precipice dropping down to the water. On the sea everything was quiet; the horizon was clear, and nothing was to be seen on the watery expanse lit up by the searchlights. Turning round, I saw the smooth edge of the hill; at an equal distance one from another, the four evil-looking mouths of the howitzers. Two minutes had passed since the last shot; everything in the battery was quiet and dark, and I was alone on the glacis. Down below stretched the town, buried in darkness, with no sign of light or life in street or house; it might have been a city of the dead. Suddenly the battery was lighted up as if it were day: a pillar of flame flashed from the mouth of one of the howitzers, and the blast swept up the pebbles from the ground and hurled them over the cliff.

I went back into the casemate, and found it hot and stuffy. The majority of officers were lying down, as was every one in the battery above, with the exception of Zeitz; but it was impossible to sleep, because of the deafening noise of each shot. I sat down to the table close to a lamp and began to read over my daily 'News' for the *Novy Kry*. The telephone rang, and orders came that we were to cease fire for half an hour. In the distance shots became fewer and fewer, and in the battery noise gave place to silence. For three hours incessantly the whole of the shore front from Golden Hill had bellowed at Ta-ku-shan.

Next day I was permitted to accompany General Smirnoff upon his inspection, and had the good luck to witness our attempt to recapture Ta-ku-shan. Before giving me permission to accompany him, however, he warned me that by being with him I should probably earn Stössel's ill-will. We first visited A Battery, where the garrison was taking cover from the enemy's rifle fire, and whence we could see the Japs moving about on the hill. Having given his instructions here, the General rode on, and we descended along the road leading from the Fortress into Dalny, where we found ourselves exposed to Ta-ku-shan, and bullets whistled overhead one after another. Smirnoff began to go slower, as if on purpose. Passing through the deep ravine towards B Battery, we saw a group of officers in the distance, amongst whom was General Gorbatovsky. On reaching the battery General Smirnoff gave orders for all the guns on the eastern front to open fire immediately, and for the companies which had been told off to advance and attack Ta-ku-shan. On the hill itself nothing was now visible; the Japanese had hidden. Our batteries were covering it with shrapnel and common shell, which we could see bursting on the slopes.

'Colonel Tokhateloff, order the batteries to shell the top of the hill and behind it: there is certain to be a number of the enemy there. What is the good of firing on the near slope?' said Smirnoff.

The Colonel dashed down into the casemate. He tried

to telephone to the further batteries, but could not manage it, as the central exchange would not answer.

'Put me on to A Battery! A Battery! I say, are you all mad? A Battery! A! A! A!'

At last the exchange replied, but time was flying, and the shells, instead of bursting on the top of the position, were still falling on the near slopes. At last those from A Battery began to reach the saddle of the hill.

'Ah! that's right; but only one battery has got the range. Pass the word to the others at once. What are they looking at?' said Smirnoff, getting angry.

Tokhateloff was beside himself; he shouted from the top to the nearest battery, and gave orders to transmit by semaphore. At last they all concentrated their fire on the top of the hill.

It was here and now that I for the first time realized practically the splendid inefficiency of our Fortress telephone system. Owing to its construction, the officer commanding a section of the Fortress artillery not only was unable to issue simultaneous orders to all the batteries under him, but could not even get through quickly to any one of them. In the central exchange they well knew that the Commandant himself was in B Battery on this occasion, and was personally directing the fire. And if it was not even possible for him to issue urgent orders in such a case, what must have happened when a mere section commander wanted to transmit an important order to one of the batteries under him? In some cases messengers actually went and returned before the stations were connected through.

The sun was fairly high when our infantry firing-line got near to the foot of the hill. Our artillery fire had intensified to prepare their way, and the hill-top was hidden by bursting shell. The moment for the assault was at hand, and we all nervously watched the attacking columns. By midday they had begun to ascend the hill, and were with difficulty climbing up the spurs under a burning sun.

'Colonel Tokhateloff, tell the guns to cease fire,' said Smirnoff. Again the Colonel dashed down to carry out the order, a by no means easy task for a corpulent person like himself, and after a long time at the telephone, and much semaphoring, the fire gradually began to stop.

The interesting phase of the attack had begun, and in the battery and far beyond, to left and to right, there was the silence of expectation—the attention of the whole front was directed on the hill, of which our infantry had now seized half. We could see them crawling up higher and higher. Suddenly, from a ravine on the left slope of the hill appeared a column of the enemy, which quickly moved against the flank of our infantry, who, not seeing them, continued to press upwards.

'Sir, sir,' shouted every one, 'look! there are the Japanese!'

'Open fire with shrapnel,' commanded Smirnoff. We watched the Japanese intently, and could clearly see them climbing up, with an officer in front waving a sword.

'Open fire, open fire quickly; a good shot would mow them down,' said Smirnoff angrily.

Captain Vakhneieff tried to get the range.

'No. 1!' It was short.

'No. 2!'

'No. 3!'

Still they dashed forward, though some were seen to fall.

'Why are the other batteries silent? Pass the word to the other batteries,' shouted Gorbatovsky.

Behind us Zaliterny Battery, high up on the hill, opened fire, as did one other battery on the left. But further to the left and on the right there was silence; either these batteries did not see the enemy, or they were asleep. Colonel Tokhateloff, despairing of transmitting the necessary order by telephone, ran out to the gorge of the battery and shouted as loudly as he could and semaphored to them:

'Fire on the column—on the C-O-L-U-M-N—F-I-R-E!'

The fire gradually increased, and shrapnel after shrapnel tore after the Japanese, but it was late; they had got cover behind an outlying spur. Our men were still climbing up—on and on—they would soon be near the top! But they never reached it, for the enemy were too cunning. The moment the attackers became exposed, a ring of musketry fire burst out from the summit. Some of our men fell back, retreating right away down the hill; others could be seen to halt, take cover behind the rocks and folds of the ground, and to crawl along the hollows. More men came up from behind, but it was no good; they stopped gradually, and crawled downwards one by one. The attempt had failed.

The attack of this huge hill could never have succeeded by daylight, nor should it have been undertaken with so few men. To take it, a much larger force—at least one regiment—should have been sent; but although advised of this, General Stössel would have his way. He considered that he knew best, and he alone was responsible for the failure.

Evening came on, and, according to the intelligence reports of the Chinese, there seemed every reason to believe that the Japanese would make a general attack that night. This information was common knowledge, and no one looked forward to the coming of night; we expected an assault, but knew not where the chief blow would fall. However, Chinese information was always most inaccurate and confused, and did not justify the reliance we placed in it.

The morning after this fight the Japanese did a thing

which surprised us: they fired on a small party of our stretcher-bearers which had gone out to pick up a wounded man who had lain all night on the slope of the hill, and succeeded in again wounding him and also one of the bearers—an action as disgusting as it was incomprehensible.

The bombardment of Arthur by land was now systematic, lasting generally from 7 a.m. till 11 or 12 noon, and then again from 2 or 3 p.m. to 6 or 7 p.m. The shooting was apparently carried out by 'squares,' as all shells fired at the same time, fell into a comparatively small space. They did their best to destroy the fleet, the port, and the harbour workshops, and their shooting was so good that after two or three 'overs' and 'shorts' they were able to get on.

And now a word as to the press censorship in the Fortress. From August 9 right up to September 8 the *Novy Kry* printed my notes, under the heading 'News of the *Novy Kry*.' These notes were based entirely on personal observations or on information received by me in the Fortress Staff Office. By the direction of the Commandant and with the knowledge of Stössel and Reuss, the following procedure was observed.* Every day, after going round the line of defences, I went to the Fortress Staff Office, where I was given all the telephone messages of the preceding twenty-four hours up to twelve noon that day. I busied myself with this budget in the office of the Chief of the Staff, in his presence, and under the supervision of Lieutenants Kniazeff or Hammer.

When my account was ready I handed it to Colonel Khvostoff for him to see, and everything that I said relating to the operations of the fleet was given to Lieutenant Mackalinsky of the Navy, attached to the Fortress Staff, to

---

* General Stössel was always very well informed of everything that happened in the Fortress Staff Office.

look through. These two then deleted such parts of it as, in their opinion, ought not to be published, and at once returned it to me with permission to send to press. I then despatched it by my orderly to Colonel Artemieff in the Editor's Office, who in his turn cut out such parts as seemed to him suspicious—*i.e.*, parts to which objection might be taken by the censors. After he had done this—it always had to be done by him personally—the manuscript was sent to be set up. Two corrected proofs were sent, one to General Stössel's Office and one to the Naval Office, to be censored. The proofs, when signed by the censors, were returned to the printing-offices, where they were checked by the assistant editor, and sent by him to the type-room to be amended. Thence a revised proof was sent to the editor for checking with the censors' original remarks. It was only after very careful checking of this revised proof with the original that Colonel Artemieff permitted it to be printed.

See what an amount of correction and checking my 'News' was subjected to before it reached the reader. However, notwithstanding all this absurd severity—the almost impossible requirements of two censors, naval and military—General Stössel deemed it so dangerous that he stopped the publication of the *Novy Kry* for one month!

CHAPTER XXIV

THE SORTIE OF THE FLEET ON AUGUST 10

FOR some time previous to the sortie of the fleet on August 10, Admiral Witgeft used to assemble conferences of the Admirals and Captains, at which the question of the fleet breaking through to Vladivostock was thoroughly discussed. The majority were in favour of the fleet putting out to sea. Some urged that we should engage the enemy's fleet, and at the same time operate by making a demonstration towards Dalny as the nearest of the enemy's naval bases. Others thought it more opportune to go out on to the line between Korea and Shantung, where, after a battle, the enemy's communications between Japan and his army might be interrupted. This plan had the advantage that those of our ships which were injured could return to Arthur for repairs. At a Council of War held on July 18 with regard to this question the majority had been opposed to a sortie, their chief arguments being that (1) the fleet would have to take away with it those of its guns which were being used on the land front, and this would reduce the power of the land defence by nearly 30 per cent.; (2) its departure would have a bad effect on the *moral* of the garrison; (3) most of our destroyers were unfit for a long voyage. Three weeks later, at a Council held on August 7, when it was evident that the enemy, by bombarding the harbour, could cause

REAR-ADMIRAL GRIGOROVITCH.

To face page 151.

great damage to the ships, not only above the water-line, but below it, as in the case of the *Retvisan*, several of those who hitherto had been opposed to the plan of making for Vladivostock altered their opinion.

The day before the fleet's departure Rear-Admiral Grigorovitch proposed to Admiral Witgeft, at first verbally, and afterwards on paper, that to force its way successfully to Vladivostock the fleet ought to be composed only of the fastest ships, and the slow ones—the *Poltava* and the *Sevastopol*—should be left in Arthur to strengthen the shore defences. Rear-Admiral Loschinsky supported this proposal; but he developed the idea by suggesting that when the squadron moved out of Arthur towards Shantung he, with the two battleships, four gunboats, and ten destroyers, should make a demonstration towards Dalny. If the larger part of the Japanese force followed the departing squadron, then his force would be able to bombard Dalny, the naval and principal supply base of the Japanese army. If by some mistake, or owing to other circumstances, the enemy's main force attacked him, then, taking advantage of the mine defences and supported by the coast batteries, he would be able to engage the enemy's force, although superior both in numbers and strength, for a considerable time. Unfortunately, Witgeft did not agree.

'My orders are to go to Vladivostock with the whole squadron, and this I shall do.'

If he had agreed to Grigorovitch's proposal, Togo would not have had a balance of advantage, and his force, being split up by reason of the demonstration at Dalny, would have been weaker than ours. Our squadron would have successfully broken through to Vladivostock without serious injury, and Dalny would have been destroyed by Admiral Loschinsky. If only we had not let slip the excellent opportunities we had had for sinking the enemy's ships, their force would have been considerably weaker than ours.

As the time approached for the squadron's departure, the Admiral and most of the officers were depressed, for the approaching voyage promised little good. They all realized that the squadron was going to sea short of guns (most of those put ashore were left there), and of very much else; they knew that our shells did little destruction, sometimes not even bursting, whilst those, even the 4·7-inch shells, of the enemy caused great havoc, and that, having superior speed, the enemy would have the initiative.

The Admiral was wounded by a splinter of shell bursting on the *Cesarevitch* the day before the sortie, and, as if foreseeing his near end, his last words to those on shore were: 'Gentlemen, we shall meet in the next world.'

At daybreak on the 10th the fleet steamed out into the outer Roads, and, forming into single-column line ahead, steered for Liao-tieh-shan. The hospital ship *Mongolia* left exactly at eight o'clock, and overtook the fleet at 8.30. Some Japanese destroyers showing themselves in the direction of Dalny, the *Novik* was sent towards them, and having rapidly driven them away, the whole fleet started at nearly full speed—a formidable array of yellow-brown vessels, brought up in rear by the *Mongolia,* glistening white, with the red cross on her funnels.

As the Commandant, from the top of Electric Cliff, watched it steam out, he said:

'May God grant it luck! If only it can vanquish the foe and gain possession of the sea, the Fortress will be saved. But evil will be the day if it is defeated and does not return. How many men, guns and shells has it not taken with it, all of which we badly want!'

* * * * *

Port Arthur's weary day of strained suspense came to an end; the night passed and morning dawned. The signal station at Liao-tieh-shan reported that our squadron was approaching. It did return; but heavens! in what a plight! By the afternoon it was drawn up in the inner roads, less four ships, the *Cesarevitch, Askold, Novik,* and *Diana,* which had not returned, and about whose fate no one knew. Admiral Witgeft had been killed. What had happened at sea has been described by others, and I will spare the reader the details of this sad engagement.

Thus weakened by the loss of one of our best battleships and three of our fastest cruisers, the rôle of the fleet might be said to have come to an end, for the sea was held by an enemy powerful in numbers as well as quality, and till the coming of the Baltic fleet our squadron would not be able to engage them in battle. All it could now do was to give us men, guns and ammunition for the land defence. Why the Pacific Ocean fleet, consisting of the best ships in the navy, had done nothing during a seven months' campaign, and why in the end it had been forced to abandon all idea of an active rôle and its chief *raison d'être*—to get command of the sea and interrupt the Japanese sea communications — are questions which demand an answer.

'Who was to blame?' There is but one answer.

The very essential and fundamental reforms in the navy, which had been pointed out as necessary years ago by the better and more enlightened officers, should have been introduced, and the prehistoric naval customs of the time of Peter the Great should have been consigned to oblivion. To blame the individual for this is impossible: it was the system that was at fault, as well as that official class which, like a thousand-headed hydra, sucks and nibbles at the really healthy organism of Russia. British and German officers will not believe my assertion that everything on Russian ships was neglected save the personnel, which was fairly well looked after materially and moderately well trained. The education of the higher ranks in staff duties, as well as their training in shooting, torpedo and other work, was so neglected that the majority of officers had but the vaguest notion of the practical application of theory. In most cases, owing to their constant transfer from one to another, they did not know even their ships. For three-quarters of the year these were in harbour and hardly any cruising was done, while the officers were made to work so little that at the commencement of the war they did not even know the shores of the Kwantun Peninsula.

The return of the squadron with its mutilated hulls, battered funnels and masts, had a bad effect, and on all sides was heard, 'The end will now soon come!'

CHAPTER XXV

OUR SECOND ATTACK ON TA-KU-SHAN—A FLAG OF TRUCE

THE daily land bombardment of the town and port made every one extremely jumpy; for after our fleet's return it seemed likely that the Japanese would again bombard us from the sea, and then our position would not be enviable. There is nothing worse than uncertainty, and it was horrible work wait, wait, waiting, for decisive events, not knowing how, when, or where they would happen.

On August 11 I again accompanied Smirnoff—who was much depressed by the events of the previous day—on his tour of the defences, and witnessed from B battery our second attempt to recapture Ta-ku-shan and Sia-gu-shan. As before, far too small a number of men were told off for this attack, and, to make matters worse, by the time they had reached the foot of the hill they took the wrong direction. Smirnoff watched the failure of this second attack in silence, but his brow was black, for it was indeed a comedy that was being enacted before us. Was it wise to attack such high, precipitous hills with the fewest possible men, when the veriest tyro in military science knew that hills of such importance to us would be held to the last by the enemy? While this foolery went on the Japanese steadily pounded the town and port.

At daybreak on the 12th the bombardment of Angle Hill and a gradual advance of the enemy towards it commenced. Smirnoff placed Kondratenko in command of the western front, while Fock was appointed to command the general reserve. He himself, being convinced that the Japanese, forcing the points on Angle Hill, would sooner or later deliver their main assault on the salient angle of the north-east front, turned all his attention to it and to 203 Metre Hill on the west. Meanwhile, General Stössel seemed to be chiefly impressed with the importance of not tiring the men. His anxiety on this account was evinced by his order of August 12:

'A tired soldier is always sleepy and dull. Men are not to be employed on fatigue for more than five hours in the twenty-four.'

At this time the enemy were putting the last touches to the iron ring which was being welded round the Fortress, and their batteries were daily growing, while our defences were far from ready. If our men were compelled to work hard, it was necessary. They dug, dug, dug without end in the stony soil, but they did it that they might the more easily be able to repulse the assaults, and that they might get protection from the rain of iron and steel which during the five long months was to be showered on them with such wonderful generosity. This was no time to think of resting: every moment was precious. The men realized it, and delved ceaselessly, willingly, knowing that the deeper the trenches, the better it would be for them. But General Stössel's order had the evil effect on their spirit that might have been expected; for, after it, when men were urgently wanted for working-parties, their commanding officers took advantage of it to protest direct to Stössel that they were being overworked.

General Smirnoff was much dissatisfied at this period with the fortification and work on 203 Metre Hill. This hill, which was destined to play such a fateful rôle in the defence of Arthur, was in the salient angle of the western front, and its top, commanding the surrounding heights, overlooked the Fortress, the inner harbour, port, town outer Roads, and the distant sea; yet it was armed only with four 6-inch guns. There were no masonry casements or earth bomb-proofs, and protection against the fire of 6-inch and 11-inch guns was given by sandbags, stones, earth, and dry cement. The guns had been mounted at the beginning of the campaign, and no strong batteries to protect the garrison from the effect of 11-inch shells had been made; now only one thing could be done—that was to dig caves into the hill.

About midday on the 13th a balloon soared up above Wolf's Hills, and our nearest batteries at once opened fire on it with shrapnel. Whether we made a hit or not it was impossible to say; but after being about half an hour in the air it descended quickly. Chinese spies stated that officers of the Japanese General Staff were making a reconnaissance in it, and had taken some photographs of the Fortress, for General Nogi was surprised at meeting with opposition at so many points which had not been fortified before the war, and which were not shown so in the plans in his possession. The works which checked him, after Smirnoff had been five months in the place, were very probably a considerable surprise.

We had no balloons in the Fortress, nor had we pigeons or wireless telegraphy! No station was rigged up there, and therefore communications were not established.

On the night of August 13 the Japanese attacked Orphan Hill, but were driven back.

As I went round the defences almost every day, I marvelled to see the healthy, happy look of the men, who all looked as if the work agreed with them. Since the beginning of the strict blockade the officers had ceased to drink as much as they did—that is to say, in the main positions, where I never saw any debauchery. On the advanced positions, on the contrary, drinking had been carried on abnormally. Stössel and Fock had deprived the men of their vodka, but the officers were drunk day and night, which, besides being bad for their own health, had a demoralizing effect on the men. Their behaviour may be explained, perhaps, by the fact that they had so poor an example set them by two of their superiors who never had any influence for good. They hated one of the Generals, who abused them on parade and played the buffoon with their men (he was known as the 'Mad Mullah'), and they feared the others. When the strict investment began, and the infantry officers mixed and lived with those of the artillery, who were on a higher plane as regards education and intelligence, all this changed. As soon as the 4th Division entered the Fortress and Fock was appointed to command the Reserve, a great change was also noticeable in that Division.

On August 14 an artillery duel was waged all day. At night and in the early hours of the following morning the Japanese began to concentrate against our left towards Angle Hill, which they attacked at 3 a.m. In spite of being repulsed, they at dawn made a second attack, which met the same fate and caused them heavy loss. After the failure of this second attempt their guns opened fire with shrapnel all along our line, and under cover of it the infantry, with desperate rushes, tried to get close to our positions, evidently with a view to a general assault.

On the night of the 15th-16th desultory firing went on all along the line. On the morning of the 16th a Japanese officer came in with a flag of truce. He bore a letter from Baron Nogi, which ran approximately as follows:

'The Russians have given signal proof of their gallantry, but Arthur will be taken all the same. Therefore, to avoid useless loss of life and any possible violence, murder or looting by Japanese troops fighting their way into the town, which it will be difficult at once to prevent, His Highness the Emperor of Japan suggests a discussion of negotiations for the surrender of the Fortress.'

A Council of War was at once summoned, at which Stössel suggested that no answer should be given, as the proposal that the Fortress should capitulate was a piece of insolence. Smirnoff expostulated, explaining that the elementary rules of military etiquette required that a reply should be sent. Stössel then said:

'Well, if an answer must go, let us send a blank piece of paper or else merely write a joke on it.'

Smirnoff insisted that an answer, and a polite one, should be sent, and he drafted one which was eventually signed by both Stössel and himself:

'The honour and dignity of Russia do not allow of overtures of any sort being made for a surrender.'

The morning of the 17th was very unpleasant, with fog, sleet, and mud. The town was already being bombarded, and the shells could be heard bursting in the harbour. With General Smirnoff's permission, I accompanied the flag-of-truce party taking out the reply: it consisted of Captain Golovan, an officer of the General Staff, and Lieutenant Mackalinsky, of the Fortress Staff. As we went out the passers-by gazed at us with curiosity and wonder, many of them thinking probably this was the end of Arthur. At last we reached the fortifications near the cemetery; on this being reported to the Commandant, he at once ordered the guns to cease fire: so that exactly at nine o'clock we were able to move on. I was told to ride in front with the flag, with one of the mounted scouts, the rest of the party and escort following a short distance behind. We passed our firing-line and piquets and went on some distance, but seeing nothing of the Japanese, I began to get suspicious, for I could not forget how they had fired on our Red Cross at Green Hills; perhaps they were now lying in the kiaoling on either side of us ready to pour in a volley. It was jumpy work.

'Sir, sir, there they are!' whispered the man riding beside me. I looked ahead, but could see nothing. At last, however, I noticed four Japanese dressed in khaki behind a sharp bend in the road on a small pass. They were difficult to distinguish from their surroundings, while we, in our uniform, were very conspicuous. Having approached to within fifty yards, we heard in Russian—

'Halt!'

We stopped.

'Advance one!'

We stood as still as statues, and a man, evidently a non-commissioned officer, came up.

'What do you want?'

We answered.

'All right.' He gave some order to one of the men, who quickly moved off.

We stood and looked at one another. The non-commissioned officer, a broad-shouldered, thick-set man, took out a note-book and, with great coolness, wrote something in it. After ten minutes, an interpreter, with a truculent-looking Captain, and a young Lieutenant, came up. At last Major Yamoaka, who had brought the Japanese message, arrived, accompanied by a mounted orderly with a flag and the Corps interpreter, who, in spite of his high rank, spoke Russian most atrociously. After we had presented our credentials, he took and gave us a receipt for our letter, and in his turn handed us one, for which we gave him a receipt. The interpreter informed us that 'this was a very,

very important letter.'* When the ceremony of handing over the letters was finished, a shell whistled past towards Ta-ku-shan. Major Yamoaka anxiously asked:

'They are surely not firing?'

To which Lieutenant Mackalinsky quietly answered:

'No, it is probably at sea.'

Later it turned out that the enemy's infantry could be seen to be on the move from one of the batteries, and the non-commissioned officer on duty, unable to restrain himself, had fired at them—a mistake he had to pay for.

Having received the letter, Major Yamoaka arranged the time and place of meeting for further negotiations. We well knew that further negotiations would not take place, but of course made some pleasant reply. We bowed and parted, and as soon as we reached the fortifications on Cemetery Hill and lowered our flag the guns boomed out again along the whole line. Once inside the line a Cossack met us and told me that Stössel wanted to see me. The General had watched us from Jagged Hill. Mackalinsky proceeded to report to the Commandant, and we, with Golovan, going on to General Stössel, found him in a casemate of the battery. He had just breakfasted, and was in a most affable frame of mind, surrounded by the young officers from the nearest batteries. Their laughter and jokes could be heard from a long way off, and the array of empty bottles showed that breakfast had not been a dry meal.

'I didn't want to answer those yellow-skinned scoundrels. I wanted to draw a caricature and sent it back. They wanted the Fortress? I'll show them the Fortress!'

There was general laughter. The youths, under the

---

* This letter was from the German Emperor to his naval attachés whom he ordered to leave the Fortress. One of them, Captain Gilgenheim, was killed by Chinese pirates on his way from Arthur to Chifu.

soothing influence of plentiful liqueurs, forgot their positions as junior officers, and shouted:

'Splendid, sir, splendid; quite right. Your health, sir.'

'And do you know, gentlemen, they took me for a foreigner—a Swiss by birth? By heavens! I am not lying. Quite recently I got a letter from Austria, from some Stössel or other who pretended he was proud of his relation in Arthur. Others write that I only became a Russian subject in 1893. I have got the letter!'

Again there was laughter. The General was in the best of form. Whether he was talking seriously or not I do not know. Presently he thought it was time to return to Arthur, and told me to accompany him: we rode through the arsenal.

'Look what a number of captured guns there are! I took all those in the Chinese War.'

All these guns passed into our hands when we peacefully occupied Arthur!

CHAPTER XXVI

DEATH OF PRINCE MACHABELLY—ALL-ROUND FIGHTING

I CONTINUED daily to send my 'News' to the *Novy Kry*, but the strictness of the censors deprived it of all interest and sometimes of its accuracy. For instance, on August 17, my article stated that work was being rapidly hurried on all along the defences. This was by no means the case everywhere, for the engineers, spoilt by six years of doing nothing or of only constructing private buildings, neglected the important mobilization works. There were exceptions, for some of the engineer officers did really good work, but the majority did nothing. Then again, as regards the quality of the food which I had praised in my article—it was eatable, but far from nutritious, and the siege had only just begun. Again, I mentioned General Gorbatovsky; but I did not venture to say that this officer, who was always to be found in the section of the defences under his command, never rested, or that he spent day after day on the fortified positions, where by his presence and cheerfulness he inspired the men with confidence. Though the men were cheerful, I had not dared to say that they were physically incapable, and weedy, which was the truth. I did not mention that when officers begged for timber, planks, iron, or material for building bomb-proofs the engineers replied that they had no transport, or else refused the requests of the 'small fry.' Neither could I hint that the only way in which General Smirnoff could make these lazy engineers work was by personally going round and seeing how his orders were being executed.

Many and many a life lies at the door of the engineer officers in Arthur. If St. Petersburg be held responsible for the mistake of cutting down the perimeter of the defences of Port Arthur, the engineers, of whom some left for Russia at the first shot and others were criminally idle, will also have to answer for much. If they had worked hard and conscientiously while the place was in our possession the mistakes committed at St. Petersburg would not have had such dire consequences.

On the 18th there was a lull—an absolute cessation of firing—all day. This was so unusual that it seemed ominous of something worse to follow, and we were filled with forebodings. Indeed, the hospitals, in which the first hints of an approaching assault were usually to be found, were preparing to meet the expected demands of the next few hours. I accompanied General Smirnoff on his afternoon inspection. Having gone round many works and said a cheery word to all he met, he went up on to Danger Hill and we climbed into the look-out station.* The sun had already sunk below Liao-tieh-shan, but from the top of the hill we could see everything quite distinctly. After last instructions with regard to the concentration, etc., of the troops on the north-east front we silently made our way back to Arthur, all of us feeling impressed with the uncertainty of what might come.

At 5 a.m. on August 19 the enemy opened fire from all their batteries on our works, particularly on those of the west and eastern fronts. Gradually increasing their fire, they made a determined attack on the foot-hills of Angle Hill. At 7 a.m. this was repulsed, and then they concen-

* It was from here that he proposed to command during the assault Colonel Raschevsky had as far as possible adapted it for this, and had connected it by telephone to the Fortress Staff Office.

trated their artillery fire chiefly on Angle Hill on the western front, and on B Battery, Little Eagle's Nest, and others on the eastern. General Stössel watched the progress of the fight from Fort No. 1, and General Smirnoff took up his position on Danger Hill, whence he commanded. At noon the fire slackened, only to be shortly renewed with increased ferocity. Having prepared the way with artillery, the Japanese again advanced, but were repulsed everywhere, though they gained possession of a ravine opposite Water Supply Redoubt, and, taking advantage of the darkness, lay concealed in an outer ditch, and fired at some of our outposts. From twilight till morning the town was bombarded, and at 6 p.m. one of the arsenal buildings was set alight. I was again with Smirnoff that day, and, amidst all the turmoil and stress, the thing that disturbed me most was that several shells had fallen into the hospitals. It was right and proper that our forts should be shelled, but that the enemy should be able so early in the siege to fire right into the centre of the Fortress augured ill for the future. Smirnoff was kept tied to the telephone, and we stayed for some time at his quarters. As we were sitting on the balcony we heard a shot fired from Golden Hill. In a few seconds, high up above us, we heard a noise. It grew louder and louder, then something flashed and struck the ground in front, scattering mud and gravel over us.

'That's luck; let us go and look at it,' said Smirnoff.

It was half of a prematurely bursting shell from Golden Hill, weighing some 320 to 360 lb. The iron shells of the 11-inch howitzers on Golden Hill were so cunningly contrived that most of them burst, not in the enemy's lines as intended, but over the town and over our own positions.

At 2 p.m. Kondratenko telephoned to say that the

trenches below Angle Hill had been abandoned, and in the evening he came in to report personally. This was the enemy's only gain that day. Night came, and the fire was continued all along the line. While we in the town were kept awake by anxiety and on account of the hideous uproar, how about the men at the front? Those narrow, deep, advanced trenches, which wound about like black ribbons on all sides of the Fortress, were full of men. If we, in the inside, could not sleep, how could these men, whom a shell might at any instant turn into blood and dust? There they lay peering ahead and whispering to each other in their unaccustomed surroundings—tired, strained, and watchful.

The enemy made great efforts during the whole of the night of the 19th to seize Water Supply Redoubt, and held the parapet till daybreak. On the 20th there was desperate fighting round Angle Hill and Water Supply and Pan-lun-shan Redoubts, in which we lost 500 men. At midday we heard that we had lost Angle Hill. When Kondratenko reported this personally, Smirnoff was very angry. It appeared that the men had retired without orders, and had left eight guns of sorts on the hills, which Kondratenko engaged to try and recapture. At 9 p.m. a series of unsuccessful attacks were made on Temple Redoubt, and at midnight on Water Supply and Pan-lun-shan Redoubts, and the enemy got possession of the north-east corner of the former. At daybreak on the 21st two companies of Frontier Guards went to the assistance of Water Supply Redoubt and surprised the enemy, who retired suddenly on their own reserves. They came under fire from Erh-lung-shan Fort, and left more than 1,000 dead on the ground.

It was about this time that the enemy wore us down and captured Pan-lun-shan Redoubt. This redoubt was so important to us that Smirnoff resolved to retake it

INSIDE A TRENCH ON THE EASTERN FRONT.

To face page 166.

at all costs, and its recapture was one of the bloodiest fights that had yet occurred. Colonel Prince Machabelly commanded the battalion entrusted with this work, and the redoubt was taken on the night of the 21st. In the midst of the hand to hand fighting, when grenades were bursting on all sides, and machine guns were firing point-blank, the bomb-proofs were set on fire. The place blazed up like a torch, and our men had to retire to trenches in rear. The Japanese could not get into it either, and so it became neutral, Pan-lun-shan Hill remaining in our hands till the fall of 203 Metre Hill in December.

Prince Machabelly, who was killed in this assault, was the *beau-ideal* of a soldier, and the circumstances under which he met his death were sad. He was under a cloud, having been made a scape-goat for the failure on Wolf's Hills, and having been deprived of the command of his regiment, the 13th East Siberian Rifles, which he had led with such gallantry at Kuen-san. In spite of this he led his companies at the attack of Pan-lun-shan as he had led his battalions on Green Hills; he won the redoubt for us, and was killed in the attempt.

At daybreak on the 21st I had gone with the Commandant up on to Danger Hill. The Japanese were pouring in a heavy fire especially on the north-east front, and General Gorbatovsky, commanding the eastern portion, asked for reinforcements. The enemy was attacking the Redoubts, Kuropatkin Lunette, the Chinese wall, and Big Eagle's Nest in force; the regimental reserves were melting away, and the position was serious. General Smirnoff telephoned to Fock, commanding the main reserve, to send up the last unit—the 14th Regiment—at the double. Fock, however, argued with him. Time was flying, and Gorbatovsky, losing patience, again begged for support, for each moment was precious. Smirnoff, appreciating the seriousness of the situation, repeated his order to Fock, who, to the anger and amazement of the officers standing round, again raised objections. The Commandant, usually calm and self-controlled, then lost his temper.

'Lieutenant Hammer,* give me the note-book.' He quickly wrote a message. 'Take this to General Fock and give it to him personally.'

Hammer disappeared. Meanwhile, reports from Gorbatovsky were coming in, each more alarming than the last. The artillery front had suffered heavily, and could only reply weakly to the enemy's guns, and the struggle was being maintained chiefly by the heavy guns of our coast batteries. Considerable bodies of infantry were seen moving out of the villages,† and it appeared from what we could see that the Japanese intended to attack, but not till evening. General Gorbatovsky arrived, and greatly excited, reported that the decisive moment was at hand, the troops had suffered terribly from the enemy's guns, the infantry were utterly worn out, and without reinforcements the attack could not be repulsed! He hadn't slept for several days, and had been continually under a very heavy gun-fire, so that he was overtired and painted things somewhat blacker than they really were. General Smirnoff, with his usual *sang-froid*, replied:

'It is not so bad as that. We must, above all, keep calm. You have been sitting in that hell, and from your immediate surroundings things have seemed to you worse than they really are. You are not quite yourself. Take it easy, we'll soon put matters right.'

'Quite so, sir, but things are very alarming. The Japs are getting possession of the Redoubts, which are in a critical state, and will in all probability deliver an assault

* General Smirnoff's A.D.C.
† Dapalidjuan, Lierre, and Wanziatenzy.

on the centre, which has suffered so heavily. Big Eagle's Nest and Zaliterny Battery are out of action; Kuropatkin Lunette is in a critical condition; B Battery has only one serviceable gun and the Naval Battery is also disabled. . . .'

'I agree,' continued Smirnoff, 'matters are very bad, but I have already taken the necessary steps. The 14th Regiment, which is in the main reserve, I have ordered up to the north-east front, to be échelonned by battalions near Big Eagle's Nest and the Ice-house. In addition to this I am getting six naval companies (1200 strong), which I will concentrate at the front in the bomb-proofs of the 9th Regiment. When night comes on the guns must be repaired; where there are none, I'll send field-guns from the general reserve, and we will hurl back the assault. You return now, and at 4 p.m. I will come and give you detailed orders as to what to do.'

Gorbatovsky departed, and at that moment up came Lieutenant Hammer with a note for the Commandant. Instead of at once carrying out Smirnoff's urgent order to move the 14th Regiment up to the north-east front, Fock had written a whole page in reply, in which he expressed his conviction of the danger of the move, especially of a concentration near the Ice-house, which the enemy would doubtless shell! The building was at the foot of the very hill from which the Commandant had issued this order; it was in a well-concealed spot, and was not even being fired at.

The Commandant was furious. 'Here, Hammer, write at once to Fock, and say that if he doesn't immediately carry out my order, I'll remove him from his command.'

At 1 o'clock the artillery attack began to slacken. The enemy, having seized two villages* began moving towards the redoubts, and the assault seemed to be near. It should be observed that from the very first, appreciating the

* Fudziafan and Dapalidjuan.

weakness of the north-east front, Smirnoff had armed it at the cost of the western, having transferred to it the 9-inch howitzers from Wolf's battery, and mounted a number of the guns received from the fleet. He was convinced that the chief blow would fall here, and more particularly because directly behind this front lay, so to speak, the heart of the Fortress (harbour, dock, commissariat dépôts, chief magazine, mills). Stössel, on the contrary, had always considered that the west side was the more important.

Having sent off Hammer and given his final orders, Smirnoff turned to the officers present.

'Gentlemen, the gun-fire is slackening, and the enemy will rest. The attack won't take place before dark; we can now rest and refresh ourselves.'

On our way down, we met the 14th Regiment, whom Smirnoff greeted, telling them that he would see them again in the evening. Later, when the north-east front was being continually stormed, Smirnoff for a long time could not find one of the battalions of this regiment, and wondered how it could have got lost. After exhaustive inquiries, it turned out that it and the scout company had, with the General's knowledge, remained in barracks! The General himself had not come with the regiment (the last one in the reserve), but had remained in his quarters in the town.

Though a great danger threatened the Fortress that night Smirnoff did not lose his head, his prophecy as to the course of events being fully justified. After giving some more orders he asked us all to breakfast. In the middle of it Stössel turned up in a very agitated state. He refused refreshment, and said: 'Redoubts Nos. 1 and 2 are being captured. Both Eagle's Nest and Zaliterny Battery are in ruins, the adjacent batteries are badly injured, the local reserves are used up, and the

GENERAL GORBATOVSKY.

To face page 171.

enemy are still pounding us. The losses are enormous. It is difficult to hold out. What is to be done?'

Just then, unannounced, in walked General Fock, and interrupted:

'Your Excellency, Gorbatovsky is a traitor. He is uselessly wasting the reserves—inviting a slaughter of them by putting them into the trenches. If he does this we'll have to surrender. He is a traitor, sir!'

Smirnoff turned to Stössel, and said quietly:

'I do not know that I fully understand. Gorbatovsky's actions do not quite tally with those of a traitor. For three days and nights he has been constantly under fire, directing the defence, and by his gallantry encouraging the men. I will see to the repulse of the attack; the reserve must be used when necessary.' Then, turning suddenly to Fock: 'And you, sir, it appears, do not intend to obey my orders? To-day, instead of at once carrying them out, you employed your time writing replies. . . . I never give an order twice. Bear that in mind.'

For his action on this day Fock was removed from his command by Smirnoff, and so, from August 21 right up to December 18, he took no part in the operations, and employed himself in writing long memoranda and giving advice to Stössel.

In the early hours of August 22 the enemy attacked the Redoubts which were held by the naval detachment, and all day long heavy fighting continued round Long Hill, between it and Divisional Hill, round Jagged Hill, and Redoubts Nos. 1 and 2. Redoubt No. 1 changed hands four times during the course of the day, and remained in the enemy's hands, as did No. 2. The Japanese cunningly managed to transfer their field-guns through the kiaoling to the east side, whilst they kept the garrison of Jagged Hill under cover by their heavy shell-fire.

At daybreak on the 23rd all was silence. The enemy had abandoned No. 1 Redoubt, and were retiring from No. 2, both of which, after five days' bombardment, had been reduced to a shapeless heap of ruins. At 11 p.m. that night by moonlight the enemy opened up with two search-lights, one from behind Ta-ku-shan, the other opposite Chi-kuan-shan Fort, and, lighting up our parties who were searching for wounded, kept on firing on them —so much so that after a few hours our humane efforts had to be stopped.

CHAPTER XXVII

STÖSSEL DISOBEYS—PROGRESS DURING AUGUST

I HAVE mentioned in an earlier chapter how General Stössel was recalled from Port Arthur in June, and I will now explain the circumstances under which this happened.

When the Japanese began landing, and in particular after the *débâcle* at Kinchou, Stössel began showering telegrams on Kuropatkin, in which he made out affairs to be very critical, and implored for help. Later he sent Lieutenant-Colonel Gurko, of the General Staff, who was on the Fortress Staff, to him with despatches. (Before this Prince Gantimuroff had succeeded in breaking through and returning with despatches.) When Gurko left he reported his departure to the Commandant, and —knowing well what Stössel was like—asked if Smirnoff wished him to give any particular reports to the Commander-in-Chief.

'Tell him,' said Smirnoff, 'everything that you have seen. And if you hear that they want to make a separate command of the District, tell him the best man for it is General Subotin, who knows the peninsula thoroughly.'

In June Captain Odintsoff was also sent to the north by Stössel with very alarming despatches, and he also, in reporting his departure to Smirnoff, was given the same instructions. After reading these despatches, and hearing from Odintsoff a corroboration of what he had heard from Gurko, Kuropatkin came to the conclusion that Stössel must be ill. But before deciding to recall him he consulted others, and after their reply he had no option left him as to how to act. He decided with great regret that he must sever his friendly relations with Stössel, which dated from the time when they had been boys together in the 1st Cadet Corps, and when he used to spend his holidays at the latter's home. Realizing that it was inevitable, he made up his mind to recall his old comrade, but before doing so he unfortunately made for him the appointment of Officer Commanding the District.

On June 18 he sent two cypher messages to Arthur, one addressed to Stössel, ordering him to hand over everything to Smirnoff and leave the place, and the other to Smirnoff. The former, having received both of them, concealed their existence. Shortly afterwards two more telegrams from Kuropatkin to him and Smirnoff were received, brought by a subaltern officer of the reserve on the *Lieutenant Burakoff*. This time General Stössel came to the conclusion that silence could not longer be kept and that he must act, so he destroyed the messages to Smirnoff, and sent the following letter to Kuropatkin:

'Your despatch of July 2 was handed to me on the positions as I was repelling an attack in force by the enemy. I was anxious to leave Arthur, but as things are at present I consider my presence here essential for the good of the Fatherland and our troops. Every one here knows me, Chinese as well as Russians, and they trust me, knowing that the Japanese will never get into the place save over my dead body. Neither Fock nor Nickitin believes in General Smirnoff, who is unknown to the officers and men, and who calls the latter cowards. He may be all right in his way, but he is a professor and not a fighting general. If you are determined that I should come to Liao-Yang, I will do so on receipt of fresh instructions to that effect from you.'

ON THE ATTACKED FRONT: AFTER AN ATTACK.

To face page 174.

Meanwhile, as might have been expected, the enemy were not going to wait for the reply to this to come, and, having cut our communications at Kinchou, they occupied Dalny, and before the letter reached Liao-Yang General Nogi had begun to operate on Green Hills. Stössel, of course, was not very sure as to its reception and whether good or evil would result to him. Taking advantage, however, of it being a time of war, he now began reporting direct to the Tsar, to whom he sent telegrams describing an absolutely untrue condition of affairs. He turned the defeats and retirements in the district into victories, and telegrams of congratulation began to come in from their Imperial Majesties.

On the night of the 23rd, the Japanese made the most desperate of all their attacks so far. They made three separate and most determined assaults on Zaredoubt Battery, on the line between it and Big Eagle's Nest, and on Ruchevsky Battery. Though temporarily successful at one or two points, they were finally driven back out of all with shocking slaughter. They then again concentrated a gun-fire on these points, and our men took whatever cover they could find, anxiously awaiting a fourth assault which did not take place. When the sun rose the heaps of corpses in front of the works were revealed. In the heat the smell from them was appalling: even the cotton wool with which our men had plugged their nostrils was not of much avail.

With regard to the firing from the battery on Golden Hill* a rather amusing incident occurred. As prematurely bursting iron shells from this battery had somewhat endangered General Stössel he gave orders that it was not to fire. Major-General Biely, commanding the Fortress Artillery, thereupon reported to Smirnoff that the 11-inch howitzers were not to be used, notwithstanding the damage they were doing to the enemy.

* See p. 165.

'Well, let us go to Stössel,' said Smirnoff; 'you tell him that in future you will use steel shells.'

They acordingly went to the Officer Commanding the District and found him very indignant about the premature bursts of the iron shells.

'May I use steel shells, sir, instead?' asked Biely.

'Will they be all right?'

'Oh, yes.'

'Very well, but are you sure?'

Smirnoff energetically supported Biely and they went out.

'That's splendid,' said Smirnoff, rubbing his hands; 'now you use the iron ones as before because you have not got enough steel shells for the battery, and remember —if there are any premature bursts they are the *enemy's!*'

Biely did this with the result that Golden Hill continued to be of great service to us, while the occasional premature bursts, which still continued, were put down to the Japanese. Stössel was quite pacified, but, unfortunately, soon found out that he had been deceived, and roundly abused Smirnoff to his suite. He did not interfere, however, as the hill was undoubtedly a great check to the enemy.

The night assault on August 23 on the centre of the north-east front was the finale of the assaults in August, and what General Nogi had said to the correspondent of the *Daily Mail* when he first saw him: 'You have arrived most luckily, just at the right time, neither too late nor too soon, you will see the end of our victorious campaign,' was not justified by the event.

The results of the eight days' desperate fighting were inconsiderable. On the western front we had lost Angle Hill and its foot-hills, and Pan-lun-shan Redoubt remained neutral. On the eastern front we had lost Redoubts Nos. 1 and 2, but only after an incessant and awful bombardment and most bloody assaults, which cost the Japanese 22,000 killed and wounded. However, they at last learnt that the capture of Arthur was not all plain sailing. They realized that Russians were not Chinese, and it was a complete surprise to them that the Fortress which in January might have been captured by a *coup de main* had grown into a stronghold against which tens of thousands of men had perished. Proud in the knowledge of their superiority, they had on August 16 suggested that we should capitulate, but upon counting up their losses at a Council of War on the 26th, they came to the sorrowful conclusion that it would be yet some time before they took the place.

Expecting to hear at any moment of the fall of Arthur, Japan had been preparing lanterns and flags to celebrate a great national holiday; but at last she had to confess that, although Russians are by nature negligent and careless, they can in moments of emergency do wonders. In the country of the Rising Sun complaints were raised that the besieging army was not making such progress as it should, and the dissatisfaction almost turned into something worse. The Government of the Mikado acted wisely and promptly, proposing that those who were discontented should go and join the besieging army in order to replace casualties and show how things ought to be done. The *amour-propre* of the proud Japanese, especially the Samurai, was touched, and whole transports filled with volunteers came to the Kwantun Peninsula.

Later, when the Chinese reported that these newly arrived recruits, which included many old men and mere boys, were being drilled and trained in the Lunwantun Valley, our battleships and Electric Cliff shelled them at long range, just to remind them that Arthur was not yet dead; when the October assault was repulsed, we found amongst the killed and wounded numbers of old and very young men. Strong, indeed, must have been the spirit of the nation, which in the moment of trial could back up its discontent by example and action. During my residence in Japan before the war, I had ventured to write that the Japanese were a nation with a great future; but I was laughed at.

On the 25th, Big Hill, Little Eagle's Nest and B Battery were bombarded, and the enemy were seen to be concentrating behind Sugar Hill. During the night a sortie was made from 203 Metre Hill to recover the guns left on Angle Hill, but we could not bring them in, so they were blown up. The Japanese were now entrenched along the foot-hills of Angle Hill, and on the ridge joining Angle Hill with 203 Metre Hill, and had mounted some thirty guns near two villages.* A force of infantry and cavalry also was concentrated north of Pigeon Bay. I rode round with the Commandant on the 25th on his tour round the north-east. The military road was a track of death and destruction. Everywhere were half-dried puddles of blood, broken rifles, haversacks, boots, carts, blood-stained clothes, wheels, horses, broken down gun-carriages, and unrecognizable corpses, and it was ploughed up with shells. The rest-house on Little Eagle's Nest, where not long ago we had spent many careless hours, was burnt to a heap of ruins. At Eagle's Nest the greater part of the bomb-proofs and parapets had been destroyed, and the infantry were sitting about, some above ground and some below; the reserve was behind the steep slope, in various shelters made of corrugated iron or anything which they could get hold of. This improvised cover might protect from the sun, but certainly from nothing else. The officers and men were reduced to shadows, unwashed, and wearing torn uniforms. They asked the Commandant for planks—any sort of timber—to help them with the aid of earth to get

* Khantsistun and Siagoklantiatun.

some protection. Smirnoff smiled as he heard them; but it was a cynical smile, for, two days previously, he had given the strictest orders that they should be supplied with the very planks for which they were now asking. His order had not been obeyed, and for this the engineers were entirely to blame.

'All right, you shall have the planks to-day. Hammer, make a note of it,' answered Smirnoff.

On the 26th and 27th the enemy continued to mount guns and push forward their works, but there was no general action. Smirnoff and Kondratenko were much exercised about our lack of heavy guns, and, through the agency of Prince Mackalinsky (naval officer attached to the Fortress Staff), arranged for the fleet to supply some. This officer was of the utmost use to us as an intermediary between the Fortress Staff and the Navy; for the Navy as a rule wanted many reasons before they would assist us.

On the night of the 26th we discovered that the enemy had abandoned Nos. 1 and 2 Redoubts, which were full of corpses; but on the night of the 27th these were again occupied by them. At 2 a.m. in the morning of the 28th there was an alarm of a general attack, but it turned out to be an attack on 203 Metre Hill, Long Hill, and Fort No. 4 only.

The 28th passed fairly quietly, with unimportant gun-fire, as did the 29th. On the night of the 29th our communications behind the main line were heavily shelled. During the preceding three days the gendarmes buried 700 Japanese dead in front of our north-east positions. This was done under fire. In the evening of the 29th the enemy entrenched near Water Supply Redoubt, and we temporarily recaptured part of No. 2 Redoubt by a sortie.

That evening, Prince Mickeladsey informed me that he was sending a post to St. Petersburg, and that I could send a telegram. He added: 'But don't talk of it, for if it is known, —— will at once hear of it.'

I wrote out two identical telegrams—one to a relative in St. Petersburg, and one to a friend:

'Arthur is enabled to hold out only by the efforts of Smirnoff and his excellent assistant Kondratenko. . . . When I can give you details your hair will stand on end. Tell the Tsar this, for it is absolutely necessary that —— should be removed.'

The Prince sent off these telegrams in a special letter with the official stamp, and in a separate packet, addressed to our consul in Chifu. The latter duly received them, but in spite of Prince Mickeladsey's request to despatch my wires to their destination, he never sent them, and gave as his excuse that they would have discredited a great name. He did this notwithstanding the fact that they were enclosed in a letter from the Chief of the Gendarmes in Port Arthur. Nor did he even consider it his duty to report the circumstances to his superiors, although he might have known that there is never smoke without fire. At the end of the siege, when I reached Chifu on the *Rastoropny*, on board of which I had been sent from Port Arthur, with the knowledge and by the direction of the Commandant and all the Admirals 'as an officer of the Fortress' (Stössel wished, as he expressed it, to 'abolish' me), the consul received a telegram from Port Arthur to the effect that I was a Japanese spy. He accordingly went to all the officers in authority and did everything he could to procure my arrest, and I was only saved by the intervention of the Chinese Governor, who declared that he would send an armed guard to protect me.

On August 30 a shell from one of the batteries blew up a Japanese magazine on the eastern front. General Biely at once gave orders for the battery to pour in a still hotter fire on to the magazine. As far as we could see the shells fell splendidly, preventing the enemy from saving the material, for groups of men could be seen running about in every direction, but at a considerable distance. To the left of Orphan Hill a big-gun battery was brought up by them, but it was very effectively fired on by one of our coast batteries. On the same day General Stössel published the following District Order:

'I have to-day had the honour to receive a telegram from the Tsar to the following effect: "To-day being the christening day of the Heir to the Throne, I appoint you and Colonel Semenoff, commanding the 26th East Siberian Rifle Regiment, to be my Aides-de-camp."'*

The following is what the late Colonel Raschevsky thought of this: 'We are all delighted with the latter appointment which is most just (the appointment of Semenoff as A.D.C.), but that Stössel should have received this honour is a proof of how often those in authority are rewarded for the deeds of others.'

By twelve noon all the official world in Arthur was on their way to congratulate the newly appointed A.D.C. I did not wish to go, but was persuaded that it was necessary.

'Go? You must go; if you don't you will make him an enemy for ever. He will put you face downwards and deprive you of the possibility of seeing and collecting the valuable historical material which you are getting,' said the experienced and canny ones. I bowed to the wisdom of this, and went and did as I was advised. In the evening I called on the Commandant. For some time he had been very ill with dysentery, and for the last two days

---

* Actually, General Stössel was appointed 'General-Adjutant' to the Tsar, while Colonel Semenoff was appointed 'Flügel-Adjutant.' Both these honorary ranks were originally borrowed from the Prussians, and can best be rendered in English by 'aide-de-camp,' though they differ in degree.—A. B. L.

had been told by the doctor that he was on no account to ride. He certainly seemed to be very much thinner than before.

The following Order was issued by General Stössel on the 31st:

'On the night of the 29th and 30th a sortie and an attack on No. 2 Redoubt was again made by the scouts and sailors. The former dashed into the trenches, but the sailors did not do all that was expected of them, and so the attack was unsuccessful and the loss of life wasted. No more such attacks are to be made without my personal sanction on each occasion. Similar sorties would be better carried out under the command of a man like the Chief of the Fortress Staff, who is thoroughly acquainted with the locality.'

With the final capture of Nos. 1 and 2 Redoubts by the Japanese—their greatest success during the month—they gained an enormous advantage. They at once constructed trenches back from both of them, which was, of course, an easier operation than throwing them forward under the gun-fire of our batteries. The Commandant considered it absolutely essential to organize sorties against them, but General Stössel, by every means in his power, opposed this.

The series of assaults culminating on the 23rd of this month were so bloody and had such a great influence on the course of the defence, that they are worthy of further description. It had been evident on the 21st, 22nd and 23rd that the Japanese were preparing to deliver the final blow by a general attack. Our difficulty, in the absence of balloons, was to ascertain where that blow would fall along the extensive front. Chinese reports were quite untrustworthy, and we could not see enough from any of the positions to judge where the enemy was concentrating. The standing kiaoling, the ravines and roughness of the ground greatly assisted the concealment of their move-

THE ASSAULT REPULSED.

ments. On the evening of the 23rd the Commandant, after long and careful inspection of the enemy's positions, ordered the last battalion of the 14th Regiment to Eagle's Nest. This left a main reserve, only two companies strong, under Quail Hill, to cover the valley of the Lun-ho. Two companies! all the rest had been sucked up into the firing-line. He then sent orders to Admiral Wiren to be ready to land a detachment of 800 men from the ships at anchor to form a reserve. It was now 7 p.m., and the darker it got the more silent became the line of front, and the more tense our expectancy.

Nogi himself, on the highest point of Wolf's Hills, was gazing fixedly towards Port Arthur hidden in darkness; for having concentrated more than two Divisions, with a strength of over 35,000 men, on the portion from Redoubt No. 2 to B Battery (three and a half miles), and having determined with one blow to seize Chi-kuan-shan Fort, B Battery, and Eagle's Nest, he was anxiously trying to pierce the bloody veil of the future. Smirnoff seemed to divine the thought of his chief enemy as if by inspiration, and despatched his force opposite where Nogi was concentrating. There was this difference, however—that while Nogi was playing with tens of thousands of men—Smirnoff had to count every section.

At 11 p.m. Nogi gave the sign, and a living avalanche of men rolled irresistibly up towards us, and from valley, ditch and ravine the Japanese appeared. Rifles cracked, machine guns spluttered, guns boomed and boomed again, and the air was turned into an inferno of shrieking missiles. The rays of the search-lights flashed up and down, rockets shot up into the sky like enormous fiery snakes, and burst in hundreds of large brilliant balls, eclipsing the light of the eternal stars and blinding the heroic little infantry-men who were attacking us. They ran forward, fell, jumped up again and pressed on, in groups together. In the shimmering rays of the search-lights, the flashes of bursting shells seemed almost blood-red. The noise became a horrible blur of sound—shouts, moans, cheers—clash of arms and detonations. But at last it ended; the clamour gradually died away; the attack had been repulsed. In front of us not a living soul remained—only dead—piles of dead and wounded men. Never shall I forget that night.

At 2 a.m. a second wave started and surged forward, despite the shower of lead and steel poured into it. With incredible efforts it got possession of the Chinese Wall opposite Zaredoubt Battery, and a hand-to-hand fight ensued. The search-light was turned on to the spot, and lit up a revolting picture; our last two companies of the reserve were sent forward at the double from Quail Hill, and every Japanese by the wall was bayonetted; then the rays glided further afield searching for the enemy, but only lit up a ground strewn with bodies.

At 3 a.m. a third attack commenced, and it seemed as if the passionless, cold-hearted Nogi had sentenced the last of his troops to death. The signal was given, and a fresh wave of living flesh and blood rolled forward. This time it was the attack—the spring—of a maddened, wounded, blood-drunk herd of tigers—not men. Our truly awful fire was of no avail; the mass roared forward with the strength of a tidal wave. On it came, though lit up by rockets and search-lights, on, on it rolled irresistibly; on, right through the breached Chinese Wall, and up on to Zaredoubt and Wolf's Battery, half of which it seized. But the timely arrival of two companies again saved everything, for after a bloody hand-to-hand fight the Japanese were thrown back; they gave way, and fell back on those in rear. It was a critical moment, but our light showed up their thick reserves taking cover

BURIAL-PARTIES AT WORK.

in the ravine between Chinese Wall and Zaredoubt Hill, and they were almost destroyed.

A reddish vapour slowly rose up over this valley of death, and screened the bursting shells and the rays of light. It grew light; the attacks had been repulsed, and not a rood of ground had the enemy got, but the scene on all sides was awful. The rising sun showed up sheaves of corpses on the ground that was still ours. Death had indeed triumphed, and had claimed 22,000 lives.

From this time forward the enemy remained content with the slower advance of regular siege operations.

CHAPTER XXVIII

AWARDS—SOME PERSONAL NOTES

SEPTEMBER opened for us with a minor success. The enemy on the night of the 1st attacked the works under construction by the sailors on Long Hill; during the attack one of their columns moved across a mine between Long Hill and Divisional Hill. The effect was terrific; of a whole mass of live men, in a moment nothing remained.

On September 3 the early morning passed quietly. From 2.30 a.m. the Japanese bombarded the Old Town, and from five o'clock they fired on the New Town, and were seen to be hard at work in Redoubt No. 1, whilst other works were quickly rising from Takushan and Palidjuan. A great parade was held in honour of General Stössel's rewards. In the evening, a submarine mine was seen to explode under the starboard bow of the *Itsukushima;* the cruiser listed some ten degrees, and a fire burst out, but she was able to steam away.

That night 500 dead bodies were buried by the Gendarmes and the Chinese, in front of Eagle's Nest and Kuropatkin Lunette. While thus employed one Gendarme and three Chinamen were wounded.

On the 4th an ineffective assault was made on Water Supply Redoubt. From the 4th to the 6th the enemy were very busy at work on Nos. 1 and 2 Redoubts. On the night of the 6th we made a successful sortie with the bayonet from Water Supply Redoubt, and 600 more dead were buried on the north-eastern front.

On September 6, the following extract of District Orders was issued by General Stössel:

'I have to-day, the 5th, had the great honour to receive from the Tsar the following telegram, sent via Liao-yang, and dated Liao-yang, August 28:

'"As a reward for the gallantry of the Port Arthur garrison, I have given orders that all ranks of the Military and Naval Services defending Port Arthur shall from May 1 till the end of the siege, count every month's service as one year. I promote you to be a Cavalier of the Order of St. George of the 3rd Class, and I await your recommendations for rewards for those who have distinguished themselves in battle.

'"(*Signed*) NICHOLAS."'

'The following telegram was received to-day from the Viceroy:

'"Prince Ukhtomsky is to hand over the command of the battleships and cruisers to Captain Wiren, and as soon as the ships are repaired the latter is to endeavour to break through to Vladivostock.

'"Rear Admiral Loschinsky is appointed to command the sea and mining defences."'

This question of the fleet forcing its way to Vladivostock was discussed at a conference of flag officers and captains, and they came to the conclusion that it was an absolute impossibility owing to the state of the ships, the shortage of ammunition and men, and to the general conditions being three times as unfavourable as they were at the time of the sortie of August 10. The squadron had indeed been greatly weakened by the transfer of guns to the land defences, by the casualties among the sailors during the assaults in August, by the impossibility of going into dock for below-water repairs, and by its inequality in speed, all of which deprived it of chances of success. The attempt must have resulted in the destruction of all our ships, as for a whole month the Japanese had been able to repair and rest. An encounter at sea with a force of double its strength, fresh, and with superior speed, to say nothing of the preponderance in destroyers, must have entailed the absolute annihilation of the fleet, and the loss to Arthur of ammunition and several thousand men, whose value had already been well proved.

The appointments of Loschinsky and Wiren met with warm approval. During the siege both had equally distinguished themselves, and had shown themselves to be the most energetic, gallant, and capable of the senior naval officers.

Notwithstanding his weak state of health, Smirnoff to-day went out to see the work on the third artillery line of defence, which had been newly armed with the naval guns. It ran from the northern part of the town wall to Stonebroken Ridge, Spur Hill, and Big Hill. Roads were being made, trees cut down, and the scene was a confusion of digging, blasting, levelling, building. He remarked:

'As soon as this line is finished I shall be happy. I am quite easy about the rest.'

On our way back we met Stössel. 'Aha! so that's it? Wherever we find the war correspondent we find the Commandant, eh . . . ?' was the rude welcome he gave the man whose energies and capabilities had gained for him the reward of Aide-de-camp to the Tsar!

Aye, and not only was he an aide-de-camp, but he was now a hero, for had he not been promoted to the St. George of the Third Class? Alas! how that Order for gallantry fell in our eyes. It was dreadful to think of the Tsar and the millions of people in Russia who had been deceived by

COLONEL RASCHEVSKY.

To face page 188.

his false reports. But for this I was forced to go and congratulate him, as for his former honour. After a few moments' conversation he turned to me.

'Who writes the "News" in the *Novy Kry*?'

'I don't know.' I had every right to say this, for, though it was not signed, I well knew that Stössel was aware I wrote it.

'What are you doing with yourself?'

'I am collecting materials with which to write a book.'

The General frowned, and his manner changed.

'And you will, I suppose, only write the truth in it?'

'Only the truth.'

'Ah! all you correspondents are liars! The one who pays most gets the truth.'

'At present and till the end of the campaign, sir, I am in the power of the censors; but later, taking advantage of the Tsar's promise to the press representative of the capital, I shall consider it my duty to write the truth—the whole truth, in order that Russia and the Tsar may be spared another Port Arthur.

'And I wish to remind *you*, sir, that my name is an unsullied one, and I belong to one of the oldest of the "noble" families.'

Two days later the following District Order appeared:

'As the *Novy Kry*, although warned more than once, continues to publish information of the distribution and movement of our troops which would be better kept secret, the offices of the paper will be closed for one month.'

Colonel Raschevsky wrote as follows in his diary of that date:

'Stössel has published a stupid order about closing the *Novy Kry* offices on the pretext that it publishes information about the sorties, patrols, etc., which might be of use to the enemy. It is utterly absurd! The paper passes through the hands of two censors—the Commander of the Port and the Fortress Staff—and suddenly to deprive us, from pure caprice and out of an evident desire to make himself unpleasant to the Commandant, of the only source of information and news from without is,' etc., etc.

CHAPTER XXIX

SEPTEMBER PASSES

WITH the capture in the preceding month of Nos. 1 and 2 Redoubts the enemy had got close up to our positions, and the salient angle of the north-east front was almost in their hands. I say 'almost,' because the ruins of these works remained the greater part of the time untenanted, neutralized by the gun-fire of both sides. As soon as they were abandoned by us, Smirnoff, appreciating their importance, decided, whatever it cost, to recapture them, and compel the Japs to retake them, and he considered the importance of this warranted the loss of even 2,000 or 3,000 men. He had accordingly arranged for a sortie in force, but Stössel intervened, and prevented this by his Order of August 31, already quoted, in which he would only permit sorties in small parties. To attack these redoubts with small numbers was quite ineffectual, and could only result in useless loss of life, and Smirnoff tried in vain to persuade Stössel to alter his opinion. Had we only been able to recapture those works the effect on the *moral* of the men would have been great, as they would have realized that they could attack as well as defend; as it was, they had seen nothing but continual retirements ever since the war began. It would not have been impossible, for we possessed an excellent *place d'armes* in rear and on the flank of these places in Rocky and Water Supply Redoubts.

The Japanese meanwhile did not waste time; they sapped right up to the glacis of the two latter, then started the first parallel, and, surrounding them with trenches, gradually endeavoured to work their way to Water Supply and Temple Redoubts. Here, again, the only course for us was to hamper and delay the enemy's steady trenchwork-advance by means of well-timed night sorties. But not only had Stössel paralyzed any attempt at a sortie in force by his order of the 31st, but he also managed to stop all small sorties by his action after one such had been attempted. Order No. 590 of September 9 read as follows:

'On the night of September 8-9, Lieutenant Endrjievsky, of the 26th East Siberian Rifle Regiment, on his own responsibility, and without even reporting it to his commanding officer, took 100 men of the Scouts and performed various pointless gallant acts. This only shows: (1) That there are officers who do not consider the lives of the soldiers entrusted to them to be of the least value, and do not consider themselves responsible for them; to such gentlemen the sacrifice of a number of men for a quite useless undertaking means nothing; this proves their youth. (2) That in some units strict discipline is not maintained; for anyone to be able to take a company away from a bivouac without the knowledge of the commanding officer is very extraordinary.

'This officer is deprived of his appointment for taking his company out without permission, and for losing 5 men killed and 19 wounded to no purpose; he will not be recommended for any rewards, and will be transferred to the 27th East Siberian Rifle Regiment for duty. Colonel Semenoff, commanding the 26th East Siberian Rifle Regiment, will be good enough to look to the internal discipline of his regiment.'

This order excited intense indignation, all that was most honourable and most sensible in the garrison was outraged. Thus was a gallant young officer, who had

PANORAMA OF NORTH-EAST FRONT.

1. Tumulus Battery.
2. Bombproof of the Officer Commanding the Section.
3. Fortification No. 3
4. Rocky Ridge.
5. Chinese Wall.
6. Fort, Erh-lung-shan.

To face page 193.

risked his life to try and assist us to hold Temple Redoubt a little longer, held up to ridicule. Individual initiative was absolutely frozen up by this treatment, and no one attempted to carry out what, after all, is one of the most dangerous of operations, for all knew what the slightest piece of bad luck would mean for them. Had its author at all considered the after-effect of this order, he would probably not have issued it.

It has been said that Stössel was liked by his subordinates, but he was feared, not loved, and he in his turn cared so much for the men under him that he did not consider it necessary to ride round the positions. And yet when telegraphing to the Tsar his thanks for his promotion in the Order of St. George, etc., he said that he had that 'day, on the positions, made the Tsar's telegram known to all.' He never went nearer the front than the barracks of the 10th Regiment, the safest spot in the whole Fortress!

On September 9 I, as usual, accompanied the Commandant on his inspection of the positions. As we went round, the men, taking advantage of the lull, were resting, having, wherever they could, burrowed under ground. The Chinese Wall had been repaired, and was held all along its length by infantry. Life at the front, though possibly exciting, was now neither amusing nor pleasant. The air all round reeked with the mingled stench of decomposing bodies, garlic and disinfectants, for on all sides hung pieces of linen steeped in carbolic acid. At first the men could not eat, but they gradually became acclimatized. Dogs had long ago fled.

On the 15th I spent some time on the splendidly appointed hospital ship *Mongolia*, and was much struck with the perfection of the arrangements, and the contrast between the comfort and cleanliness on board and the squalor and filth at the front. I met one of the nurses who had served with the Red Cross in the late war in.

South Africa. I asked her which she thought was worse, this war or the other.

'There, in comparison to what is going on here, things seem trifles: the wounds there were generally small; here they are dreadful.'

Meanwhile, on land, the enemy were, generally speaking, quiet. The reconnoitring patrols of both sides frequently came into contact, and each tried to snatch surprises and ambush the other. But the results were small. They shelled our defences, and we in turn did our best to foil them and delay their siege-works. On the 17th I accompanied Smirnoff on a visit to Colonel Yolshin, who had been wounded, and a good deal was said about the inactivity of our engineers.

If we had only had good men here, in six years what might we not have done, seeing what had been accomplished in four months? Our senior as well as junior engineers entirely forgot that enormous progress has been made of late years in ballistics, and apparently had no knowledge of modern artillery. They quietly pursued the prehistoric dogmas of ancient manuals.

In a fortress with a stony soil like Arthur—soil which cannot be touched with entrenching tools—all the mobilization defence works, especially those of heavy profile, should have, to guard against such assaults as we had experienced, been prepared beforehand. The mobilization works in Arthur were only begun on the arrival of the new Commandant on March 17, up till which time they had not been touched. The whole attention had been directed to the central wall, and on the forts and intermediate works.

There was no mobilization scheme in the Fortress. Perhaps General Bazilevsky knew of one, as he had seen the gradual development of the Fortress works, which had gone on for over ten years. Unfortunately, all records of these matters had been despatched to Harbin, and no one in Arthur, not even the Commandant, knew anything of them. It may be asked why the new Commandant was not entrusted with the plan of mobilization works? Why did General Bazilevsky—if he had such a plan—not give it to Stössel? Why did Kuropatkin when he went round the Fortress not ask for the plan of its works, even though only roughly drawn out? Because in all probability one never existed. As to General Stössel, it is quite possible that he did not know that a fortress ought to have a mobilization scheme, or did not even appreciate what a mobilization scheme was. He knew nothing about the works of the Fortress; they had been entirely under the control of Bazilevsky, who worked absolutely independently, and was subordinate only to the Viceroy. For him, it was a sufficiently important duty to dismiss and abuse the cab-drivers on the streets, to order private soldiers who were improperly dressed back to barracks, and to order men walking about in the streets to keep step. To march out of step he considered such a crime that he thought it necessary even to make a special report on this subject to the Viceroy. He was therefore very busy, and of course could not trouble himself about a defence scheme.

During September 18 and 19 heavy firing took place all along the line, and the attack on Water Supply and Temple Redoubts was fiercely pressed. The enemy mounted artillery within 100 yards of the former, and after changing hands six times, it remained on the 19th a smoking ruin, in the enemy's hands. Temple Redoubt was captured on the 20th, on which day furious attacks were made on Long Hill and 203 Metre Hill, and Pan-lun-shan was shelled. In the evening the first was seized by the Japanese. With the capture of Water Supply Redoubt the town was deprived of the usual water-supply, but Fresh Water Lake and the wells dug by Smirnoff's orders gave us plenty of water for the requirements of the garrison and civil population.

From the early hours of the 21st the Japanese attacked 203 Metre Hill, upon which their gun-fire was also concentrated. The whole of the western front and part of the eastern replied by massed fire. The assault increased; column after column rushed forward on to 203 Metre Hill, covering all its fore hills and slopes with heaps of dead, but at 8.45 a.m. they were repulsed. This assault was distinguished by particular obstinacy. I myself saw how, when their attack was repulsed, instead of retreating, the enemy began to build parapets of their dead and wounded comrades on the granite slopes of the hill, for they had no sand-bags. From this parapet they kept up rifle-fire all day on 203 Metre Hill and its spurs, on Fort No. 5, and on the Military Road, making all communications impossible. From morning till late in the evening the Japanese guns kept up a constant bombardment on 203 Metre Hill, and its position became more critical with every hour. Having got three-quarters of it, they meant to get possession of the rest at all costs: they slowly crawled upwards, fell dead, rolled back, and others dashed forward; they lay concealed and waited for reinforcements, nothing would drive them back. All their thoughts, all their endeavours were to get possession of this hill. Our men began rolling down great boulders from the top. These bounded down, flattened out the dead, and sought out the living, who, in trying to dodge, exposed themselves, and were shot by our men on the look out.

There you have the poetry of war—the reverse of a battle picture.

The following is what Colonel Raschevsky wrote on the 21st: 'In two days, the 18th and 19th, we have fired 70,000 rounds. As we have for long been short of shells, batteries were often unable to reply to the enemy.

A CANET GUN MOUNTED ON FORT V., SEPTEMBER 22.

To face page 197.

From May 26 (the battle at Kinchou) our losses have been: killed, 3,200 men and 59 officers; wounded, 8,500 men and 286 officers. Of the wounded, up to the present not less than 2,500 to 3,000 have recovered and returned to the front.'

During the night of the 21st about 900 corpses were collected under 203 Metre Hill. At 2 a.m. on the 22nd Colonel Tretiakoff reported that the enemy were again advancing on to it, and that our men had great difficulty in holding on. Fort No. 5 was bombarded all day. On the 22nd the town and part of our line were being bombarded, when Smirnoff started to reconnoitre 203 Metre Hill himself. Under a hot fire we reached Fort No. 5 (by courtesy a 'fort,' for it had no masonry shelter, and was even now a ruin), but had to wait until the fire slackened at the enemy's dinner-hour before we could venture to watch over the parapet; he then saw how 203 Metre Hill was surrounded. To relieve Fort No. 5, which was being heavily shelled, he decided to telephone to Electric Cliff to turn their fire on the enemy's guns, but the time taken to get the telephone message through was disheartening. (I have seen an article in the *Voenny Sbornik* by a M. Timchenko-Ruban, to the effect that the Fortress was supplied with materials for telegraph and telephone construction on a *luxurious scale!*)

The General was disturbed about the position of 203 Metre Hill, though for that front, as a whole, he had no fear. He thought that the enemy would storm this hill that night, and that they must therefore have large masses of reserves collected somewhere close by: he wanted to find those reserves. His theory was justified, for at 1 p.m. a report was received from an observation post at Pigeon Bay that, from a small peak half a mile away, a good view could be had of a deep ravine running to the foot of 203 Metre Hill, and that in it the enemy's reserve of almost two regiments was hiding, waiting apparently till dark to make a fresh attack on the hill.

Smirnoff at once telephoned to Colonel Khvostoff to send a section of quick-firers from Liao-tieh-shan or Fort No. 6 to shell them, and at the same time told him to warn all guns on the west front to be ready to sweep the south-west foot of 203 Metre Hill, where the enemy were bound to first show themselves on leaving the ravine. The section of quick-firers moved cautiously towards the ravine without being seen from the enemy's siege-batteries. It then suddenly opened rapid fire on the crowd of reserves massed in the ravine, and caused great loss. They were surprised, and, as had been foreseen, bolted out on to the slopes, where they came under the fire of the guns of the west front and scattered in panic, leaving great numbers of dead behind. It was a most skilful and daring operation, for these guns advanced to within one and a half miles of the enemy's outposts and four miles of their siege-guns; the gunners must have been so taken aback that they did not at once open fire, and it was evening before our section was forced to return to Liao-tieh-shan, after a brilliant piece of artillery work.

On that night a pyroxyline mine was rolled into the attack trenches, and caused awful havoc, a number of the enemy being literally blown to atoms and many burnt and wounded. The remainder bolted, and, falling into our wire entanglement, were hurled down the hill. After this they again made two mad efforts to storm the hill from the north-west, but both assaults were repulsed with loss.

On the morning of the 23rd another Japanese battalion, which was in this same ravine, came under the fire of our guns, took to the slopes, and in about ten minutes was also wiped out of existence.

The initiative in thus checking the attack on the almost

captured 203 Metre Hill was the conception and work of the Commandant alone, and was due to his true grasp of the situation and his taking the risk of sending guns where most other commanders would have feared to send them.*

In Stössel's order of thanks to the troops for their work on this occasion, all the seniors were mentioned by name —except Smirnoff!

From the moment this assault was beaten back, the trenches in front of 203 Metre Hill were gradually evacuated, and the enemy went to earth only on Angle Hill. All their sapping was confined to the north-east. On the western front of the Fortress there now remained in our possession only 203 Metre, Flat, and Divisional Hills.

There was now more interference than ever with Smirnoff's arrangements. No sooner did the Commandant give an order (based on his personal acquaintance with the state of affairs) than it was altered. It was only through the mediation of Kondratenko that a deadlock was prevented; in fact, Kondratenko's chief work now consisted in persuading Stössel that the opinions of one of his friends—always diametrically opposed to Smirnoff's—were detrimental. Every morning and late every evening, after going round the fighting-line, Kondratenko, Biely, Grigorenko, and Khvostoff used to meet the Commandant. All questions as to the defence which were pending were then decided, and the programme of future work for armament, fortification of positions and distribution of troops and their supply was worked out. Each of those present received detailed instructions, and at the following day's meeting reported results. Stössel and his staff never took part in these meetings. Indeed, he, as a rule, did

* Several of the general officers in Arthur claimed that it was due to them.

not interfere till after Smirnoff had issued his orders; he then altered them or by his own made it impossible to carry them out. But, notwithstanding this, work continued, for all knew that it was necessary, though the District Staff's interference often caused hopeless confusion, hindered success, and demoralized the garrison.

The following is what Colonel Raschevsky wrote in his diary on September 28:

'What strikes one most on inspecting the fortifications on 203 Metre Hill is the impossible arrangement of the trenches which encircle the whole of the top and have apparently been made under the influence of our "Mad Mullah." Those placed on the steep slopes are deep, narrow, and have a very thick roof. They resemble long dark corridors with narrow slits in the front wall. To hold such trenches is difficult, for they are quite unadapted for defence. The loop-holes have been made tight under the roof, so that to look out of them in a downward direction is impossible, and the field of fire is consequently very small. In fact, all beyond 20 to 25 yards is dead ground, so that an attacking force can get up almost to the position without loss. They are difficult to aim from, as the men cannot stand up straight and have to fire stooping. Generally speaking, their arrangement is such that the attacker is able, with small loss, almost to fall on the defender and take the top of the hill, whence the defence can be driven from under the bomb-proofs. It is only the pluck and coolness of our men in making the most of the 25-yard field of fire, coupled with the indecision shown by the Japanese in the last moments of an attack—for they have not yet displayed dash or made a rapid attack with the bayonet—that has enabled us to hold the hill so long.'

There was none too much ammunition in the Fortress to waste, and yet while we were trying to husband it, the

A COMPANY IN THE TRENCHES.

To face page 200

following absurd note was written by Stössel to General Smirnoff. The author's amazing ignorance of the functions of big guns and his want of foresight is by it strikingly illustrated:

'Groups from three to five men can often be seen running about on Pan-lun-shan. The artillery does not shoot. Why? They should never wait for orders to fire at infantry on the run. The artillery seems to want waking up, and it is not the first time this has come to my notice.'

The enemy did not lack humour. I find a note in the diary for the 24th. 'It is said that the Japanese have dropped a letter for us recommending Electric Cliff to fire more carefully lest they should hit Kuropatkin!' Considering his many promises to come down and help us, this was rather smart. But all the same, even our friends the enemy had their disappointments. As Smirnoff said, 'Their General Staff had furnished Tokio with a detailed plan of the Fortress, upon which the plan of the attack was carefully worked out. They expected everything to go as had been ordained, and so have run up against some "snags." Where they never suspected any defences they have found works of strong profile. They have now fought for two months without doing much, though, till the naval guns had all been mounted, I feared for the north-east front. They have fixed upon our weak side all right—the north-east—behind which is our heart.'*

The September assaults had contributed their quota to the hospitals, where life had now been very sad for months: not only were the patients suffering, but the whole staff were worn out.

On the 28th the besiegers' attention was turned towards Erh-lung-shan and Chi-kuan-shan Forts and Kuropatkin

* For the detail of the guns taken from the navy and mounted on shore see Appendix II. All these must have been surprises to the enemy.

Lunette, towards which they were burrowing, while the former and Tumulus Battery were bombarded. That day also we were favoured with visitors. In the morning the look-out post on Golden Hill sighted a Japanese destroyer on the horizon from which a boat, flying the French flag, put off in the direction of Arthur. Admiral Loschinsky sent out one of our destroyers, which brought the stranger into port. In her were two men who said they were correspondents of a French and an American paper.

While the Fort Commander, Admiral Grigorovitch, was telephoning their arrival to the Commandant, they informed the officers around them that Kuropatkin had been defeated at Liao-yang and that the Baltic Fleet had returned to Libau. We had received no news for a long time from outside, and this, of course, quickly spread throughout the Fortress, producing an overwhelming impression.

The Commandant at once ordered an aide-de-camp to meet the new-comers and take them to the Fortress Staff Office to be examined, and he requested the Chief of the Staff to let him know the result. He then busied himself with his work. Not hearing of them for two or three hours, he telephoned to the Staff Office for information, and was told that they had been met on the road to the Office by Stössel's aide-de-camp, and had gone to his quarters. Before half an hour had passed in came the orderly with the cards of X. ——— and Y.——— ! The correspondents were inspecting the Fortress, accompanied by Lieutenant Malchenko, and, happening to pass the Commandant's house, they thought they ought to pay him a visit! He did not receive them, needless to say, but rang up the Staff Office.

Colonel Khvostoff arrived, and reported that the foreigners had been with Stössel, had lunched, and had been sent round the Fortress works with Malchenko. They had shown no papers when asked for them by the Port authorities, but had produced a letter they had brought for Stössel, the address of which was most ungrammatically written. Having arrived at Stössel's, they gave him this, which turned out to be a letter from Christoforoff (Christoforoff and Prince Radzivill had brought Stössel the telegram about his appointment as Aide-de-Camp to the Tsar). Stössel asked them to lunch, and after the wine the conversation became intimate. He openly told them the condition of the Fortress, the shortage of ammunition and of supplies. After the feast he gave them permission to go round the works. Excusing himself on the grounds of work at the front which could not be postponed, and to which he had personally to see, he went for a walk in the town (instead of his usual after-lunch snooze).

The Chief of the Staff finished, and every one was for the moment silent. A whirl of ideas flashed through the Commandant's brain. Stössel was interfering in his arrangements, and would make the defence of the place impossible, and his authority was being undermined at every step. This state of things must be stopped.

'Gentlemen, I am going at once to General Stössel, and will try to persuade him that suspicious correspondents must not be allowed to stroll about the town and Fortress. They must be arrested and examined.'

Having reached Stössel's, he pointed out that the arrival of these men, apparently with the blessing of the Japanese and without any papers, necessitated our looking upon them with suspicion, and that they must on no account be permitted to inspect the defences. Stössel replied it was nonsense; that they had brought a letter to him. When it was remarked that this letter was so very badly written that it was hard to believe that a Russian officer could be the author, he replied that neither Christoforoff nor Prince Radzivill were great scholars!

Smirnoff, feeling that Stössel might not wish to compromise himself in the eyes of foreigners, said:

'If, sir, it is inconvenient or awkward for you to arrest them after they have been your guests, I will undertake it as Commandant, and will have them examined. Let all the unpleasantness fall on me. Later, when we find out there is no reason to suspect them, they will blame me, and not you, and will take me for the Russian barbarian.'

'Pooh! they will see very little of the Fortress. There is no harm in it. They will go back and write that we are not yet eating earth, as most of the foreign press seems to think, and that bands are always playing. How could they be spies, when they asked me to let them enlist in the volunteers that they might bark at the Japanese?'

On the 29th, loaded with letters and requests, they left the hospitable shores of Arthur, and when they had gone a short way they were taken up by a Japanese destroyer.

I afterwards met X. ——— in Tokio. He showed me a passport given him by the French Consul at Chifu, which was signed by the District Staff on September 28. Beneath was the signature of General Nogi's Staff, dated the 29th! From Nogi, Y. ——— went to Nagasaki and X. ——— went to Chifu, whence he telegraphed untruths about Stössel to his paper.

The day of their departure Stössel stupefied us. We had become hardened to most things, but the following order by the District Staff, dated September 29, was in its way a gem:

'Yesterday, the 28th, two foreign correspondents, French and German, arrived from Chifu. They were allowed to land without the permission of the Commandant, and without a careful inspection of their papers. They had letters of credit from the Consul, but no official permission to act as war correspondents from the Staff of the army. They came, of course, to ascertain the condition of Arthur, for while in one paper it has been said that we are already eating earth, another has it that bands play and we want nothing. Having detained them for twenty-four hours at the Staff Office under the supervision of an officer, I ordered the Chief of the Staff to examine their papers, and afterwards to send them at once out of the Fortress, as I couldn't permit them to remain.

' Much nonsense is printed in foreign papers, from the capture of Port Arthur to the retirement of Kuropatkin almost as far as Harbin. We are inclined to believe all this, though it is utter nonsense. For instance, we are ready to believe that Kuropatkin has retired to Harbin, till we look at the distance, and see that he must in two days have gone a hundred miles; but our people still believe these things because they appear in a newspaper— a foreign paper at that.

' For the future the Port authorities are requested not to allow anyone to land without the Commandant's or my permission, or without a careful inspection of papers. The Commandant will be responsible for this.'

I think comment on the above is unnecessary.

At this time a rumour was current among our men that Arthur had been sold to the enemy. It was founded on letters from the Japanese saying: ' Why do you hold on? Arthur has been sold to us. We have it here on paper.' For the ignorant masses this was quite convincing.

CHAPTER XXX

MOLE WARFARE

OCTOBER 1 was an epoch in the history of the defence of Port Arthur, for it was on that day that the first of the 11-inch shells fell into the Fortress, and so changed the aspect of affairs.

It was during a conference held on the positions that a message was received that an 11-inch shell had fallen in Chi-kuan-shan Fort, destroyed the masonry, and killed and wounded several men. Those who were present suggested that a bombardment had again begun from seaward.

'No, no. These are newly mounted land guns—big guns. I am afraid they will do for the forts and the fleet.'

The majority of those present doubted it.

'You doubt it? It is no use. You will soon see.'

I walked with General Smirnoff back from this conference along the hills. As the bullets were whistling over the deep trench along which we were walking, I could not help thinking that there was nothing worse than this whistling—one got used to shells, but not to this ceaseless squeaking of invisible birds. We had scarcely got on to Mitrofanieff Hill when a pillar of smoke, sand, and stones rose up out of Chi-kuan-shan Fort, as if a gigantic tree had sprouted up and been thrown down. Then, with clockwork regularity, fantastic trees grew up every few minutes in different directions along the north-east front, and we heard the roars of dreadful explosions. Eight of them occurred in Erh-lung-shan and Chi-kuan-shan Forts this day and did great damage to the casemates. They were different to anything I had yet seen.

About two o'clock in the afternoon a bombardment of the town began; the fire was concentrated near the Tifonty Mill and grew heavier every minute. As the area of the falling shells gradually contracted, it became clear that the target was this mill which supplied us all with flour. This was the first day of a special bombardment of the town: there were no 'shorts'; it was a deliberate cannonade. The fire continued steadily, and the mill was struck by several shells.

The result of the foreigners' visit to us was apparent!

The conditions in the besieged Fortress—the wearing, trying uncertainty, the want of confidence, and the constant, unavoidable danger began to tell. The younger men lost their nerve, and suicides commenced.

On October 2, nine 11-inch shells fell in Fort No. 4, and it was reported that a large howitzer was mounted to the right of, and in rear of, Sugar Head.

On October 5 a fire was caused on Tiger's Tail by the enemy's shells. In the morning we attacked Signal Hill, which we had abandoned the day before. After a fierce and bloody fight we recaptured it, and it remained ours till the end of the siege. On this day Raschevsky's diary says:

'The parallels and approaches of the gradual attack against Chi-kuan-shan Fort, Open Caponier No. 3 and No. 2 Battery, have got much closer. The Japanese are working with great perseverance, notwithstanding our fire and occasional sorties. It has been decided to make these oftener and of greater strength.'

And on the 7th he continued:

'... The approaches also are being pushed forward with greater perseverence than ever toward our works; we can, in the daytime, even see the men digging, while we are not strong enough to concentrate our gun-fire on them. The situation of the approaches is particularly dangerous in front of No. 3 Open Caponier, where the distance between the enemy and ourselves is only 50 yards.'

In the afternoon the enemy suddenly began to shell the quarters of Stössel and Smirnoff by *rafales* from their small guns. Their sudden and extraordinarily accurate shooting is proof that they had learned from the 'correspondents' where Stössel and the Commandant were living, for up to this they had always fired on the Viceroy's house. As soon as the first shells began bursting near Stössel's quarters he at once gave orders that General Volkoff's house, which was at the foot of Quail Hill, should be got ready for him, and he began to move. However, an 11-inch shell happening to strike this house, compelled him to abandon the idea.

On the 8th Raschevsky wrote:

'Since 9 a.m. their big howitzers had been busy firing at our howitzer batteries Nos. 20 and 21. By 1 o'clock they had fired about fifty-five shells at them. The left half of the masonry battery, No. 21, afterwards presented a picture of complete destruction: the concrete is in many places destroyed, and has fallen down in great masses.'

For six days now the town had been bombarded with 11-inch shells—great masses of metal of awful destructive power. Nowhere could we find real safety from them except, perhaps, in the bomb-proofs of Madame Subotin, dug out of the rock. The concrete of the forts, the armour on the battleships, were penetrated clean through. From October 1 life in Arthur was any-

BOMBARDMENT: JAPANESE SHELLS BURSTING ON HILL.

To face page 208.

thing but pleasant. On the evening of the 9th the enemy seemed to be concentrating near Rocky Redoubt, Water-Supply Redoubt, and the village close by.* We had made an attack, but as they were in great force, we had to withdraw. They were also active on the west front. The following is the entry in the diary for the 9th:

'It was quite quiet up to 12 o'clock. Exactly at noon a salvo was fired at the town. After a short time it was repeated, and then, at 2 o'clock, the enemy turned all his nearest batteries on to the trench in front of Erh-lung-shan Fort, which we had recently recaptured, and we were obliged to abandon it again. To-day a sortie was ordered on the Redoubts with the object of seizing them and some of the Japanese trenches in front. In the event of success the enemy would, of course, have had to evacuate his parallels and approaches to Chi-kuan-shan Fort, from which they were now only 150 yards distant. The attack failed.'

On the 10th the 11-inch shells did much damage on the north-east front. General Stössel published the following order this day:

'On the 7th instant I received the following telegram from the Commander-in-Chief, dated Mukden, September 20:

'"I have received your despatch of September 16, and I congratulate you warmly on your fresh success. We are making energetic preparations for an advance. The 1st Army Corps has already arrived. God be with you! Trust to me to succour you."'

When Kuropatkin received General Stössel's piteous despatch asking that he might be allowed to remain on in Arthur, he had forwarded it to Petersburg, asking what he was to do (Stössel had by this time been made Aide-de-Camp to the Tsar, and had been promoted to the Third-Class Order of St. George), adding that he had already twice recalled him from the Fortress. Petersburg replied that it left the matter entirely to him. Kuropatkin naturally did

* Dapalidjuan.

not think that Stössel had changed his spots by having had the above distinctions conferred on him, but being a clever and experienced diplomat, he did not wish definitely to recall a newly-appointed Imperial aide-de-camp, and so kept silence.

On the 11th and 12th there was fighting round Chi-kuan-shan and Erh-lung-shan forts on the east, as well as Fortification No. 3 and Tumulus Redoubt, where the enemy gained ground. On the west they were entrenching on the slopes of 203 Metre and Long Hill. The following is an extract from the diary for October 12:

'The enemy's approaches are getting closer up. With wonderful energy and perseverance they are digging them towards Chi-kuan-shan Fort, Open Caponier No. 2, and B Battery. Early this morning two additional approaches were made towards Kuropatkin Lunette, and parallels were begun. Our artillery fire is not continuous enough to stop them. Sorties are not often made, and when made few scouts go with them, so that they are carelessly carried out, and have little result; consequently the siege-works are progressing rapidly. In the last parallel in front of B Battery the Japanese have built a thick bomb-proof with a covering of Chinese wood, apparently with the object of protecting the gun crews from hand-thrown grenades.

'We are all alarmed for the condition of the caponier of the main faces of Chi-kuan-shan. They have mined behind the counter-scarp, and evidently mean to blow it up. In anticipation of this we are making two counter-mine galleries from the corners of the caponier, which, running for twelve yards, ought to hit their main gallery, but as the soil here is almost rocky, progress is slow, and we may be late in intersecting the enemy's gallery. In order to ascertain the position of their shaft, and the direction of their gallery, orders have been given for a sortie to-morrow, in which the sappers will take part.'

RESULTS OF A BOMBARDMENT.

To face page 210.

This sortie failed through the clumsiness and noise of the men who were not specially trained scouts.

From Chi-kuan-shan we made another sortie on the night of the 15th. This also failed, owing to the majority of the men turning tail. Stössel's order about sorties undoubtedly had a good deal to do with the poor spirit shown on this occasion. An attempt was also made to stop the work on the sap-head by firing the war-head of a torpedo charged with 70 pounds of pyroxiline out of a torpedo-tube on the parapet. On the 17th General Gorbatovsky took the place of General Nadein as commander of the right flank of the defences.

In some places now the enemy were face to face with our men, with only a distance of twenty to thirty yards between them. Taking cover behind sand-bags, the Japanese were doggedly continuing step after step, yard after yard, and fresh earth was constantly being thrown up out of the deep saps which hid the men working. Occasionally one would see the glint of a spade, or a black forage cap, and along the communicating trenches here and there would run a Japanese dressed in black.

On the 20th Raschevsky wrote:

'At 3 a.m. a sortie was made from Chi-kuan-shan. Its arrangement was entrusted to me, as its main object was to reconnoitre the enemy's works nearest to the fort: 40 infantry and 5 sappers took part in it. Owing to the failure of the two preceding sorties, this one was most carefully prepared. The men were ordered to go round the foot of the glacis and its slopes, and to dash on to the head of the enemy's three approaches. If possible they were to destroy the works, and not attempt to pursue, but immediately to return. A party of 25 infantry and 3 sappers, under the command of Ensign Marchenko, were to go round the fort from the left, and to lie concealed on the glacis. The other portion, under the command of a non-commissioned officer, was to break through the wire entanglement placed along the glacis of the right face, and to lie down there silently and wait for the signal for the general attack by both parties. The signal was to be a ray of search-light thrown on to the nearest peak of Ta-ku-shan. The first flash, at 2.45 a.m., was to be a warning for the men to be ready: the second, at 3 a.m., was to be the signal for the general attack. Both parties were then to dash simultaneously down the glacis right on to the appointed place. By doing this we hoped partly to escape the fire of the enemy's machine-guns, which in the previous sorties had fired along the direction of the salient angle of the glacis, and along the slopes under the flanks of the fort. Our men were not to fire till discovered, but directly the Japanese opened fire, the guns and infantry from the neighbouring works were at once to concentrate their fire on their near trenches—not, however, closer than a certain given direction towards the foot of the glacis—in order to divert their attention. At the same time a demonstration was to be made from the covered way of the salient angle by raising dummies up above the glacis, and throwing stones tied with string on to the wire entanglement to make it appear as if we were trying to advance from the centre and not from the sides.

'As all the members of the sortie parties knew beforehand where to go and what to do, everything turned out almost as we had hoped. The sortie was a complete surprise to the enemy, and, when our men dashed on to the heads of their approaches, they were seized with panic. From the glacis I could hear their shouts of fear distinctly, and their fire was comparatively weak, no machine-guns being used. After these shouts we heard a few cheers, and then, after five or ten minutes, our men appeared at the caponier, where they rushed, fearing that the Japanese would recover themselves and get to work with their machine-guns. However, they successfully went down the ladders into the ditch and got round the caponier. They had ascertained that the Japanese were making galleries under the caponier of the fort. The direction of one was along under the axis of the caponier; the direction of the other we did not discover. The heads of their galleries were found covered by bomb-proofs, into one of which a sapper managed to throw a six-pound bomb. We lost 3 killed and 7 wounded, amongst whom, to our great regret, was Marchenko, very dangerously wounded. The result of the sortie was so far very successful, and our countermining will now no longer consist of groping blindly.'

Colonel Raschevsky was inclined to judge our men severely, because they dug slower than the Japanese; he called them absolute children. I cannot agree. The Russian soldier, when he came to Port Arthur, was physically strong, though intellectually starved. By this time he had become physically starved as well. No soldiers of Western Europe would have done what he did.

Extracts from Colonel Raschevsky's Diary.

October 22.—'The Japanese approaches are being particularly developed these days in front of Kuropatkin Lunette. There are scarcely any new ones in front of Chi-kuan-shan, but the men saw from Caponier No. 2 that stones were being carried out from under the glacis; they were evidently from mine-galleries.

'To-day, for the first time, was heard a suspicious knocking in our counter-mines. I myself listened for a long time from both galleries, but could hear nothing. I think it must have been a mistake, and the noise was probably made by some one in the caponier. However, I have told the miners to listen oftener and more carefully.'

'*October* 23.—The enemy have not yet done anything to seize Open Caponier No. 3, and the position there is most curious. We have dug a trench and are holding two branch ends. At these ends are our sentries; the Japs are behind the sand-bag traverse. Occasionally our men throw hand-grenades at them, but they haven't as yet replied. At this close range it is impossible to prevent constant firing, each trying to spot the other and shoot first.

'Our men resort to the following ruse: one fastens a pole on his back, on this is put a fur cap and round it a great-coat. He then crawls on all fours along the trench. The Japs at once open fire on what they think is a man, and, exposing themselves, give us a target. Generally speaking, the men are in excellent spirits, though things are daily getting worse. It is becoming colder—almost freezing at night, and in the thin bomb-proofs it is uncomfortable, and in the trenches horrible. The danger from the enemy's fire is daily increasing and the food is wretched. But our men don't seem to notice it; on the contrary, they seem to be more light-hearted and full of life.

'A chicken costs 12 roubles, a goose 20, an egg 1, a pound of flour 1, a pound of horseflesh ½ rouble.'*

The Colonel was to-day kinder to the men. His engineer heart had grieved at the slow progress made with the works, and it was quite comprehensible. His one desire was at all costs to interfere with, to delay, the enemy's works, not to give him a chance of seizing the trenches of the fort. In Chi-kuan-shan the men felt uneasy, expecting an explosion, but the countermining was in Raschevsky's capable hands.

On the 24th he wrote:

'Yesterday morning the noise of the enemy working was heard in our left gallery in front of Chi-kuan-shan; this time it was more easy to be certain of than yesterday.

* About 10 roubles go to the English sovereign.

Judging from the loudness of it, the enemy cannot be further than 20 to 25 yards away, and are advancing. However, the sounds are very indistinct,' etc.

On the 25th he wrote:

'Since 4 a.m. the enemy has ceased work in front of Chi-kuan-shan, and has not recommenced up to the present. This is very suspicious. We must in any case not stop our work, but must shove on our two galleries and sink two new ones.'

On the 26th:

'At 4 a.m. we suddenly heard the Japs working from the left gallery in front of Chi-kuan-shan, and the thud of their tools seemed much nearer and more distinct. When I listened to it about 9 a.m. it seemed as if they were at work almost 5 feet to the left and a little above. The calculations for a camouflet* to destroy their gallery worked to a charge of about 320 pounds of powder, and I at once gave orders for a chamber to be dug out and all the necessary material for tamping it to be got ready.

'After listening most carefully, we all came to the conclusion that the enemy was sinking a shaft from the surface of the glacis with the object of destroying our left gallery. At 8 p.m. the Commandant arrived, and, having listened attentively, said that he wished to fire the first camouflet himself.'

The besiegers had driven a long gallery under this fort so as to blow it up, and the defenders dreaded an explosion any moment. The dangers were much exaggerated, for some one spread a rumour that the Japs were laying a charge of thousands of pounds of dynamite, and the whole fort would be blown into the air. Though this

---

* A camouflet is a mine calculated to break down and shatter an enemy's underground gallery without causing any crater at the surface.—E. D. S.

was of course absurd, in their hearts the men believed it and it acted on their spirit.

It was a calm moonlight night when the Commandant went to inspect the fort and the progress in mining. Having received the report of the officer commanding, General Smirnoff went to look at the destruction to the masonry work, which had just been badly breached by 11-inch shells. Then he descended into a subterranean casemate, where he was met by Colonel Grigorenko, the Fortress Chief Engineer, Colonel Raschevsky, Colonel Tretiakoff (an expert in mining), and some junior officers. Having gone down into the low subterranean gallery and crawled to the end, he listened attentively to the work being done by the enemy. From this gallery he crawled through to the next, where he again listened. Not more than 3 to 4 feet of granite can have been between him and the enemy. Every one looked at each other in astonishment; this daring act of Smirnoff's surprised us. Amongst the men the word was passed in an instant: 'The Commandant himself has crawled into the gallery.' Some believed it, some did not; but it made a great impression.

At a conference in the officers' casemate (where General Kondratenko was killed later on) it was decided to load the camouflet without loss of time. The condition of the fort was indeed serious; any hour, any minute, an explosion might take place. It was a question of who could explode their mine first—a game, and a dangerous game! All were nervous; but General Smirnoff calmed every one by a few words.

Heavy and continual bombardment of the position was carried on on the 26th and 27th. At 11 a.m. on the 27th the Commandant, accompanied by Lieutenant Hammer, arrived in the fort, where everything was ready for firing the camouflet. All the Fortress guns were ordered, in case of a successful explosion, at once to open fire on the

GENERAL SMIRNOFF FIRING THE CAMOUFLET.

To face page 217.

enemy's batteries if they should concentrate their fire on the fort. At this time the enemy were methodically shelling this fort, Kuropatkin Lunette, and B Battery with 11-inch shells, which were detonating every two or three minutes. After an inspection of the tamping,* the electric leads were extended from the station in the casemate to the outer parapet, when, taking advantage of the interval between the shells, the General went on to the parapet and pressed the firing-key.

Above the caponier rose a cloud of dust and smoke, out of which projected planks, stones, and bodies. We had succeeded,† and the garrison breathed again. The awful, weary hours of waiting had passed. Congratulating every one, the General went down into the inner courtyard. His presence as Head of the Fortress at the most dangerous place in the defences soon became known, and inspired every one to further efforts.

On the 28th the Japanese blew a breach through the wall of Caponier No. 3. They followed this up with an assault, but were repulsed. The same afternoon batteries were shelling the road from Little to Big Eagle's Nest, from the saddle of Ta-ku-shan. This only emphasized what the loss of that hill meant to us. One cannot help asking why, when Velichko drew out the plans of the Fortress, he did not insist on Ta-ku-shan being fortified? It was a natural fort! Could he not realize the difficulty of defending a fortress when its roads are under shell-fire from the very commencement, and he our leading Professor of Military Engineering? On the western front there was considerable activity towards Wolf's Hills, the trenches of Siu-shuing village.

* To 'tamp' a mine is to fill up the gallery by which it is loaded with earth or other material, so that the force of the explosion shall not be dissipated in that direction.—E. D. S.

† From the description it seems that this was more than a camouflet.—E. D. S.

So far, Smirnoff had endeavoured to imbue the men with the idea of no surrender, but General Fock now wrote a memorandum in which he persuaded General Stössel to lay mines under our forts in order that they might be blown up when it was decided to abandon them! Smirnoff protested most vehemently, trying to show that mining our own forts (to say nothing of the danger to the men in them) would sap at its very roots the principle that a fort might perish but must never surrender, and would consequently demoralize the troops.

Stössel believed Fock, and insisted. The Commandant then sent Grigorenko to him, who submitted a detailed report, in which he pointed out most clearly that the results of the explosions of such mines would, generally speaking, be inconsiderable, whilst the mines, if laid, would constitute a great danger to the garrison, as a chance 11-inch shell might cause a premature explosion. But Stössel had made up his mind, and ordered chambers to be made in the forts for the laying of charges. In Chi-kuan-shan, however, the Commander, Lieutenant Floroff, said point-blank that so long as he was in the fort it should not be mined.

General Stössel was in the habit of issuing frequent orders direct to General Biely, Commanding the Fortress Artillery, and gave the strictest instructions that not a gun was to be mounted without his special sanction. As he never visited the fronts attacked, and, therefore, could not judge of the state of affairs himself, the result of this order could have been merely to make unpleasantness for General Smirnoff and to interfere with his work. Though things were usually done in the end as Smirnoff wished, all this hindered progress and made matters very difficult. When systematic attacks began before the general assault of October 30, Stössel, ignoring the Commandant, told General Biely to open fire from the northeast front on to the ground near to the fortifications at sunset—at first at intervals, more often between 7 and 8 p.m., and again intermittently from then till 10 p.m. His ostensible reason was that the enemy would attack at that time. Of course, they did not do so, but despite the protests of Smirnoff, Biely, and Kondratenko, he insisted upon this cannonade—an utter waste of ammunition, when every shell was valuable.

To fire away our ammunition pointlessly in this manner was unjustifiable, nay suicidal, and the motive for doing so is difficult to comprehend.

The following were some reports received on the 29th:

'There has been gun and rifle-fire all night. A fight is now being waged for the trenches. In Chi-kuan-shan the enemy have blown in the roof and outer wall of the caponier, and are making use of iron shields in the attack. From the opening they have dug a trench to their trenches. The fire is increasing on Erh-lung-shan, Fortification No. 3, and Tumulus.'

On the night of the 29th a heavy bombardment of the position took place, and on the 30th there was a general assault. The following telephone messages will show the progress of the fighting:

From Colonel Naumenko.

11.50 a.m.—'The artillery-fire is increasing. Shrapnel has begun. We are awaiting the attack.'

From Sub-Lieutenant Vonliarliarsky.

12 noon.—'The Japs are storming B Battery.'

12.30 p.m.—'A bayonet fight is going on in B Battery.'

12.50 p.m.—'A Japanese flag has been planted on the parapet of B Battery. It has been torn down, but the Japs are near the guns.'

From Captain Golovan.

1.55 p.m.—'Fortification No. 3 is on fire. Our men are holding the gorge.'

2.10 p.m.—'Fortification No. 3 is burning and the face has been occupied by the Japs. Our men are in the gorge. Chi-kuan-shan, Fortification No. 2 and Kuropatkin Lunette were captured, but have been retaken.'

2.23 p.m.—'Fortification No. 3 has been recaptured.'

From Colonel Semenoff:

11.30 a.m.—'The Japs are in force under Erh-lung-shan.'

12.25 p.m.—'Water Supply Redoubt and trenches are strongly occupied by the Japs.'

1 p.m.—'The Japs are moving in force on Erh-lung-shan.'

2.5 p.m.—'The Japs were driven out of B Battery at 1 p.m. They are on Wolf's Hills in force.'

2.25 p.m.—'From Wolf's Hills the Japs are moving in front of Water Supply Redoubt.'

5.15 p.m.—'The Japs are entrenching themselves in front of the obstacles of Fortification No. 3. They are laying sand-bags along the trench that was ours. They have got storming ladders.'

The third general assault on October 30 was preceded for four days by a cruel bombardment, which began at midday on the 26th, and gradually increased till the night of the 29th. For forty-eight hours the works on the north-east front were incessantly pounded, the enemy deciding to break down and annihilate everything with their fire, and then to dash on the defenders with the bayonet. The night of the 30th was black, and the sky cloudy. Morning came, and the fire increased, and by 10 a.m. the whole front was enveloped in dense smoke: the hills were literally reeking. The whole destructive energy of hundreds of guns was thrown on the portion

KUROPATKIN LUNETTE AFTER THE ASSAULT IN OCTOBER.

from B Battery to Fortification No. 3. It seemed as if everything there must be destroyed—every living thing killed, that no one could be left to defend, and that any moment the enemy would dash in to fight in the very streets. Further opposition seemed useless, inhuman. The fire slackened, and then again broke out; shrapnel was poured on to those points that were to be stormed; the other works were paralysed by high explosive shells. The assault began, and the Commandant quickly moved the reserve companies along the ravines to the attacked points. The enemy dashed in with the bayonet, and hand-to-hand fighting ensued. The Commandant followed the progress of the assault and defence on the telephone, and the reserves were massed in time at all the most dangerous points successively.

At last the front was again clear. We had survived the third assault, and the crisis was over.

The October attacks were short, but most determined and bloody. As regards their success, it was but slight. The enemy had gained some dozens of yards—no more. Our total loss was Open Caponier No. 2, already quite destroyed by the bombardment. The Japanese had fired over 150,000 shells.

CHAPTER XXXI

JAPANESE VIEWS. GENERAL FOCK'S MEMORANDUM ON FORTRESS DEFENCE

THE October assaults had been repulsed. The third obstinate attempt to get possession of Arthur had been a complete failure, and had cost the enemy more than 10,000 killed and wounded. We breathed freely again. Though tired and utterly worn out, the success instilled fresh life and energy into the whole garrison, and revived their hopes. After all, the Japanese were only human beings, and they must eventually become tired out and have to confess that Arthur was too much for them. The long months of bombardment, the anxious days of assault, the death and the suffering of thousands of our nearest and dearest, as well as that of the enemy, had somehow made us feel attached to these inhospitable mountains and the mournful ocean which silently lapped against the shores of the Kwantun Peninsula. Arthur had become near and dear to us, almost as if it were our native land, in which we had passed our lives. It was painful to think that perhaps the time would come when the Japanese might break in and become masters of it all. Each of us felt in greater or less degree that he was taking part in a historic drama; he realized that the whole world — civilized and uncivilized — was keenly watching every phase of this bloody struggle, and was impatiently waiting the conclusion: for whatever the end was to be, it would have an influence, not only on the future of Russia, but on the future of the world.

But to continue with our chronological narrative: On October 31 the enemy on the eastern front were making preparations to assault Fort Erh-lung-shan and the intermediate works near. They were repulsed in their assault on Chi-kuan-shan, but that fort was in a most critical condition. On the west their assault on Fortification No. 3 was beaten back, with a loss of nearly four companies to them from our gun-fire. On November 1 Stössel excited much indignation by accusing a most excellent officer—Colonel Murman—against whom he had a grudge, of malingering. He appointed a special medical board to examine him, but similar publicity was not given to the finding of this board—an acquittal—as was given to the accusation. On November 2 the following entry was made by the late Colonel Raschevsky in his diary:

'It is interesting to spend a night in Fort Chi-kuan-shan. Here we are all in good spirits, though rifle-fire never for a moment ceases. In the darkness of night, broken only by the detonation of a pyroxyline grenade, the flare of a rocket, or the flash of shrapnel, the dark figures of soldiers doing their best to repair the damage caused by the bombardment of October 30 can be seen swarming about. Wood fires are kept burning in the ditch of the caponier, in order to prevent the enemy breaking through unseen along the ditch towards the gorge. We are waiting to be attacked to-morrow, the Mikado's birthday. It is a strange coincidence that to-morrow is also the anniversary of the Tsar's accession to the throne.'

Raschevsky mentioned wood fires. In properly built forts in Western Europe a number of well-protected electric lights are arranged in the wall of the counterscarp to light up the whole of the outer ditch of the work. Of course, such a luxury was not to be expected in Arthur, where the Fortress was defended by primitive means and all was left to the bravery and inventiveness of individuals. In many ways the defence suggested mediæval days, when human life was of little value. The Japanese, heroically throwing away their lives in front of Arthur, strewing the ground with their bodies as if they were sacks of earth, showed that we had to deal with enlightened barbarians, inspired by great patriotism and a deep conviction that a victorious campaign, in particular the conquest of Arthur, would give them a permanent economic position on the continent of Asia. I know that I shall be told that I am wrong, but, still, I venture to express my opinion that the Japanese are savages, but enlightened savages, for they knew that they could by their blood relieve an economic crisis in their country. In Japan before the war I often talked with one of the best educated of Japanese. On my asking if Japan really meant to fight us (I was then under the delusion that Arthur was ready and that our War Office was capable), he thought deeply in an apparent effort to answer me. The question was a serious one, one which every Japanese invariably tried to avoid. I had long intended to put it, but had refrained, knowing from experience that I should only receive the kind of reply of which every Japanese is a past-master—a reply —but not an answer. He thought for five minutes and then said: 'Our nation works differently to the way you work in Europe. Our poor do not know what it is to rest. They are thrifty and sober; they have little to eat, and that little is bad; yet most of them are fairly educated. Machinery is beginning to be largely used everywhere, so that small industries are failing, and the proletariat is increasing daily. Our nation is fond of its country and of the Mikado, and wishes much to eat, drink and read, to multiply and to educate their children, etc.—in fact, to live under conditions of certain refinement.'

(He was quite right. I have travelled much, and, with the exception of among the English, I have never seen such refinement and culture in domestic life as with the Japanese. Japan is called the 'Country of the Rising Sun'; I think I should not be far from the truth if I called it the 'Country of Children that Never Cry.') 'Politics have taken a serious turn. We have begun to negotiate with Europe. We commenced to watch, to listen to and to learn from Europe: now we have learnt all that there was to teach. On all our ships and in our factories English engineers have for several years gradually been replaced by our own, and we are running these things ourselves; but what we want is land for our growing population and markets for our industries. In Tokio they have been doing their best that the masses should hate the Russians for taking Arthur, and they have been working on the national pride. The school-teacher and the priest have educated and are educating the nation to this end, and every Japanese knows his own national history well, and knows, for instance, that in olden days Korea belonged to Japan, and that one of our Empresses had of her own freewill given it up.'

I listened attentively, and said that Japan would never succeed if she tried a fall with Russia, for that Colossus would crush her. In a couple of months the clamour of war was heard. Having arrived in Arthur, I, like others, at first believed in a happy issue of the campaign. I was convinced that Japan would be annihilated, and I was sorry for her.

The day before the anniversary of the capture* of Arthur, Colonel Tirtoff, who was in charge of the *Novy Kry* till Artemieff's arrival, had asked me to write a leading article. I took one to him the same day, out of which he cut everything unpleasant that I had put in about the English.

* From the Chinese.—E. D. S.

(I used then to write against them very strongly.) 'Admiral Makharoff is opposed to attacking the English in the press until the war is over. He does not doubt how things will end, but till that time he wishes to be polite; and in Petersburg they are of the same opinion. We must not commit ourselves,' was the advice of Colonel Tirtoff, as he handed back my corrected MS.

The following extract from Order No. 780 issued by General Stössel, published at this time, will not be without interest to the reader:

(1) 'The detachments in each fort and battery will be told off in three reliefs. The first will be on duty and ready for any emergency, being relieved every two hours, between 6 p.m. and 6 a.m. If there are two officers, each will take half the night. Additional to officers commanding sections of the defence, the following officers will be responsible that this order is carried out, and will take steps accordingly: Generals Nickitin, Tserpitsky; Colonels Reuss, Savitsky, Khvostoff and Nekrashevitch-Poklad. General Nickitin, being the senior, will arrange for the tours of duty, and will indicate the sections to be visited and the hours for visits.'

Notwithstanding the fairly heavy losses we had suffered during the bombardments and assaults, especially in the last one, Smirnoff had not abandoned a single important work of the main line. With the exception of Nos. 1 and 2 Redoubts we had held our ground. Yet General Fock continually endeavoured to convince General Stössel and the garrison that Smirnoff did not know how to conduct the defence of the Fortress, and what could have been more subversive of discipline than the following memorandum published at the time by him?—

MEMORANDUM, DATED PORT ARTHUR, NOVEMBER 3, 1904.

'A besieged fortress can be compared to a man suffering from gangrene. In the same way that he must sooner or later succumb, so, too, must a fortress fall. The doctor and the commandant should realize this fact from the very first day that the former is summoned to the bedside of the patient, and the latter placed in command of the fortress. This, however, does not prevent the former believing in miracles, or the latter hoping for a happy issue by external relief. And this belief is more necessary for the latter than the former, provided it is not so great as to make him careless. Gangrene attacks a man in his extremities—*i.e.*, in the toes—and it is the doctor's duty to separate the part affected. His task consists in prolonging the patient's life, and the commandant's in postponing the date of the fortress's fall. The doctor must not allow the patient suddenly to die, any more than the commandant must allow the fortress to fall suddenly through some unforeseen circumstance. The patient should succumb gradually, beginning with the extremities, and so should the fall of the fortress be gradual, beginning with its outworks. Successes with the first, as with the second, will depend upon the extent to which the infected member is in time removed, or the attacked position is abandoned. This task is no easy one; the doctor must be a skilled professional to be able to fix the moment when the diseased organ is more harmful than useful; but this alone is insufficient, for the patient must first be persuaded to agree to amputation, as without his consent the operation will be impossible. Who cares to lose a leg or an eye? Some would prefer to die, and the doctor must be able to persuade the invalid that it is possible to get about without a leg, that an American artificial leg will enable him to dance. Nor is it easy for the commandant, who must have a thorough grasp of the situation, to be able to know when an attacked position has inflicted all the loss that it can inflict on the attacker, and to recognize the moment when the balance of superiority passes to the enemy. The skill *consists in being able to abandon a position before the final blow is delivered*, and at the same time to sell the enemy his success dearly. It must be borne in mind that fortress warfare resembles rearguard fighting, a fact which does not seem to be appreciated by everyone. But besides eyes the commandant must have character, for commonsense and conscience will call out " Retire !" while sentiment and anger will cry " Hold on !" He does not know what he can get—like the artificial leg—in place of what he loses. With the doctor it is different, because his medical store contains false limbs, the commandant's does not. The doctor amputates the infected organs so as not unnecessarily to waste the life's blood, keeping it for the heart. The commandant abandons by degrees the enceinte of the fortress so as to preserve strength for the keep. The length of a defensive line should correspond to the strength of the garrison. No doctor would torture a patient by attempting to reunite the amputated organs, even though it be a tooth taken out by mistake. And, similarly, no commandant should waste his men in an attempt to recapture a position once yielded to the enemy, even though it were abandoned through carelessness. At Sevastopol we held firmly on to what we had, but we did not once attempt to retake a position; the redoubts Komchatsky, Selenginsky and Volinsky are good examples. Osman Pasha, the celebrated defender of Plevna, never attempted to retake a position; on losing one he hastened to hold out another to our blows. Thus, when we seized Grivitsa Redoubt, he got ready another for us which he named Grivitsa Redoubt No. 2, with which he checked our onslaughts. Would he have held out long if he had attempted with his army of 40,000 to retake the redoubts from us? He was careful of his men, and they served him with their spades. A doctor to perform his task successfully must have more than a true hand and eye; he must make his assistants conform strictly to his requirements, and must also know in detail all their work, and be able to direct them while doing that work. Who could perform a good operation if his assistants did not know how to help him, or through stupidity were to pull the thread or the wool out of a wound? To that there would usually be but one end—death. And so for a commandant, it is not sufficient for him merely to select the site of positions and indicate the style of fortification. What use is a fortified position if its loopholes are unsuitable for firing, or, instead of giving the firer cover, expose him? The Germans assert that with modern rifles a flying sap cannot approach closer than to within 800 metres, etc., etc.'

This is a sufficiently long quotation to show in which

direction Fock's mind was working, and how he took Smirnoff's disinclination to surrender anything. It was poison—slow—but certain poison, which even in October had begun to demoralize the garrison, which was beginning to suffer from scurvy, induced by bad food. The Commandant knew that this memorandum was known to the whole garrison, for copies had been lithographed and freely distributed. But how could he deal with this enemy of the Fortress? He had done everything that was in his power; he had already removed him from duty, and could do no more. The reader must not forget that General Fock had great influence over Stössel, that what he said at this time he said 'by order.' There was only one thing to do, namely, to arrest both of them. Why did Smirnoff not do this? may be asked. Because the garrison was already demoralized. It was tired, it was morally and physically worn out; and if he had arrested Stössel—'the Tsar's Ambassador,' as Fock called him—he would not have had the full sympathy of the garrison, but would only have created more dissension and scandal. For what would these partisans of Stössel—the all-powerful —have said in Arthur, if they had found out that he had been arrested by the hated Smirnoff? For he was then literally omnipotent, and the future hopes of many depended on him. When he arrived in Russia, instead of going into confinement as a prisoner of war, hundreds of his friends thought that he was the hero and Smirnoff the intriguer. Read their evidence before the Committee of Inquiry, and you will be amazed to see to what extent men can lie to save their own worthless skins. Therefore, keenly as Smirnoff felt the baneful influence of this effusion of Fock's, he was powerless. To have such a spirit fostered in the Fortress was truly an alarming symptom.

On November 3 there was a heavy bombardment,

which resulted in a tremendous fire in the oil stores, covering the surrounding country in dense black smoke.

The following are some entries in Raschevsky's diary:

November 9.—'To-day the Japanese succeeded in blowing up the magazine on Zaredoubt Battery with their 11-inch shells. The explosion was awful, but luckily our shells were not damaged. On B Battery two casemates have again been penetrated by an 11-inch shell which burst in the lower floor.'

November 10.—'To-day we fired from Fortification No. 3, with the mortar improvised by Lieutenant Podgursky, a pyroxyline bomb weighing about 40 pounds. This mortar is very convenient: it makes hardly any noise in firing, but it is difficult to regulate. In any case the effect of the bomb is very great, and with luck should cause the enemy much damage. They have for quite a long time fired at us in the forts from similar guns, and this is the first time that we have retaliated in kind.'

November 12.—'The Japanese seem to be doing nothing. In places where formerly we could not show ourselves without being fired on we can now pass with impunity. This gives rise to the hope that they are in a bad way, and will leave Arthur.'

It was not only Colonel Raschevsky who thought this. Many buoyed themselves up with a firm belief in a speedy relief. Unfortunately these hopes were not destined to be fulfilled.

November 14.—'Chi-kuan-shan Fort, Kuropatkin Lunette, and B Battery are in a most critical state. The latter has been broken down and so battered by 11-inch shells as to be useless. The masonry of the casemates is all crumbling away, and the commandant of the battery is asking that it may be tied together by a wire hawser! I daily get similar original suggestions.'

On November 18 the following telegram from Lieu-

B BATTERY.

tenant-General Sakharoff to Stössel was published in orders:

'Admiral Alexeieff is leaving for Petersburg. General Kuropatkin is appointed Commander-in-Chief of the army and fleet. From the troops in the theatre of war and the corps which are now arriving three armies will be formed. The following are appointed to command them: First, Linevitch; second, Gripenberg; third, Kaulbars. The Baltic Fleet has passed the Spanish coast. The Manchurian army commencing to advance on October 5 compelled the enemy to fall back; but, afterwards, having met considerable opposition, and after a series of obstinate battles from October 9 till 17, took up its position on the bank of Liao-ho, in very close touch with the enemy. All three Japanese armies are in front of us in fortified positions. The Commander-in-Chief hopes to attack the enemy and advance, and he is confident that the gallant troops in Arthur will hold out.'

And so the Viceroy went away, and Arthur had to work out its own salvation. His departure from the army added to the depression produced by Sakharoff's telegram. In the garrison it was no secret that between him and Kuropatkin strained relations had for a long time existed, but it was thought that from the date of the retirement at Liao-yang they had assumed a better character. It was well known in the Fortress that Liao-yang had been splendidly fortified, and as regards preparation conceded little to Arthur. It was known that in front of Liao-yang we had 25,000 more men than the enemy, and that Alexeieff had asked for, or insisted on, a forward movement whatever it might cost, in order that the Fortress might be relieved. The Viceroy had strained every nerve towards Arthur, as he well knew that, as well as attracting the attention of a large army, it was a sanctuary for the fleet, which would be a decisive factor in the campaign. He feared the destruction of the fleet in Arthur, for in that he read a bad ending to the war. He knew that upon the fall of the Fortress the fleet would be destroyed, and that once it was destroyed the campaign would be lost, for we should never obtain command of the sea. So long as the sea was not ours, so long as the Japanese could feed their armies from Japan without hindrance, it was useless to think of a successful issue. He realized all this, but whatever the cause his wishes were not accomplished.

CHAPTER XXXII

HINTS OF SURRENDER. MORE ASSAULTS

FROM Raschevsky's diary, November 18:

'We have to wait and wait, which makes things very difficult. It is far easier to fight a fierce action which would be decisive than to waste away by slow degrees. Sickness has already begun to break out. The troops seem to be losing their energy, and there is a shortage of supplies; in fact, the state of affairs is daily becoming unendurable, and we are not in a condition to endure any ill-fortune.'

In reality the position of the Fortress, owing to the decrease in energy, was getting alarming. Writing these lines, I can plainly see before me Raschevsky's well-built figure, as he used to report to the Commandant about the progress of work at the front. If the energetic, indefatigable Raschevsky began to feel tired, what must the faint-hearted have felt? Raschevsky did not live, he seemed to boil over with energy, and his eventual loss to the army was irreparable. Arthur was indeed being burned in a slow fire, but no one had been heard to talk of a surrender except *chez* Stössel. We all longed for a fierce, decisive battle and a quick end—better death than a shameful surrender. Meanwhile the enemy were on the whole silent, occasionally firing at us, gathering together their strength for the future. This lull, this weary uncertainty, was hard to bear. To continue quoting from the diary:

'News has been received from Chinese spies that the seven guns which were lying on the shore of Louisa Bay have been mounted at Nangalin. They also say that the Japanese, annoyed at their want of success in the north, have decided to seize Arthur between November 21 and 26, whatever it may cost, and that if this assault, for which they have about 40,000 men and will use their fleet, is not successful they will not attempt another.'

At this time there occurred one or two episodes which seemed to be indicative that the idea of surrender was already held in certain quarters.

General Smirnoff was now paying special attention to the third line of defence, already armed with naval guns, and having excellently laid out redoubts and deep trenches. On this it was intended to oppose the enemy should we have to withdraw from the second line, and Admiral Wiren was to be appointed to command it. In the middle of November the Commandant unexpectedly received a definite order to cease work, not only on the third but also on the second line (the Fortress works), and at the same time to send men from the main reserve direct to the first line of defences — the forts, and intermediate works — of the north-east front. Though General Smirnoff thoroughly appreciated the important rôle which the second and third lines must play in the future defence, he obeyed the order and also sent the Chinese coolies to the first line, but at the same time continued to carry on the works on the second and third lines energetically, so that by the middle of December they were almost finished. Stössel's definite order to cease work on the second defence line, which was most important, could only mean that he either did not understand the importance of this line, or that, under the influence of General Fock, he had an ulterior motive. The course of later events forced me to suppose that the order was founded on a previously formed conclusion that the Fortress could no longer be held, once the enemy should have established themselves on the part of the first line between Tumulus and B Batteries, from the highest point of which — Eagles' Nest — they could observe and direct the fire of their guns on to any point up to the sea. Another incident, which took place directly after the interruption of communications in April or May, possessed in conjunction with the one just described a curious significance. From the moment when the railway was cut, the majority of the inhabitants had wisely withdrawn their deposits from the Russo-Chinese Bank, and consequently scarcely any ready money remained in hand. The Defence Fund deposit could not be drawn upon, but in the treasure chest of the 3rd Corps there was £120,000. As the Chinese labourers had to be paid almost daily, cash was a necessity, and General Smirnoff asked the Officer Commanding the District, through Colonel Grigorovitch, to advance him £5,000 in order to pay them; but Stössel declined. Then the Commandant himself went to Stössel and tactfully and politely explained to him the absolute necessity of paying the labourers, and he said that if this was not done all the work on the defensive lines would be stopped. The reply he received was: 'The money belongs to the 3rd Corps, and should stay at its credit.'

'But, sir! I have absolutely no money with which to pay the Chinese, and shall have to stop work altogether in two or three days. And, if they find they can't get work here, they'll all leave the place. At present great progress is being made with the defences; the labour is absolutely essential, and I must have money.'

He argued, and tried for a long time to convince the Officer Commanding the District, but when he had done speaking Stössel bluntly refused his request with the words:

'It is nothing to do with me.'

Realizing what menaced the Fortress if money for these labourers was not forthcoming, the Commandant sent General Kondratenko to Stössel to endeavour to get something out of him, if only a small sum. Roman Isidorovitch* went and, after great difficulty, eventually got Stössel to lend £1,500 to the Defence Fund. Later it was found necessary to borrow several more thousands of pounds from the Corps treasure chest, but to each request Stössel at first gave a refusal, doing everything in his power to hinder and prevent the money being lent, though the Corps did not require it, the men having nothing to spend their savings on. It was due to this difficulty of getting money, that right up to the strict investment, the works were not made on the liberal scale on which they should have been, but were constructed from hand to mouth according to the money available. It was due to this action of Stössel's that much in the Fortress was found unfinished and unready at the beginning of the blockade. Everything which was incomplete had to be finished anyhow—by the superhuman efforts of men who, since May, had begun to feel the effects of being on short rations.

Early in November, Field-Marshal Oyama joined the besieging army, with orders to ascertain on the spot the reasons for the siege being so long protracted. The enemy were alarmed at the vision of the approaching Baltic Fleet, for, so long as Arthur held out and afforded protection to what remained of the Pacific Ocean Fleet, this, after uniting with Rojdestvensky's squadrons, would shake their position at sea. They were accordingly most anxious to take the place, and at a council of war it was decided that Nogi must seize it at any cost. Fresh troops were pushed up to the front and the tired ones relieved;

* Kondratenko.

more guns were mounted, and ammunition was replenished.

All along our front men lived just like every one else—they ate, slept, hoped, and died. To the noise of bursting shells and firing they had long got accustomed. A shell burst; a man—perhaps two or three—were killed. Up came others to separate the wounded from the dead; but there was no bustling, no excitement; it was nothing unusual—merely routine! Habit is indeed wonderful! When a fairly long lull took place we at first enjoyed it, but after a bit began to feel the want of something. It was thus all along, except on the extreme flanks and on the shore-line, where there was almost absolute safety, especially on Tiger's Tail and on Liao-tieh-shan. Of course, in some parts of the front, where the enemy were within 15 to 20 yards of our parapets, life was a little *difficile*. Neither side dared show up to the other; each was always waiting for a shot. It was particularly so with Erh-lung-shan, Chi-kuan-shan, and Fortification No. 3. Here the merciless, dogged struggle never relaxed for a moment. It was our most vulnerable point, to which the enemy stuck like leeches, daily establishing themselves more firmly. They dug, dug, dug, and burrowed like moles, laid fougasses, exploded mines, pounded us with shells, and showered bullets.

We now started the November 'assault season,' which began on the 20th. It was begun by a bombardment, followed by an assault of several companies, which dashed into the ditch of Fort Erh-lung-shan. After a desperate struggle they were repulsed by 4 p.m., and by dusk all was quiet. The men were so used by now to death and fighting that, except for the conversation in the casemates being afterwards perhaps a little more animated, no change was noticeable. Among the staff-officers alone one saw unusual activity, and telephones were busy. An alarming message was received, also, to the effect that the enemy had fired a mine in the caponier of Fort Chi-kuan-shan, and we had been obliged to withdraw some 8 yards behind the traverse. We had actually given them 8 yards! This was at once reported to the Commandant, who, as usual, when not riding round the defences, was studying the chart on his table or at the telephone: he never had a spare moment, for he was the slave of the telephone. When in his house he could never leave the instrument day or night. He used to doze beside it, always ready to make decisions and give orders, for he was the nerve-centre, the brain of the Fortress.

On November 21 they built a new battery on the north side of Ta-ku-shan. The importance of the hill and its command over the north-east front was always being brought home to us. Had we only fortified it well, and been able to retain it, what a difference it would have made to the Fortress! On the 22nd the enemy hurled themselves at dark against Kuropatkin's Lunette and B Battery, but, being seen in time, were repulsed by reserves taken from the flanks. At midnight they again attacked, and again were hurled back.

The following is an extract from Raschevsky's diary of November 23:

'As usual, we found it very hard to drive the Japs out of the trenches; it took nearly half an hour. It is clear proof of the faulty way in which our trenches are built. They are narrow and deep with revetted banquettes, on which the men firing are like hens on a perch, and it is impossible either to shoot well from them or to give support to any place broken through. Men who want to move along have to squeeze past those manning the trench; it is agony to a wounded man to pull him out along behind the firing-line, and it is very difficult for an officer to get past to control the fire. Generally speaking, our trenches are beneath contempt, and yet new ones are being dug, on the same pattern, and we are forbidden to let the men build them in any other way!'

On November 24 our guns were busy all day destroying the crowning of the glacis of Fort Erh-lung-shan and Fortification No. 3. The enemy continued to advance, and mounted a gun in the ditch of Fortification No 3, with which they battered the caponier, and built a bridge across the deep ditch of the Fort, which was only destroyed with great difficulty. There was heavy firing all night on the 25th, and at dawn on the 26th every gun on the northeast front was in action. The whole line from Tumulus Hill to B Battery was enveloped in thick black smoke from the shells of hundreds of guns concentrated on to a comparatively small space.

The assault began. Living waves of infantry rolled forward against the ruined front, and the moments of the Fortress seemed numbered. Bayonet fighting was the order everywhere, as attack was met by counter-attack. Time after time the enemy threw themselves with extraordinary gallantry and persistence on Forts Erh-lung-shan, Chi-kuan-shan, and B Battery. Thousands were mown down, but the living surged onwards. But it could not go on for ever, and at 3.30 the infantry attack slackened and ceased. We had lost nothing save Caponier No. 2, but the enemy kept pounding us with their guns, and we awaited a fresh attack. At 8 p.m. our search-lights showed up dense columns behind the railway near Tumulus Hill. On they came, and hell was again let loose. Their effort was to break through Cossack Square towards the central wall. They got the hill and reached our guns—on, on they crept. It was the moment for a counter-attack. Bayantseff's Company, commanded by Lieutenant Misnikoff, doubled to the rescue and reached the foot of the hill.

'Company—halt!' shouted Misnikoff. 'Men—in front is glory or death. Pray.' The men crossed themselves. 'Forward!'

It was the work of seconds. The men climbed upwards. 'Hurrah!' 'Hurrah!' was heard, and the Japanese were hurled backwards, bayoneted, and swept from the battery; but again they crept up. A section of quick-firers came to the rescue and saved the day, leaving the hills in our hands. The Fortress had survived a critical moment, for the firing-line had not only sucked up into it the whole of the naval detachment, but the latter's reserve also. All next day and night an incessant stream of wounded poured into Arthur, our losses being more than 1,500 men. In many companies but sixteen men remained. A strange sight could be seen that day, for the slopes below and beyond Tumulus Hill were thickly spread with dead Japanese. A thick, unbroken mass of corpses covered the cold earth like a coverlet.

On the day of the assault the following order had been issued by Major-General Nakamura, who commanded the Japanese force told off for that forlorn hope—a force composed of the bravest men of the whole of the enemy's left flank.

'Our objective is to sever the Fortress in two parts. Not a man must hope to return alive. If I fall, Colonel Watanabe will take over the command; if he also falls, Colonel Okuno will take his place. Every officer, whatever his rank, must consider himself his senior's successor. The attack will be delivered mainly with the bayonet. No matter how fierce the Russian fire, our men will not reply by a single shot until we have established ourselves. Officers will shoot any men who fall out or retire without orders.'

This order shows excellently how relentless our enemy could be in his determination to gain his end. It was issued to a force of brave men—all volunteers. It was read on the threshold of death, and each of those who read it knew well that it was not a joke, but the end. Each well understood that there, on the steep slopes of Tumulus Hill, was his grave. They knew there was no return; that the only issue was death—the death of a hero or the shameful fate of a coward. That is the kind of foe we had to fight.

On the 26th the enemy unexpectedly began to force their way forward on the western front, in front of 203 Metre Hill. On the morning of the 27th they attacked in superior force the hill at Little Pigeon Bay, north of the village of Shan-yan-tau, capturing a small hill in front of the big one. This led to the idea that an attack on the highest point of the western front was intended, and Smirnoff accordingly began to strengthen that flank by bringing up the reserves. On the 27th an attack was delivered between Flat Hill and 203 Metre Hill. During the day a magazine in Fort Erh-lung-shan was exploded. The noise was awful, but the casualties were few.

About 4 p.m. on the 27th a group of Japanese carrying a white flag were seen near Tumulus Battery. The 'Cease fire' sounded, and the parapets of our works were dotted with those who had for long been hiding in the trenches and other holes. Men seemed once again to become men, and the past was forgotten. Captain Spredoff went out from Fortification No. 3 to meet the flag party, whose leader handed over a letter written in French asking permission to carry away their wounded. The staff was telephoned to, and while waiting, those who had been deadly enemies looked at each other with unconcealed curiosity and admiration. Around on all sides the dead were lying—endless rows of them. The sight was horrible. They lay, as if alive, with open but glazed, fixed eyes. On their faces were expressed horror, entreaty, agony, anger, and even laughter. They lay face downwards, doubled up, with nails dug into the ground in a last convulsion. They lay with thoughtful, earnest expressions on their faces, upturned to the heavens. They lay on their sides naturally, as if asleep. They lay with clenched fists and wide-open mouths, showing all their teeth. They lay in heaps together, one on the top of another, some looking at others as if in amazement. They lay side by side in several rows. Arms and legs were torn off, heads split in half; some were headless, some were cut in half. . . . The Japanese looked and looked again, but could find no wounded among the dead, and they slowly and sorrowfully retraced their steps. . . .

CHAPTER XXXIII

THE FIGHT FOR 203 METRE HILL

WE now come to the culmination of the tragedy, and perhaps the bloodiest scene of carnage of the whole war—the fight for, and capture of, 203 Metre Hill. For now the enemy, foiled in their desperate attempts to precipitate matters in the north-east, confined themselves on that side to the slow but sure progress afforded by mine warfare, and turned the whole fury of their attack on to our western front, of which 203 Metre Hill was the key. It was of this hill—the scene of eight days of the most desperate fighting—that Stössel had said in May:

'Why are heavy guns being mounted here? They are quite unnecessary. When necessary, I will send a field battery up, and the devil himself will not be able to come near it: all the approaches to it can be distinctly seen.'

But the Japs knew its value, and knew that if they could take it they would be able to destroy the fleet, which would practically mean the end of the war. Nogi, under pressure from head-quarters, decided to take the hill at all costs, and to take it quickly. He was not afraid of losses; he only wanted 203 Metre Hill.

In November, at the beginning of the attack, the place, though covered with fire and communicating trenches, was, as regards fortification and armament, very weak. Everything possible had been done by Colonel Tretiakoff to protect the 6-inch guns mounted on its highest point by means of improvised protection of rails, beams, sheet-iron, stones, and earth. On the 27th the attack commenced and followed the usual course. For some hours the top of the hill was enveloped in the smoke of the shells bursting over it; then the Japanese quickly, and in lines, crept up the steep slopes, and the assault began. They fought and fought like fiends—fought till exhausted, till they lost consciousness, one of their battalions being literally swept from the face of the earth. It was dark before the last of them was driven off and the fighting ceased; but there was no rest, for all dug throughout the night—in many cases dug their own graves. At dawn a single shot echoed forth from the besieging lines, and in a few seconds the hill was again a smoking crater—the focus of the concentrated fire of many guns, whose shells were bursting in clusters. Then the assault commenced and continued the whole day. The Commandant, keenly observant of what was happening all along the front, was always ready with reserves to forestall the enemy in strength wherever the latter chose to deliver his blow. With a defensive line of eighteen miles the initiative was, of course, with the besiegers, but the Commandant was able to counter. The messages from the hill became more and more urgent. Kondratenko asked and begged for reinforcements, but the local reserves had already all been absorbed into the firing line: only one thing was left—to combine forces; and Smirnoff sent échelons from the main reserve to Tea Valley.

And what were Stössel's staff doing all this time? Some were reading copies of telephone messages sent to the Commandant, and Stössel was breakfasting, writing orders, eating, sleeping, eating again, and again sleeping. What happened at the front he only heard at fourth-hand. He had no telephone to his house—he hated telephones—and having nothing to do, he now took an interest in the Town Guard, and decided to send them up to the trenches on the hill. General Smirnoff protested. He fully appreciated their worth, but he could not allow them to go into the advanced positions, for though very keen and brave, they were ill-disciplined and had little training, so that they could not be expected to take the place of regulars. The Commandant always regarded them as his last military reserve. Having, through the mediation of Kondratenko, persuaded Stössel of this, he insisted on their being appointed to the hospitals as attendants, to replace the regulars, who were sent to the front. Stössel hated these civilian soldiers: why, I do not know.

On the night of the 28th, 203 Metre Hill was still ours, and from dawn next morning it was again the object of the same artillery fire. The whole of the defensive line anxiously watched to see what would take place on its top. For two days now it had withstood the fiercest and most insistent attacks of our gallant foe. Its garrison, already reinforced from the reserve, in spite of bravery which equalled the enemy's, began to melt away. Assaults were delivered first from the left and then from the right. At last the enemy seized the left peak (it is a two-humped hill), and the flag of the Rising Sun fluttered in the smoky air—a few more efforts on their part and the hill must be lost. From the officer commanding the western flank—Colonel Irman—the Commandant received a message that the Japanese had captured the hill. Before taking action, Smirnoff wished to corroborate this, for Colonel Tretiakoff (who was actually on the hill and really conducting the operations there, as Irman, though a most gallant field artilleryman, was ignorant of fortress warfare, and moreover had not that precious gift of a military leader—the gift of quietly and sensibly weighing the surrounding circumstances) reported that a hot fight was being waged on the top, but that he hoped, with the assistance of the reserves, to keep possession of the right and disputed peak. He said the local reserves were exhausted, and asked earnestly for help from the main reserve. Smirnoff, after confirmation, at once sent up a fresh body of men. I must mention that a spectator got a different impression of the progress of the fight, according to his point of view. One onlooker reported that the enemy had seized the hill and our men were in full flight. Another, watching from a different place, reported at the same time that the enemy were falling back. A third said the fighting was over and the hill was ours. Anyone watching from the direction of Pigeon Bay would have said the Japanese had taken it, as the western slope hid the whole field from view. Moreover, the attackers and defenders themselves could not see everything going on — they were too busy in hand-to-hand fighting to observe more than a few yards around. Smirnoff had to sift out the various messages coming in in order to arrive at the truth, and it was not till he had done this, and was sure that we could still hold on to the hill if reinforced, that he threw more men into the fight.

Suddenly an officer arrived in a tremendous hurry, and said that he was instructed by General Stössel to summon General Smirnoff at once to the District Offices for an 'extraordinary' conference. The District Staff had also received Irman's message, and it had made a great impression on all those assembled at the office.

'Irman reports that the Japs have seized 203 Metre Hill,' commenced Stössel at once.

General Fock chimed in :

'It's absurd to try and hold out there longer : we must think of the men. It's all the same : sooner or later we shall have to abandon it. We must not waste men ; we shall want them later.'

To Fock Smirnoff replied :

'It is premature to think of abandoning the hill at

RESERVES WAITING UNDER 203 METRE HILL.

present. I am pouring in reinforcements, and it is still ours.'

'But Irman—Irman reports—and he knows what he is saying—he reports that the hill is in the enemy's hands, and it is essential for us to take steps to get the men away, to save our reserve, to, to——'

'I repeat, there is no particular danger; I have already taken the necessary steps,' said Smirnoff.

'But Irman, who commands that front, reports steps must be taken. The enemy will break through; he'll force the line, and there'll be a street massacre,' said Stössel and Fock together.

'They cannot break through the line of forts and intermediate works,' answered Smirnoff.

'Oh yes, they can. You must retrench—cut off Tea Valley—and thus prevent a possible dash through.'

'I have already said that to you,' said Fock to Stössel, 'and I urge it being done. It is absolutely necessary to retrench, to cut off into compartments.'

'I quite agree—I quite agree,' echoed Nickitin.

Fock turned to Stössel.

'Sir, won't you order Tretiakoff to remain on the summit of the hill all the time? Let him sit there. Let him see for himself how the men are faring.'

The latter turned to Reuss and told him to telephone to Colonel Tretiakoff on no account to leave the top of the hill.

Smirnoff looked helplessly at those around, his glance now angry, now contemptuous.

'But Tretiakoff is always there! He is himself in immediate command of the fighting.'

This reply changed the current of Stössel's thoughts, for he replied:

'And so with the loss of this hill the days of this place are as good as——'

'Gentlemen, I guarantee that 203 Metre Hill will be ours as long as it can be reinforced without risk to the north-east front. You may feel at ease; I promise you that by morning-tea to-morrow I will give you the hill,' interrupted Smirnoff, his voice trembling.

'But it is all the same necessary that Tea Valley be partitioned off, or they will be able to break through,' was the reply.

'I have not enough men; if I do that I can't hold on to 203 Metre.'

'Take the Town Guard—make use of them,' said Stössel.

Smirnoff, seeing that the only way of getting away was to agree, said:

'All right; but I promise you by morning-tea to-morrow the hill shall be yours. Good-bye,' and departed.

Meanwhile, on the place itself the fight was desperate. One moment success was ours, the next it passed to the foe. At times it seemed as if all were lost. But no! not yet. Gathering themselves together, inspired by their officers, reinforced from the reserve, our men made a final effort and hurled the enemy down. The hill was again ours. What took place there cannot be written of with an ordinary pen — it could only be described in blood. The hopes and fears, the gallantry, the—— words fail me. Some of the details are perhaps known to General Tretiakoff, the hero of that spot, and those under him. It was just now, when it seemed to be touch-and-go with the hill, that a rumour was spread to the effect that Kinchou had been recaptured by Russians—by Trans-Baikal Cossacks. It was nonsense, of course, but the men were so worn out and so hungry for good news from the north that the hope of relief by General Kuropatkin, cherished deep down in their hearts, made them believe. The third day's fighting came to an end; darkness set in, and the position was not yet lost. At tea-time on the morning of the 30th it was still ours—Smirnoff had kept his promise.

The fourth day was but a repetition of the preceding three. Shells of all sizes, from 11-inch to small quick-firers, rained upon the place. All cover, or anything that looked as if it might afford shelter, had long ago been turned into heaps of stones, iron, beams, rubbish, and mangled bodies. During the night shelters of sorts had been scraped up, only to be swept away by the first breath of iron which accompanied the morning light. The fury of the assault reached its zenith at 4 p.m. Fortunate it was that the enemy's demonstrations on the east were weak, and so enabled us to withdraw troops from that front to assist here. Bayonet fighting again took place for some hours, but at four the Japanese were compelled to fall back. The hill was still ours, but its slopes were thickly strewed with more dead, more dying. In four days we had, excluding dead, lost 37 officers and 4,000 men wounded. Among the dangerously wounded was the gallant Colonel (now Major-General) Tretiakoff, of the 5th Regiment, wounded in head and chest. When those near him implored him to go to the rear to get his wounds dressed, he refused, muttering, ' I will die where my regiment dies.'

On the morning of December 2, Colonel Irman, on receipt of a message from the top of 203 Metre Hill, telephoned to Smirnoff:

'All the assaults have been repulsed, and the hill is completely in our hands.'

This glad news was soon known, and the town rejoiced, for the enormous importance of this spot to Arthur was recognized by all, and Smirnoff's intention to hold on to it, even though thousands of lives were sacrificed, was appreciated. The north, south, and east fronts had, however, been considerably weakened, every available man that could be moved from them being taken—this hill had greedily swallowed up all, even the reserves of the reserve. The Commandant went to Fort No. 5 to make a detailed reconnaissance of the position, and after a thorough inspection of the enemy's approaches and distribution, he became more than ever convinced that things were in a most critical state. The enemy had got possession of almost all the slopes, and apparently had no idea of withdrawing. They were merely resting—bracing up for a last and final blow. The slope towards the western front, as well as the road joining it to the hill, were in our hands; all the rest was theirs. There was not the slightest doubt that the assault would be renewed with greater force and fury. Four hours Smirnoff spent in the fort, and returned in anything but a happy frame of mind, for the attack might be renewed at any moment. Exactly at midday, after an anxious respite, the bombardment again broke out.

That evening the garrison read the following order (No. 865, of December 2, 1904) by Stössel:

'I have just returned from seeing Colonel Irman. [Stössel had gone to Tea Valley, and made a speech to the men, not apparently realizing that it was no time for words.] 203 Metre Hill is all ours! Let us thank God for it. You—heroes that you are—have done what was impossible, what was only possible to brave men like yourselves. From November 20 to December 2 —*i.e.*, for twelve long days—the enemy has repeatedly launched his columns to the attack on A Battery, on B Battery, Kuropatkin Lunette, Erh-lung-shan, Chinese Wall, Chi-kuan-shan, Fortification No. 3, Tumulus Battery, Pan-lun-shan, ending with 203 Metre Hill and the position at Pigeon Bay—*i.e.*, from sea to sea. Day and night they have come on, not sparing themselves; they have fallen under your heavy blows, but you have not yielded to them a rood of ground. What was ours on November 20 is ours to-day. In the Tsar's name, as his aide-de-camp, I thank you. You have delighted him. May God preserve him! Hurrah!'

A white flag was raised on the north-east front this day, and the Japanese asked for a truce to bury their dead. The Commandant at once gave permission, fire ceased, and friend and foe mingled amicably. All at once shots rang out from Erh-lung-shan Fort—it was an awkward moment for us. It turned out that Stössel, annoyed that his permission had not been asked for the dead to be buried, had therefore ordered the firing to recommence. Smirnoff was quite within his rights in not referring the matter, but Stössel's dignity had been hurt. He was now formally asked for permission, and granted one hour's armistice.

On the north-east front a white flag was again raised by the enemy in front of Kuropatkin Lunette. The fire gradually ceased, and we put one up in reply. From both sides officers and men moved out to meet each other, and they met like old friends.

CHAPTER XXXIV

THE LOSS OF THE HILL

WHILE men were slaughtering each other in thousands on this hill the civilized world watched the tape, wondering who would win, what the end would be. How many protested or were even indignant at this legalized butchery? It is said, of course, that war is necessary and inevitable, that it freshens and invigorates national organism. This may be so, but it also brings a step closer the realization of the socialistic dream. Of this I am certain.

December 3 arrived and passed under similar conditions, except that the fight on the hill was, if possible, more exasperated. In the Fortress the feeling of alarm was intensified, and all unemployed men had been got under arms (at the time of the surrender the number of armed men had been increased by 9,000), and the other points denuded, in order to feed the maw of 203 Metre Hill. Even the hospitals gave their contribution. December 4—bright and frosty—ushered in a fresh hell. It was now hardly a fight between men that was taking place on this accursed spot: it was a struggle of human flesh against iron and steel, against blazing petroleum, lyddite, pyroxyline, and mélinite, and the stench of rotting corpses. It was the last day but one of the long-drawn agony.

A shell to-day fell into one of the hospitals full of wounded men, but perhaps the scene of horror inside was hardly increased. Were the enemy getting ferocious in their exasperation, and beginning to ignore humanity? It looked like it. By night our feelings had become deadened by the continued strain; we were almost apathetic.

On the hill our men still held on under the gallant leadership of Colonel Irman, but in spite of his bravery he did not really replace Tretiakoff, and Butusoff, by now well known to the reader, had just before this fight been given a week's leave to rest—a rest which he sadly needed. Captain Veselovsky, of the 26th Regiment, was actually commanding on the hill. The officers with him were Lieutenants Obolensky and Rafalovitch, of the same regiment. While the first-named was calmly doing his duty a splinter tore away his face right down to the lower jaw. On his body there was left a chin fringed with beard and some teeth. Rafalovitch, who was standing alongside, was untouched, being merely covered with earth and blood; but he was quite upset, and asked Semenoff to relieve him for a few hours. The latter telephoned permission, but 'not for more than two or three hours,' as the waste in officers was very great. Rafalovitch appeared at the Staff Head-quarters. He was dirty; his clothes were torn and covered with blood and spotted with whity-red bits of something. This handsome, healthy young fellow was quite unstrung by what he had been through. He was trembling as if in a fever; his eyes were bloodshot and wandering, and he could scarcely speak.

'What's happened? Your face is covered with blood. Are you wounded?'

'No, sir, I am—I am not wounded. It's not my blood; it's Captain Veselovsky's brains,' was the stammering reply jerked out.

'What! Veselovsky killed?'

'Yes, sir. His head was carried away—only not quite:

the lower jaw and beard were left—and I was covered with his brains, right in my face. It almost blinded me. I thought I was wounded. Can I go and rest a little ?'

'Yes, go, and God be with you. Go and rest, but remember we are short of officers.'

After a few hours a message was received that Obolensky had been killed with a bullet in the head. There was now not a single officer left in the 5th Company of the 26th Regiment; there was only the sergeant-major. He was promoted by telephone to be acting ensign, and Rafalovitch was sent for.

The telephone rang.

'Sir, General Kondratenko wants to speak to you.'

Semenoff took the receiver and listened.

'I think the position so serious that Colonel Butusoff should be sent there.'

'Sir, Butusoff is exhausted, and asked a few days ago for leave to go and rest. I gave it him on the condition that he would at once come if wanted.'

'Tell him that I do not order him to go to 203 Metre Hill, but I would ask him to. We want him there; he is irreplaceable. Say it is my particular request.'

He was at once summoned, and went up to the hill. We knew we should not see him again, and sure enough next day Butusoff, the pride of the Frontier Guards, was mortally wounded in the stomach, and suffered frightful agony till he became unconscious before death.

As the sun rose on December 5 it lit up the two-humped summit of 203 Metre Hill for the last time in the possession of Russian soldiers—a handful of gunners, sappers, and infantry hiding among shapeless mounds of rubbish. This was the last day. On it occurred an incident which might be for ever quoted as an illustration of the 'fog of war.'

That morning Semenoff was watching through a telescope from Obelisk Hill. At ten o'clock he saw that the fighting was at the very top of the hill. At noon he saw our men retiring; the Japanese had gained the top, and our men were dashing down the hill. The enemy did not follow; they did not even open fire, but more and more of them were collecting on top and working as hard as they could, throwing sandbags together and entrenching themselves. Their flag fluttered in the breeze. A parapet grew up; our men were getting further and further away. It was all quite clear and distinct. Every minute was precious. It was essential to concentrate a heavy fire on the hill and prevent the enemy establishing themselves, or all would be lost. He dashed to the telephone.

'Put me on to the Officer Commanding the Artillery.'

An answer came from the exchange that the line was engaged.

'In General Stössel's name put me on to General Biely.'

He got through.

'Sir, the Japanese are entrenching on the top of 203 Metre Hill. We are retiring; the artillery must shell the hill. Every minute is precious.'

Biely calmly answered that, according to the reports from Irman, the hill was still ours.

'I assure you, sir, the Japanese have got the hill, and are throwing up a parapet. I can see it through my telescope.'

Biely answered as before, and suggested that Semenoff should communicate with the Fortress Staff. Meanwhile the Japanese were feverishly, rapidly continuing to work, and time was going—precious time that never would return.

Semenoff rang up the Fortress Staff. They replied

that, according to a report just received from Kondratenko, the hill was still in our hands. Semenoff assured them that our men had abandoned it and the Japanese had seized the summit.

The artillery remained silent: without an order through 'the proper channel' they could not open fire. No one else either saw or knew what was happening. It was only from Semenoff's observation point, and by aid of an excellent telescope, that it could be seen that the Japanese had taken the hill. Semenoff again rang up Biely:

'Sir, open fire on 203 Metre Hill, or it will be too late. There are many Japanese there now. They are entrenching themselves on the top, and we shall not be able to get it back.'

'Perhaps you are mistaken. Why doesn't Irman, who is commanding the western front, send us any word? I——'

But Semenoff rang off. It was already 2 p.m. He rang up Irman's staff and spoke to Kondratenko:

'Sir, the Japanese have occupied the top of 203 Metre Hill, and are building a parapet. We have retreated. I can see it all in my telescope. Fire must be opened on the hill.'

'How is it that I can still see our men in a bomb-proof? And Irman tells me that the hill is ours. I will ask him now,' said Kondratenko.

'I assure you, sir, that the Japanese are on the top.'

'Well, I'll ask Irman at once. If it is so, we must open fire immediately, although I myself clearly see our men, and have asked the Commandant not to fire.'

This muddle can be very easily explained. It was all caused by the 'point of view.' The Commandant had received information that the Japanese were on the hill,

GENERAL BIELY.

To face page 256.

and that our men were retiring; he had been told so often before. However, being convinced that 203 Metre Hill was in possession of the enemy, he ordered Biely to open fire on the top. The order was given, but it took at least an hour before it reached the battery commanders by telephone. Meanwhile Kondratenko telephoned to him and implored him not to open fire, as some of our men were still concentrated on the hill! The Commandant, upon receipt of this message from the Officer Commanding the Defences, at once ordered Biely not to fire. Kondratenko was correct in reporting as he did; he saw what was happening on the hill from his own point of view, and there certainly were some men in the bomb-proof. Semenoff from his position could see well that the Japanese had occupied the top, and were entrenching. So it went on.

Later Kondratenko telephoned to Semenoff and asked him to go to him to arrange a withdrawal of the troops. This was Irman's duty, not Semenoff's. But the former was now useless: after all the strain and confusion, he had quite lost his head. There was again some misunderstanding about the withdrawal. In the evening an unsuccessful attempt was made to regain 203 Metre Hill, and after its failure, Smirnoff decided to abandon it altogether, but to cling on to Flat and Divisional Hills. However, by an error of Kondratenko's, all three were abandoned at the same time. It did not much matter, as with the fall of 203 Metre Hill the two others had no real value. The withdrawal began at dusk, and was carried on without a hitch till 6 a.m. Notwithstanding the fact that every one in Arthur well knew that it must fall sooner or later, that it was not strong enough to resist siege-guns, or to repulse for ever assaults which were constantly being reinforced by fresh columns, the actual end created a deep impression. The lull which now ensued, though, as usual, made the garrison believe in its own strength, in spite of the fact that the last days of the Pacific Ocean Fleet had come.

203 Metre Hill was lost, and with it more than 5,000 Russians.

CHAPTER XXXV

A RETROSPECT ON THE POSITION AT SEA

As soon as the enemy had established themselves on 203 Metre Hill, they began to build an observation station, and connected it to their siege batteries by telephone. December 6 passed in comparative quiet, but towards evening the enemy began to shell our ships. These were lying helplessly under Quail Hill, hoping to get some protection there from the 11-inch shells; but in vain, for from the summit of 203 Metre Hill could be seen the harbour, every ship, and every bursting shell. The huge projectiles could be seen falling one after another, either in the water near the ships, raising great pillars of water, or else striking them. The punishment began. The enemy's siege batteries set to work to destroy the squadron, which perished under the eyes of the whole Fortress, and the sailors now holding the land positions watched, helpless and with sad hearts, as their ships were struck, and one after another our great giants went to the bottom. A column of smoke was seen to shoot up from the *Pallada*, an explosion was heard, and a fire broke out on her. She struggled for life, Admiral Wiren himself superintending the extinguishing of the fire, but efforts were in vain, and she slowly perished. The *Bayan* was sunk under Golden Hill; close to Quail Hill lay the *Retvisan* on her side, and beyond, again, were the *Pobieda* and *Poltava*, turrets half a-wash, guns pointing dumbly to the sky. Alongside stuck out the masts of the *Zabiyak;* the inner harbour was, in fact, a cemetery.

With the loss of 203 Metre Hill, Stössel's determination to surrender the Fortress ripened; in this he was much influenced by ———. The latter, for some incomprehensible reason, did not like the navy; his dislike reached such proportions that, when the sad news of the destruction of the last ship came in, he crossed himself, and, as if greatly relieved, said, 'Thank God—that's the end.' This was said in Stössel's intimate circle, but it soon became known in the garrison. And so Stössel, when the destruction of the ships began on December 7, wrote a letter to Admiral Wiren, in which he categorically insisted on the sunken ships being destroyed, and on those that were able putting out to sea, giving as his reason that with the loss of 203 Metre Hill the defence of Arthur was nearing its end. (The fall of this hill had an enormous significance for the fleet, but was only of secondary importance with regard to the defence of the Fortress.)

To General Stössel's letter Admiral Wiren replied as follows:

'*From the Officer Commanding the Squadron of Battleships and Cruisers in Port Arthur to the Officer Commanding the Kwantun Fortified District.*

'I have the honour to reply to your letter, No. 2,241 of 7th instant, as follows:

'The sortie of the fleet on August 10 of this year, in order to force its way through to Vladivostock, was made in accordance with an order from the Tsar, communicated in a telegram from the Viceroy, though the opinion of the majority of Admirals and Captains was against such an operation, for—taking into consideration the superiority of the enemy, both in ships, guns, independent cruisers, divisions of destroyers, and speed, as well as the distance to Vladivostock without ports *en route*, and the necessity of passing the enemy's straits near the island of Tsushima—they deemed it impossible.

'If everything went well, our ships, having expended their ammunition in fighting the enemy's battleships and repelling torpedo attacks at night, or being disabled like the *Cesarevitch*, would have had to seek the sanctuary of a neutral port, and would have become useless for the rest of the campaign. It was doubtful if any ship would ever have reached Vladivostock; the *Novik*, which was the quickest of them, even though she had great luck, was unable to do so.

'All our ships would have been lost in the middle of August, at a time when the enemy's fleet would have been able (thanks to its above-mentioned superiority and to the fact that, while steaming parallel with us, it was making towards its own ports) to operate so that none of its ships were rendered *hors de combat*. As the enemy's ships would not have been seriously injured in these fights, they could have renewed, refitted, and repaired at ease before the earliest possible arrival of Admiral Rojdestvensky's squadron in the beginning of January, and could have met it in as good condition as now.

'With the return of our fleet to Port Arthur, after the battle of August 10, with less than half its ammunition, with battered ships, and many disabled guns, this operation of breaking through to Vladivostock became still more impossible. A few days after the squadron's return began the August assaults, in which our naval detachments played an important part, and in which several officers and men were killed. At a conference of flag-officers and Captains on August 19 a minute was drawn up, a copy of which I have the honour to attach. In accordance with this it was decided to assist the Fortress in every possible way, and we have most conscientiously endeavoured so to do. All the guns asked for for the positions have been taken off the ships and mounted, shells of all calibres have been expended on the land batteries, all ratings have worked according to their special calling for the defence of the Fortress, and have taken the most active part in repulsing the attacks in September, in October and, finally, in November on Tumulus Hill, B Battery, and 203 Metre Hill, where many of all ranks were killed.

'Till the capture of the latter the ships were, as far as possible, kept in repair, but they could only have been of assistance to Rojdestvensky's fleet *after the relief of Port Arthur by land*, which would have enabled us to get ammunition and guns and to refit. Rojdestvensky well knows this.

'The ships of the fleet are now sunk. Save for a small quantity of 47-millimetre and 12-inch ammunition, all the rest has been put on shore. The officers and crews have been sent ashore. The torpedo officers and men are employed making hand grenades and small shells, and many of the engineers are making ammunition; the remainder of the crews, numbering about 500, form the last reserve, and so the squadron to the very end of all its *matériel* and *personnel* is helping the Fortress to defend itself. With regard to the sinking of the ships, steps have been taken that uninjured guns should not fall as trophies into the enemy's hands if the Fortress falls. The *Sevastopol*, which is the only uninjured battleship, I will try to anchor near White Wolf's Hill, where, however, she will, of course, be subject to torpedo attacks and risk being sunk. It is naturally sad to have to lose the fleet thus, but if God enables us to hold out in the Fortress till relieved from the land side, I am sure that impartial men in Port Arthur will say that without the assistance rendered by the fleet it would long ago have fallen into the enemy's hands.'

To show clearly the state the fleet was in in the middle of the strict blockade, when the Viceroy ordered it to break through to Vladivostock after the unlucky attempt on August 10, I will quote an extract from a report of Admiral Wiren's, which fully illustrates its pitiful condition, and clearly shows that it had not a chance of getting through. The report was written after the fight of August 10:

'I have the honour to report that at present the ships of the squadron under my command are in the following state:

'(a) *Hulls.*

'The repairs to the *Peresvet, Pobieda, Retvisan,* and *Pallada* are finished, and to the *Poltava* and *Bayan* are being finished. The *Sevastopol* is being repaired with the aid of caissons, and will be ready in six to seven weeks. External damage to the sides has been covered with sheets, and her interior has, as far as possible, been repaired.

'(b) *Guns.*

'Since the commencement of the operations two guns have been absolutely disabled.

'After the conference on August 19, the following were put ashore for the land defences: One 6-inch, ten 75-millimetre, nineteen 47-millimetre, eight 37-millimetre, and three searchlights.

'(c) *Personnel.*

'Captain Boysman of the *Peresvet* is recovering from wounds, and is on the *Mongolia*. In the fight of August 10 two officers were killed; in the assaults two more were killed; eleven are wounded and sick.

'In reporting the above-mentioned state of the fleet, and in stating that all my thoughts and desires are aimed towards carrying out the Tsar's orders and your wishes, I consider it my duty to represent the following facts:

'Our fleet, and particularly my squadron, not being able to steam faster than thirteen knots (*Sevastopol* and *Poltava*), cannot possibly get through to Vladivostock without a fight, and the result of a fight is not hard to foresee, even if the ships were better than the enemy's in point of fighting—*i.e.*, straight shooting. Even supposing that the fleet steams out of Port Arthur without accident through the mine-fields, which have become more dangerous during the last month, as the enemy have constantly been laying mines (our dredging flotilla, though it has daily trawled, is very weak, has few pinnaces, and what with the destruction of a dredger, a port barge, and two destroyers, has not been able to do much), it is impossible for it to escape notice. Our greatest speed is only thirteen knots.

'The enemy would meet us in three or four divisions:

1. Division of battleships and armoured cruisers ... ... 6 ships
2. Division of fast second-class cruisers and one first-class cruiser (*Yakuma*) 5 ships
3. Coast-defence battleships and one armoured cruiser (*Tokiwa*) ... 7 ships
4. Several divisions of destroyers and small torpedo craft.

'We cannot take the initiative in action, as the enemy, having superior speed, can steam away if they do not wish to fight, and can accompany us until it suits them to engage in battle—*i.e*:

'(*a*) When our fleet is some seventy miles from Arthur.

'(*b*) When they can concentrate all their force.

'(*c*) When they are occupying a favourable position with regard to the sun and the sea.

'As on August 10, the real fighting would again probably commence in the afternoon; and each of the enemy's ships which were seriously injured would be able to fall out for repairs or to make the land without risk, at a time when each of our ships falling out of action, though only temporarily damaged, might become a prize to two, three, or four of their vessels, or at best might run on to a neutral coast, or steam into a neutral port, and be interned for the rest of the campaign.

'Thus they can easily beat us without losing a single big ship, and all damage to ships or guns could be quickly made good in port, after replacing the disabled guns and supplementing the crew. At sunset the big ships would cease fighting, to rest, while two, three, or four destroyer divisions would attack or menace us all night, so that the crews would get no sleep, and we should be forced to waste ammunition till morning. The speed of our fleet would in all probability diminish, as the battered funnels (one of the principal destructions on August 10) increase the expenditure of coal and prevent proper pressure being maintained. If steaming thirteen knots, the voyage to Vladivostock takes four days: it will take longer at less speed—*i.e.*, at eight knots the passage would take six days. On the morning of the second day the enemy's battleships, having repaired and rested, would again, whenever it suited them, fall on our tired fleet, and so on repeat their tactics till the island of Tsu-shima, where a fresh division of four armoured cruisers and destroyers would be waiting for us; and there, close to their shores, their fortresses and ports, the enemy would try and bring on a decisive action. We could not ram, as this operation requires superior speed. Indeed, it would be a miracle if we got to Vladivostock, and, having lost the remainder of our Pacific Ocean Fleet, we would be giving the enemy a fresh victory, and, what is more important, depriving the Baltic Fleet of the possibility of destroying them, since it is weaker than the enemy, both in numbers of ships and of guns, in its many types of vessels, in speed, and in the fact that it will have to force its way through to a base—Vladivostock—without which no fleet can operate.'

CHAPTER XXXVI

A COUNCIL MEETING

On the 8th was held a meeting of the Council of Defence, a meeting which is historic in the annals of this unique body. Up to now at previous meetings many things had been discussed. The plan of the forts and the fortifications had been criticized generally and in detail. The uselessness of our engineers had been pointed out *ad nauseam*; the disgraceful nature of the concrete work, which, though designed to resist 6-inch shells, was easily destroyed by them, and the insufficiency of the munitions of war, had been discussed. It had been reiterated in no measured terms that Arthur was in no sense a Fortress, but only an entrenched camp. General Fock generally spoke more than the others; his speeches were verbose and not convincing. Each successive meeting was a repetition of the preceding one and the minutes were of no value, as the resolutions entered in on them by Stössel, some of them dictated by others, were at variance with the opinion of the members, and were made with 'one eye on the gallery,' for future use. They were, later on, characterized by Lieutenant-General Froloff, Chief of the Head-quarter Staff, as being 'an apologetic document submitted betimes with a view to later on justifying the surrender.'

The Commandant, knowing from experience that nothing would result from these meetings except endless discussion and waste of time, was unwilling to summon them. He used to do so once a month simply to satisfy General Stössel. Instead of this Council, Smirnoff used to hold daily conferences with the general officers commanding the land defences, the Fortress artillery, and the Fortress engineers, at which all urgent questions were quickly decided.

On the morning of the 8th, Stössel and Reuss went to Kondratenko's quarters. General Biely, commanding the artillery, saw this from the veranda of his hut, and could not understand why they should visit Kondratenko. After a couple of hours they came out, conversing eagerly. Stössel went home, but Reuss went up to Biely. He talked to him eloquently of the critical state of the Fortress, drawing a dark picture of the future. He asserted that, with the destruction of the squadron, Arthur's importance as a fortress had ceased, and that therefore, on account of the suffering wounded and of the exhausted and scurvy-stricken garrison, matters should be put a stop to. Biely was dumb; the object of Stössel's visit to Kondratenko was now clear. Reuss then spoke openly about surrender, and did his best to persuade Biely to agree to it. At last, declaring he was going on to the Commandant, he said good-bye, but he went off in the opposite direction, and shortly afterwards Smirnoff received a note from him to the following effect:

'Owing to the great change in the conditions since the loss of 203 Metre Hill, the Officer Commanding the District requests that you will summon a meeting of the Council to discuss future action for the defence of the Fortress.'

On receiving this, the Commandant presumed that the Council was to meet in order that Generals Fock and Nickitin, who had no duty, might be acquainted with the scheme for the future defence. At 5 p.m. the members met in Smirnoff's room, all except Kondratenko, who was telephoned for. He was unable to come at once, so the discussion went on without him. Smirnoff opened the proceedings:

'As Roman Isidorovitch [Kondratenko] thoroughly knows the scheme for the future defence, I will begin without waiting for him. Well, gentlemen, 203 Metre Hill has fallen. With its fall began the bombardment of our warships, which have been destroyed. Nevertheless, the loss of the hill has not altered the position of the defence. So long as we held Angle Hill, 203 Metre Hill was, with regard to that, a *réduit*.* As soon as we abandoned Angle Hill, 203 Metre Hill became a salient on the western front, which the Japanese had to attack. This salient no longer exists. Our lines over this hill were large, but the enemy's were incomparably greater. For us 203 Metre Hill was only an advanced point, the defence of which was mainly important in order to ensure the safety of our fleet. This defence, on which we had to concentrate all our available strength, gradually weakened us all along the line. I held on to it till the denudation of the other fronts, especially of the north-east, in order to provide reinforcements, became dangerous. From the moment I felt that a further expenditure of men on 203 Metre Hill was more dangerous than useful, I decided to give it up. From what I have said it is clear that, with the fall of the hill, we are forced back on to positions on the main line of defence. The western front, in addition to the permanent and intermediate works, which have hardly been touched, has a lot of ground behind it. To reach this front from 203 Metre Hill by systematic approach (the enemy could not do it by assault) will take at least a month and a half. I have no fear for it.'

'It is essential to strengthen the defence of Liao-tieh-

* Keep.

shan, which is the keep of Arthur. The enemy will now turn all his attention to it. It is necessary to strengthen it and defend it,' interrupted Fock.

Kondratenko then entered.

After telling the new-comer what had been said, Smirnoff continued:

'And so, I repeat, I have no fear for the western front, as I am almost certain that Nogi, being for the present satisfied with the capture of 203 Metre Hill and the destruction of the fleet, will not force his way any more in that direction. What he does there will be in the nature of a demonstration; he will turn all his real attention to the north-east front, which has cost him so dear, to the half-destroyed forts and works whose parapets are now almost occupied by him. This is obvious, because, having conducted with the greatest pains a gradual attack against this front for more than three months, and having at last reached the parapets of our works after immense loss, he will never abandon them in order to commence a fresh attack on the almost untouched side. Besides, the enemy know well that behind this front are all the vital parts of the Fortress—the dockyard, workshops, mills, supply depôts, arsenal, magazines, etc. On the western side, however, there is no such attraction for them; on the contrary, there is everything to put them off, so I repeat that I do not fear for it. Our north-east front, from Tumulus Battery to B Battery, however, causes grave anxiety. Chi-kuan-shan Fort and Fortification No. 3 are the most critical, and that is where we must pay all our attention. Owing to this, it is essential to take some of the troops from the west and send them to the east, after drawing on the garrison of Liao-tieh-shan and the forts which have not been attacked. At present on the north-east front a second line has been got ready, running from Tumulus Battery across Vladimir and Mitrofanieff Hills to Nameless Redoubt. The third line on Stonebroken Ridge will soon be finished. I have paid special attention to this, and it will shortly be extremely strong. At present, with the forts and Chinese wall still with us, the naval guns mounted on the third line and the shore front will enable us successfully to carry on an artillery duel, notwithstanding the fact that the enemy is within the Fortress area. But, in any case, it is necessary to concentrate as many men as possible on the north-east front. The main reserve is now a little more than a thousand men. General Gorbatovsky also has a fairly strong reserve, but, owing to the great losses one way and another, we must take troops from Liao-tieh-shan and the forts on the western front. That is the position. I am ready to hear any suggestions that may be put forward.'

Fock replied:

' I urge the importance of strengthening the defence of Liao-tieh-shan. I have already pointed out its strategical importance to the Fortress. It is the keep, you understand, gentlemen—it is the keep of Arthur.'

Smirnoff replied:

' I say that Liao-tieh-shan at present is of no importance to the Fortress. Even if the Japanese occupy it, it will only be of use to them as an observation point, as it is so far away. It will take a very long time to mount guns there, and they will never attempt it, for the simple reason that to shell the Old Town and the north-east front from there is impossible. The Old Town is seven and the northeast front is nine miles away as the crow flies. But let us now get on to those points which are closely connected with the strength of the garrison.'

Fock returned to the charge:

' I urge the necessity not only of holding, but strengthening, the defence of Liao-tieh-shan. It is the keep of Arthur '—but Smirnoff continued:

' At present dysentery is on the decline; typhus, though

it exists, is stationary; what is worst of all is the increase of scurvy—that is the scourge that we must fight. The most rational, and the only thing to do is to increase the allowance of meat. This may not stop the epidemic, but it will weaken it. Scurvy is a slow disease, and by increasing the rations we may yet be able to make use of the men who have only got it in the initial stage. We have about 3,500 horses. According to my calculations, not more than 500 are required for the works. The munitions of war and food-supplies are now concentrated all along the defences, and so long-distance transport of them will not be necessary; besides, the Décauville light line,* connecting the Old Town with Cossack Square, will to a considerable extent relieve the transport of supplies to the front. I think that, with luck, we may take for food, without harm to the transport of supplies, more than 3,000 horses. I therefore propose to issue to the garrison ½ pound of horse-flesh per man. I have not worked it out exactly, but, roughly, for a garrison of 40,000 men that means fresh meat for forty-eight days at ¼ pound per man per day.'

After some discussion it was decided to issue a ½-pound meat ration to those in hospital and ¼ pound to the combatants.

Biely, who knew what was coming, could not for the life of him make out why Smirnoff was beating about the bush so long instead of coming to the main subject of the meeting. Gorbatovsky, in complete ignorance, was quietly awaiting the end of the meeting. Khvostoff was hurriedly writing down notes from which to draw up the minutes. Reuss, who looked as if he were sitting on tin-tacks, suddenly jumped up.

'The Officer Commanding the District has instructed me to ascertain the opinion of the Council as to how long they consider the Fortress should be defended.'

* Tramway.—E. D. S.

'Excuse me, sir; that question does not permit of discussion. Although we have not an overabundance of ammunition, we have sufficient to repel at least two more heavy assaults, and if the big-gun ammunition runs out we shall have more than 10,000,000 rounds of small-arm ammunition left. When *all* the ammunition is finished we shall still have our bayonets. Such a question is quite inopportune, premature, and does not permit of discussion. As to the question of how long we *can* hold out, that is easily decided for us by the Supply Returns.' And, getting up, Smirnoff moved towards the table on which the books were lying. 'Let us see what the Fortress Intendant has to say as to the amount of supplies in the depôts to-day. I see that flour, groats, green food, tea and sugar, will last for more than a month. The question of horse-flesh we have just settled. In addition to this we have sufficient biscuits for more than a month and a half.* The question of surrender cannot at present be considered. I cannot allow any discussion with regard to a capitulation before the middle of January at the earliest.'

There was a general movement of assent amongst the members. They all loudly declared the raising of the question to be quite premature. Reuss remained sitting, looking extremely disconcerted.

'Yes, yes; the raising of this question is premature,' said Fock.

Reuss looked at him with unconcealed astonishment.

Smirnoff continued sarcastically:

'At home they are just preparing to celebrate the jubilee of Sevastopol. Our fathers held out for eleven months! We shall not have completed eleven months till January 8, and only then will the son be worthy of his father.'

---

* A few days after this the steamer *King Arthur* arrived with 2,000,000 pounds of excellent flour.

When they went out into the street Kondratenko turned to Biely.

'What has happened to General Stössel? Has his wound really made such an impression upon him?'

Khvostoff alone was left in the room, scribbling hard at the minutes. Next day these were sent round to all the members for signature. They all signed, but Reuss attached his dissent, in which he protested that the Commandant had decided the question of surrendering the Fortress purely on the basis that Arthur had not held out so long as Sevastopol. With regard to the actual facts he said nothing.

When the minutes were sent to Stössel for his confirmation he first wrote repudiating the instructions which Reuss said he had given about raising the question of surrender; then, agreeing with Fock's opinion as to the immense importance to the fortress of Liao-tieh-shan, he gave definite orders that its garrison should not be weakened, and that it should be defended to the last. He also expressed great astonishment at the Commandant's ignorance in thinking that guns, rifles, and bayonets were used in succession one after another and not together!

'Every soldier knows that guns, rifles, and bayonets are used *together*. As to surrendering the Fortress, I shall know when the time comes, and I will not permit a street massacre.'

The most important resolution of the meeting—namely, the question of increasing the horse-flesh ration on account of the spread of scurvy—he did not confirm. The garrison continued to be fed on fish for five days per week, receiving ¼ pound of horse-flesh per man only on the other two days.

How can one account for such a decision concerning men suffering from scurvy? Not only was the deprivation cruelty to the sick men, but it tended to reduce the garrison to a state of impotence through disease.

With General Stössel must unquestionably lie the responsibility for the fact that the whole Fortress was slowly converted into a living cemetery (scurvy increased with great strides), and that the way for surrender was thus prepared. Finally, he, to every one's amazement, issued an order that day by which he endeavoured to prevent the Commandant getting in touch in any way with the outside world. This order was as follows (No. 904, dated December 9, 1904):

'Should any Chinese junks approach the shore, the nearest picquet or gendarme post will take steps to guide it into a safe place, and will put a guard on it to see that no one goes near it. Its arrival must be immediately reported to the District Staff, whence further instructions will be awaited. All correspondence found will be at once despatched to the District Staff Office. No junk will be permitted to leave without permission of the District Staff, and permission for anyone to go on board the junks must also be obtained from that office. The despatch of any correspondence whatever in junks is strictly forbidden. Before their departure junks will be carefully inspected, and any correspondence found on them will be confiscated, and the authors will be held responsible.'

The gendarmes were placed in the most impossible position by this order, but their chief, Prince Mickeladsey, knowing what the Officer Commanding the District was worth, and being, properly speaking, subordinate only to the Commandant of the Fortress, continued to obey the orders of the latter.

Admiral Grigorovitch, as before, continued to communicate with Chifu.

CHAPTER XXXVII

KONDRATENKO'S DEATH AND SOME RESULTS

On December 11 regular winter set in, accompanied by a searching wind. The garrison began to suffer greatly, owing to the bad food and the want of protection from the weather. Scurvy increased very much, in spite of the efforts of the doctors, who were helpless in the absence of a proper food allowance. All that Stössel would vouchsafe to their representations on this subject was: 'As to the surrender of the Fortress, I shall know when that should take place, and I will not permit a street massacre.'

For the next two or three days there was much anxiety in Arthur about Fort Chi-kuan-shan. The enemy had even got into the counterscarp gallery, whence they had driven our men back with poisonous gas, and so obtained possession of a portion of it. Many were the earnest consultations between Smirnoff and Kondratenko.

The night of the 15th was unusually wild. The snow was driven across the gaunt hills in clouds by the vicious gusts of an icy wind, which moaned as it swept up the gorges — suitable accompaniment to the more deadly sounds in the air, for the Japanese were not resting. Pitch dark though it was, there was sufficient light to distinguish the mass of Chi-kuan-shan Fort as it lay under patches of snow, with the bare rock showing on the lee of the slopes and scarps. The fort seemed deserted, for, save the few sentries on the parapets, not a soul was about—all were under cover, snatching what rest they could. Of the enemy also, busy as they were, nothing could be seen—they had all burrowed. From some casemate below two young officers came up to the main parapet, behind which they stood listening to the enemy delving in their saps. Presently there was a movement in a Japanese trench, and a shower of sparks came fizzing over: a warning shout among our men, and then the detonation of a grenade. The two officers having amused themselves thus for a short time, went down to the countermine galleries to listen for the enemy, who were now very close. Meanwhile down below in the bowels of the great fort a different and more pleasant scene was being enacted. General Kondratenko, who had come out to see things for himself this evening, so critical were they, was decorating a non-commissioned officer for gallantry. Warmly congratulating the soldier, he kissed him and pinned the Cross of St. George on his breast.

The concrete casemate in which this little scene took place was a haven of rest after the turmoil above, for here few sounds could be heard, and there was comparative warmth. After the ceremony Kondratenko sat with his head on his hands, silent and apparently depressed; the others discussed matters. Behind a wooden partition a party of sailors were busy filling hand-grenades by a lantern, and cases of pyroxyline were lying strewn about.

' Listen, gentlemen! It is coming!' and all were suddenly silent, for even down here the whistling roar of an 11-inch shell could be heard. It arrived and fell into the ditch behind, destroying the bridge, and the groans and shouts for stretchers could be heard.

When supper was served, Kondratenko would eat nothing. A consultation was started, much being said about Smirnoff's orders for work and Stössel's counter-orders as to not using up the men. In the corners of the casemate some were sleeping, others were quietly talking. Of all the officers present, Colonel Raschevsky was particularly cheerful and talkative.

'Well, gentlemen,' said he, 'this casemate is about the only place in this fort where one can feel fairly safe. The underground shelters are none too satisfactory when 11-inch shells are flying about, though they are good enough against splinters.'

It was now near nine o'clock, and again the noise of a rapidly approaching shell was heard—the fifth since Kondratenko's arrival.

A—a—a—ah ! ! !

All was confusion, dust, smoke, noise of falling concrete, stones, and splinters of steel, cracking of bursting grenades, cries, the stench of blood, the suffocating gas of high explosives. . . . In the corner where Kondratenko, Raschevsky, Senkevitch, Zedgenidsey, and Naumenko had just been sitting at the table poring over the map, a bluish flame flickered for a moment over a heap of bodies half buried in débris. All was still, save for the groans of Lieutenant Kraiko (one of whose legs was torn off) and of Potapoff—buried under the ruins. Under this heap of rubbish the others lay dead, killed while in the execution of their duty.

Kondratenko had perished, but wherever Russian is spoken his name will ever be synonymous with duty, unselfishness, bravery, and honour.

It was about 10 p.m. when Smirnoff received the news on the telephone from Khvostoff. He felt it bitterly. In one moment his best and most reliable assistant had been swept away. Not only was it on account of his skill as a soldier that Kondratenko could not be replaced: there were other ways in which he had been invaluable. His

MAJOR-GENERAL KONDRATENKO.

death meant more difficulties and a fresh struggle with Stössel. Roman Isidorovitch had always contrived to smooth over things, thus annulling, to a certain extent, the conflict of orders. But now the inevitable had come to pass: he was no longer there to help.

About eleven o'clock Khvostoff himself arrived, and briefly confirmed his telephone message:

'Sir, an 11-inch shell burst in the officers' compartment in the casemate of Chi-kuan-shan Fort. Generals Kondratenko, Raschevsky, Zedgenidsey,* and Senkevitch were killed on the spot. Colonel Naumenko was alive when brought out, but he has died since without regaining consciousness.'

Looking at the practical side of things, Smirnoff's first words were:

'We must go to Stössel at once. ——— is next in seniority to Kondratenko, and Stössel will certainly try to give him the vacant appointment. This must at all costs be prevented. I will myself take over the command of the land defences in addition to my duties as Commandant, difficult though it will be. The state of affairs on the north-east front is so serious that I cannot under any circumstances allow ——— to have charge. He can be sent to the western front, where the enemy are still a long way off, and he can't do much harm, and where, much as he may want to, he won't be able to surrender anything to them. It is different on the other front, where the Japs are almost sitting on the parapets. There he would undoubtedly surrender one position after another, carrying out his theory of the doctor and the gangrenous patient.'

Arriving at Stössel's house, they found the place locked up; even the orderly supposed to be on duty was asleep. Only after much knocking was he aroused sufficiently to open the door.

* One of the most distinguished Engineer officers in Arthur.

'Tell General Stössel that the Commandant has come to see him on urgent business.'

'The General is asleep, sir, and has given the strictest orders that he is not to be disturbed on any pretext whatever. I cannot go to him, sir—I dare not.'

This, if you please, was the man in command of a besieged fortress!

'Let us go to Fock. I will talk to him and tell him what I intend to do,' said Smirnoff.

Stumbling along in the dark, they at last reached Fock's quarters. An orderly appeared, but here again the Commandant was to meet with failure, as after a few moments the man returned to say: 'The General has ordered me to say that he is very ill and in bed with a temperature of 102. He is in a high fever and cannot possibly see you.'

'Let us try Reuss, then,' said Smirnoff quietly.

On the way they met Dmitrevsky (Chief Staff Officer of the 4th Division).

'Colonel, General Fock is on the sick list; meanwhile I propose to appoint Nadein to the western front, and you are to go there as his Chief Staff Officer.'

They arrived at the District Staff Offices, and found Reuss just sitting down to supper. He was surprised and alarmed at such a late visit from the Commandant, who at once said:

'I have just been to Stössel and Fock, but was unable to see either of them. I want you to tell Stössel in the morning that I consider the state of affairs on the northeast front so bad that I am going to command there myself. I have decided to appoint Fock to the western front, but till he is off the sick list (he is very ill at present, with a temperature of 102) I will send General Nadein there, with Dmitrevsky as his Chief Staff Officer. Please tell Stössel of this to-morrow, early, so that there may be no misunderstanding about orders.'

'Very good, sir. I will report it first thing in the morning.'

Next morning a Mass was held for the souls of the departed, at which a great number of officers were present to pay their last tribute to the men they had so respected and loved. The Commandant was there, of course, but Stössel, Fock and Nickitin were conspicuous by their absence. Thinking that the first named would surely come, the priests waited some time before commencing the service, but in vain. While waiting Colonels Semenoff and Kilenin went up to General Smirnoff and said:

'We wish to inform you, sir, that, on behalf of the officers of the garrison, we are sending a deputation to General Stössel to ask that the command of the land defences be left entirely in your hands. We are convinced that only in this event can a successful issue be counted on. If the command should by any chance go to General ——'

'Yes, yes, gentlemen—yes! But you need not worry. I have already taken the necessary steps. Everything will continue as before. Report direct to the Fortress Staff, as you have been doing. . . .'

The service began.

As soon as the service was over Smirnoff and his Chief of the Staff went to see General Stössel, but again found him out. From his house they went straight to ——, whom, to their amazement, they found in the best of health, with no apparent trace of the high fever he had said he was suffering from the previous night. In fact, they had never before seen him in such high spirits.

'Good morning, sir—good morning! What can I do for you? Won't you sit down?' (He had just returned from being with Stössel and Nickitin, and knew full well that he had been put in orders to succeed Kondratenko.)

'I have just been at General Stössel's, but found him out; he had apparently gone to Nickitin's. I must see him to talk over your appointment. The fact of the matter is that Kondratenko has left an unenviable legacy behind him in the state of affairs on the north-east front. I have decided to make use of your military knowledge by sending you to the western front, and I will take command of the eastern myself, as I did during Kondratenko's life.'

'Very good, sir; only you had better inform General Stössel. I hear he thinks of putting me in to command all the land defences, and you will have to hurry or he may have issued the order, and it will then be difficult to get him to change it. The front most certainly ought to be divided up.'

Stössel had already gone to the District Staff Offices and had issued two orders. The first (No. 920) announced the death of Kondratenko and his comrades; the second (No. 921) appointed Fock to command the land defences, vice Kondratenko, and Nadein to officiate in command of the 4th East Siberian Rifle Division, vice Fock. [Colonel Raschevsky was succeeded by Captain A. V. von Schwartz, of the Engineers, an excellent officer who had been in charge of the fortifications of Kinchou.] His deep sleep and Fock's illness together frustrated Smirnoff's good intentions as to the appointment.

However, Smirnoff, knowing nothing of this and never dreaming that he was being fooled, left at once and went again with Khvostoff to Stössel's house. This time they drew him. He received them very coldly and without sitting down.

'What can I do for you, General? You have already been here once to see me.'

'I have decided, sir,' said Smirnoff, 'now that Kondratenko has been killed, to take over the command of the eastern front myself. General Fock is the next senior to Kondratenko, but the state of affairs there is so critical that he would not be able to deal with the many questions there in addition to those arising all along the eighteen miles of front. The western side does not give such cause for anxiety, so I propose to put Fock in command of it, and myself to run the eastern in addition to my duties as Commandant. This is, I think, a sound arrangement, as Fock knows the western and has never been on the eastern front, while all my energies, as you know, have always been directed towards the latter.'

'The defence scheme of the Fortress lays down that one officer shall command the land front. Kondratenko was able to manage it!'

'I always kept him on the western, and myself ran the eastern. This was the case, you will remember, in the assaults during August, September, October, and November . . .'

'I have already appointed General Fock in place of Kondratenko,' replied Stössel, raising his voice. 'The order is published. You should know by now, General, that I never alter my orders. I never'—shouting—'alter my orders!'

'But, sir, his appointment——'

But Stössel only roared again, 'I never alter my orders!'

What could Smirnoff do? The reader must remember that, by an order issued in March, Smirnoff was made subordinate to Stössel; that the latter had been appointed Aide-de-Camp to the Tsar, which in the eyes of the troops vested him with great authority, as he could speak in the Emperor's name. What, I ask, could he have done? How should he have acted? It is easy to say now what he should have done, but, taking his position at the time and everything else into consideration, I personally do not see what would have been best to do. Even now, disgusted as he was, the Commandant knew nothing of the official deceit of which Stössel was guilty. [The first that Smirnoff heard of the concealment of the orders was from Kuropatkin himself, when he returned from being a prisoner of war.]

After this interview the two men went totally different ways. They only met once again—on the day on which the last council was held.

More than once when I accompanied Smirnoff on his inspection he said to me:

'I am hindered and opposed at every—literally every—turn in the defence, and if Arthur falls all the shame and all the responsibility will be thrown on me. But, no; I'll defeat them. If Arthur falls, I and all the other Generals will die with it.'

But he did not; the eventual capitulation was for him —the Commandant—as complete a surprise as it was for the rest of the garrison.

Extract of December 17 from Colonel Raschevsky's Diary.*

'From 2 p.m. the Japanese have bombarded Chi-kuan-shan Fort and Little Eagle's Nest. An 11-inch shell struck the casemate of the former, wounding three more officers. . . .

'It is rumoured that Fock has issued an order decreasing the garrison of the forts by half, withdrawing half to make up a reserve. This is exactly contrary to General Smirnoff's principle, but Fock seems to think that the inaction and monotony of fort life breeds disease. . . .'

General Fock's first act after taking up his new ap-

---

* Colonel Raschevsky's diary was found after his death by Captain von Schwartz, who continued to enter it up, so that its value should not be lessened by being an incomplete record.

pointment was, indeed, to decrease the strength of the garrisons of the forts and intermediate works. By degrees he reduced them very considerably. 'It doesn't do to have the men too thick, or one shell will have too many victims, and we shall have no one left to defend Arthur!'

He had always said this, and now his words took shape in deeds. His predecessor, on the other hand, thoroughly agreeing with Smirnoff's principles and wishes, had endeavoured to keep the garrisons at full strength, particularly in places where the forces were at hand-grips. In such places it was absolutely essential to have enough men on the spot to hurl back the enemy at once, should they breach the parapet and storm the works. The moments between the explosion of a mine and the crowning of the crater were so precious that immediate action was necessary with such men as were at hand; there was no time to await reinforcements. The side that crowned a crater first obtained an immense advantage.

CHAPTER XXXVIII

THE LOSS OF FORT CHI-KUAN-SHAN

THE 18th was a lovely day—bright, sunny, and calm. Silence reigned all along the front, save for the usual intermittent rifle-fire, and on the forts the sentries alone were to be seen.

Fort Chi-kuan-shan was still in a very critical state. The Japanese held the counterscarp, and the explosion of their mines was momentarily expected. The garrison had been greatly decreased, and were tired out. It was impossible to find reliefs for the ordinary duties even; much less could this exhausted, weakened body of men be asked to make any special effort that might be done by fresh troops. The feeling among them at the appointment of Fock, who had for long been nicknamed 'The General of Retreats,' was apathetic. He didn't consider it necessary to go to the fort himself to encourage his sorely-tried men; they only knew him by his prophesies of their death and the awful pictures he had painted of the destruction of the forts by the enemy's shells.

It was the day upon which the Japanese had decided to make an end of the fort, and for which they had made all preparations. At 11 a.m.—a time when the trench-guards were usually relieved and there was always noise and movement—their troops told off for the storm-

NORTH FORT, CHI-KUAN-SHAN, SHOWING GREEN HILLS IN THE DISTANCE.

To face page 285.

ing were quietly moved up and collected in the last approaches, where they awaited the explosion of the mines. The men told off for this 'forlorn hope' were divided into two parties. One party, who had red bands on their arms, was moved towards the caponiers; on the explosion it was to storm the interior of the fort. On their shoulders the second party from the last approach were to climb. If these did not manage to drive out our men, they were to be reinforced by all their available troops, who were to overcome the garrison by sheer weight of numbers.

Just about a quarter-past one a volcano seemed to burst from the parapet, and with a roar and the shock of an earthquake a huge black cloud of dust and smoke shot up to the sky. This was followed by a second eruption. For a moment there was comparative calm; then the sky commenced to rain beams, boulders, stones, masses of concrete, sacks, bodies, while on the rear of the fort (to catch our reinforcements) fell a hail of shells. Our men, shaken for a moment by the suddenness of all this, and expecting a third explosion, dashed for safety; but they quickly rallied behind the parapet of the prepared retrenchment, from whence they opened a heavy fire on those madly gallant stormers with red bands, who showed themselves on the fort. So impatient were they, and so quick was their advance, that our men could see them being buried under the falling stones and masses of masonry hurled into the air by the explosions.

The nearest batteries—Tumulus, Laperoff's, Zaredoubt, and B—opened a murderous fire on all the approaches, thus paralysing further assaults and preventing the enemy from crowning the craters of their mines. Consequently, this face of the fort, with its destroyed revetment, became neutral ground. Our gunners, shooting splendidly, glued the enemy to the spot, and did not allow them to advance a yard; but their skill was wasted, for General Fock took no advantage of it. He did not reinforce the garrison, as he should have done, and thus enable them to crown the craters, and so again establish themselves on the outer parapet. Meanwhile the enemy were holding on, preparing themselves for another assault, and our men behind the thin parapet of the retrenchment were suffering heavily.

It was the psychological moment, the crisis. Had reinforcements been sent up, they would have turned the scale, and Chi-kuan-shan would have been saved, but General Fock seems to have made up his mind at the first explosion that the fort must be abandoned. To be exact, a reinforcement of a company of sailors from the *Pobieda* and *Peresvet* was sent up by Smirnoff; but coming under a heavy fire on their way, few reached the fort, and they were not sufficiently numerous to render much assistance.

So it continued till night. When darkness came on the enemy again dashed to the attack, at the same time turning all their guns on to the ground in our rear to prevent the approach of supports. A hand-to-hand fight ensued. Both sides fought like lions, or rather devils; but the more of the enemy that we killed the more seemed to appear. They even dragged two mountain guns up on to the parapet, and got to work with them at close range, and then the scene, lit up by the cold beams of the search-lights and the dazzling glare of star-shell and rockets, indeed seemed like hell let loose. The fort's hours were numbered, for without reinforcements it could not last for ever—and no reinforcements came.

While it was in its death agony, the higher authorities were engaged in correspondence.

Telephone Message from General Fock to General Gorbatovsky.
7.40 p.m., December 18, 1904.

'General Stössel has given orders that the casemates of Chi-kuan-shan Fort are to be at once mined, and then, if the Japanese do not withdraw from the fort—*i.e.*, from the parapet—the garrison is to retire and the casemates are to be blown up. The enemy are not to be allowed to establish themselves on the parapet, which must be fired on by the guns and the torpedo tube. In view of Captain Stepanoff's report, to the effect that before sunset he and Colonel Mekhmandaroff could see from Big Eagle's Nest only one Jap officer and three men on the parapet laying sandbags, I leave it to you to hold on to the fort so long as you think necessary. In giving this order, based on my report, General Stössel came to this decision only because he thought that under present circumstances no other course was possible. At sunset a sailor came to me and reported that by the explosion of a bomb thrown by the enemy we had had 15 casualties.'

Telephone Message from General Gorbatovsky to the Staff of the General Officer Commanding Land Front (Fock).
9.35 p.m., December 18, 1904.

'From Chi-kuan-shan it is reported that heavy casualties are occurring from grenades thrown by the enemy. We have not been able to reoccupy the parapet. I therefore propose to avail myself of your permission to blow up the casemates, and I have ordered the garrison to hold on till our sappers have got the mines ready. As a precautionary measure and to cover the garrison during the retirement, please move one company temporarily from the main reserve to the Ice-house. I am just going to Colonel Glagoleff to give the necessary instructions on the spot.'

Telephone Message from Colonel Dmitrevsky (Chief Staff Officer to General Fock) to General Gorbatovsky.
9.40 p.m., December 18, 1904.

'General Fock fully concurs in your opinion about Chi-kuan-shan. He trusts that you will see that the repairs to Kuropatkin Lunette are energetically carried out.'

At 11.30 p.m., in accordance with orders received direct from General Fock, commanding the land defences, the garrison, after destroying the entrance bridge, abandoned the fort, which for four months had been held, despite much desperate and bloody fighting. Although General Gorbatovsky in his message at 9.35 p.m. on December 18 proposed to avail himself of the permission given in the previous messages and to abandon the fort, he never, in fact, gave the order.

At 11 p.m. he visited the fort to ascertain personally the state of affairs, and met the men already retiring. When he told them to go back, they said General Fock had ordered them to withdraw.

Only after four months' awful fighting, tens of thousands of deaths, countless numbers of wounded, a sea of spilt blood, a hell of human sufferings, tears, and sorrows, and owing to the difficulties in which we were, did the enemy succeed in capturing the first of our permanent forts. And even then it would not have been theirs if Fock (this is the deliberate opinion of all the most experienced officers) had reinforced it in time, and had not, on his own responsibility, determined to abandon it when he did. He carried out his theories in practice, and made this unnecessary surrender.

Smirnoff—the Commandant of Port Arthur—only learnt of this deplorable surrender after it had been carried out; for Fock, in direct contravention of the first principles of discipline, did not even inform him of his intention. He knew better than to let Smirnoff have any suspicion of it, and, ignoring him, communicated direct with Stössel.

This is not fiction, but the plain, unvarnished truth.

Early next day General Fock went to the Commandant to report the loss of the fort.

'Who, may I ask, gave you permission to abandon it?' asked Smirnoff.

'I received a direct order to that effect, sir, from General Stössel. It was he who gave the order. How could I have dared to do such a thing on my own responsibility?'

'Perhaps you are unaware, General, that I have been appointed by His Imperial Majesty the Tsar to command this fortress. You, as commanding the land defences, are immediately subordinate to me, and without my permission you have not a shadow of right to abandon anything in my fortress. I am its Commandant, and I alone am responsible.'

'I hunted for you last night, sir; I went to your hut to look for you, but couldn't find you anywhere.' This was incorrect; he had not done so.

'You must have known it was useless to look for me there—I do not follow the example set by some amongst you, and change my quarters every time a chance shell comes near them.* Every one knows that I live here, and I only leave this to go out on to the defences. I repeat,' continued Smirnoff, 'you have not the slightest right to give up a fort without my approval. I can reinforce it as much as seems advisable to me. There are more than 30,000 men at this minute bearing arms in the Fortress. Under no circumstances should the fort have been abandoned; it might very easily have been held. Moreover, its surrender has had the worst effect on the whole garrison. You have undermined the principles I have always instilled into the men—that a fort may perish, but never surrender; you have done untold harm. I cannot tell now but what the men will take it into their heads to retire from forts of their own

* General Stössel had now taken up his quarters in the barracks of the 10th Regiment.

accord. The garrison is worn out and underfed, and to men in this condition an example of this sort is paralysing, and may fatally injure the further defence.* Men are but human; they wish to live, and the instinct of self-preservation is always strong in them.'

From Smirnoff Fock went off at once to Stössel. On the 18th a secret meeting of the District Staff was held. The result was the publication in a District Order of an entirely inaccurate version of the circumstances relating to the loss of the fort.

After the sudden abandonment of this strong fort, which was made without permission of, or even reference to, the Council of Defence, the Commandant despatched the following cypher telegram to Kuropatkin, No. 1,282, dated December 20, 1904:

'*To the Commander-in-Chief of the Armies and the Fleet.*

'On December 15 Major-General Kondratenko, commanding the land defences, was killed. To succeed him General Stössel has appointed Lieutenant-General Fock, though I requested that only the western portion of the front should be entrusted to him, and that I should take, in addition to my other duties, the direct command of the eastern front. My reasons were that on the west the enemy are still some 1,200 yards distant, while in the east they are practically sitting on our parapets. Fock's first action on assuming command was to blow up the casemates in Chi-kuan-shan Fort and abandon it, taking advantage of instructions given to him directly by Stössel. This was done without reference to me, without my knowledge, and without asking either my opinion or that of the Council, and despite my previously expressed views on the subject. General Stössel's systematic ignoring of my rights as Commandant of the Fortress, in particular with regard to administrative matters and the hospitals, has been constant since September; but though my authority is being continually undermined by various orders issued in the Fortress without reference to me, the actual defence has till now suffered little, thanks to the complete agree-

* Erh-lung-shan Fort was surrendered ten days later.

ment of the late Officer Commanding the Land Defences, the Officer Commanding the Artillery, and the Officer Commanding the Engineers with my views. Now, however, that so serious a matter as the surrender of a fort has been decided on without reference to me, and, as it was in my opinion most injurious to the defence, I have the honour to ask that either General Stössel may be ordered to recognize my rights as Commandant at once, in accordance with fortress regulations, and may be forbidden to interfere, or else that I may be relieved of all responsibility for the further defence of the Fortress and of my duties as Commandant.'

Having sent this telegram, General Smirnoff hoped that Port Arthur would live till an answer could be received, which would be at longest in about three weeks; if it should be favourable to him, and the defence should pass entirely into his hands, he felt sure that, in spite of the harm already done by Fock, he would be able to hold out till the end of February.

Alas! the end came just twelve days after the despatch of the above message.

CHAPTER XXXIX

THE SAPPERS—REWARDS

THE provision of technical troops in Port Arthur, their employment, and their reward for the work done are points which deserve some mention. Their provision is a matter which it is in some ways difficult to separate from the ludicrous idea of the way to defend a fortress which held with those in authority.

It was, one would have thought, patent that to defend Port Arthur it was necessary to defend the peninsula from sea to sea and from Kinchou to Liao-tieh-shan, or an area of some eighteen miles in breadth by forty in length. As it was unlikely that an attacking enemy would advance on the Fortress held by a civilized power such as Russia with the same impetuosity as was shown by the Japanese in 1894 against an effete nation, it was equally obvious that as many delaying positions as possible, from the most excellent one of Kinchou right away back to the actual enceinte of the place, should be held. Such is the nature of the country that there is a whole series of positions. Even if general principles were not to be regarded, it might be thought that the manœuvres of the years preceding the war would have shown in actual practice how valuable these positions were to any force defending Port Arthur. The enemy were evidently of opinion that we would take every advantage of what Nature had given us, and would supplement these natural advantages with all the resources of art. It follows, therefore, that in the preparation of these successive positions, quite apart from the defence of the Fortress proper, there was an immense amount of work to be done which would necessitate the skill of technical troops.

Within and round the place itself also, even supposing that all the permanent defences had been ready at the commencement of war, [which they were not by any means], there would be during a siege great scope for the employment of technical troops. It is largely for siege-work that such troops are included in the organization of an army. On the whole, therefore, both the more distant defences of the district and the closer defence of Port Arthur appear to have called for the provision of a very large number of sappers. The district was large, from a point of view of the amount of defensive work that was necessary, and the Fortress was large. Let us see what the higher authorities in St. Petersburg and the local authorities in Arthur apparently thought sufficient.

Of sapper officers not with units there were altogether fifteen in the Engineer Department of the whole district. Of these, the following were not available for general sapper duty: six officers employed in the Naval Construction Yard, and six others specially employed, thus leaving three officers available for sapper duties over the whole area. Of troops for the work over this huge area there was one sapper company—the gallant Kwan-tun Sapper Company, consisting of 9 officers and 450 non-commissioned officers and men. Even from this number 2 officers were detached and sent up north to Manchuria, and 50 men detached for special duties; that leaves 7 officers and 400 men at the commencement of hostilities! Had the subject ever been considered in St. Petersburg? This number was all that were available for the defensive works on miles of field and semi-permanent positions, on many permanent forts and intermediate works, and for the construction and repair of all defence buildings.

It must be remembered that under the Engineer officers trained technical foremen are required, and that these have to be paid according to their skill. Stössel regarded the more expensive article as unnecessary, and thought it sufficient to employ the ordinary sappers from the company as foremen. The proper employment of these technical troops seems also scarcely to have been grasped. As a rule, for defence works the sappers, both officers and men, do little unskilled manual labour themselves; they organize, supervise, and direct the unskilled labour of the troops or of hired civilians. The extent to which the capabilities and powers of sappers was understood by some of the staff in Arthur is illustrated by the following incident:

When the enemy were on the eve of their assaults on Kinchou the Officer Commanding the Sapper Company got a telegram on May 24 from Arthur:

'*To Colonel Jerebtsoff.*

' General Stössel directs me to request you immediately to arrange for the blowing up of the southern wall of the town of Kinchou. It should be carried out at once.

' KONDRATENKO.'

The next morning Jerebtsoff went with his subaltern to inspect this wall. Kinchou was situated in front of the left flank of the position of that name. Like the majority of Chinese towns, it was surrounded with a loopholed stone wall, like a tower of mediæval times. Upon inspection this wall proved to be a solid erection of stone laid in mortar, 19 feet high, 21 feet thick at the bottom, and 19 feet thick at the top. This was what Stössel wanted blown up 'immediately.' To demolish it meant blowing up some 1,435,000 cubic feet of stone masonry!

When Colonel Jerebtsoff went into Arthur to report the impossibility of demolishing this wall *at once*, he was told:

'We will give you as many men from the 5th East Siberian Rifle Regiment as you like.'

'But, sir,' said the Colonel, 'I shall want more than two men to lay the charge in every chamber. For 1,200 yards of wall I should want not less than 500 chambers— that is, about 1,000 men—and anyhow, even if you give me the men, it is impossible to do the work *at once*.'

The answer was amusing.

'There's no time to talk, Colonel; you must please go and carry out General Stössel's order.'

Jerebtsoff left by rail that night, but the train was unable to proceed beyond Inchenzy, as the line was fired at by the enemy's gunboats. He therefore had to ride from there to Nangalin, whence he again proceeded on by train. But he never even reached the position at Kinchou, for it was already in the enemy's hands.

Without understanding the rôle of sappers, Stössel during the whole siege threw the Sapper Company about like a ball from hand to hand. It was within this period put under the orders of four separate officers, without rhyme or reason. This anomaly of passing a most valuable technical unit from one officer to another was not only not called for, but did absolute harm, as it enabled people who were totally ignorant of its duties, qualifications and capabilities to issue to it utterly irregular and impossible orders.

That the organization of the sappers in the Fortress in the event of war was not sufficiently thought out and foreseen is shown by the fact that this company, though 'a Fortress Company,' was allotted to work not only in the Fortress, but in the whole district (which was the reason it was not called the 'Port Arthur' Company). It was therefore given a civilian complement, which put it on a different footing to other fortress companies—*i.e.*, it consisted of a field sapper company supplemented by a telegraph detachment of half the strength of a field telegraph company. In consequence, when hostilities commenced, there were neither fortress nor telegraph sappers in the Fortress itself.

The Sapper Company also affords an example of Stössel's system of bestowing rewards. These men had done many gallant deeds, and by May had won thirty Crosses of St. George. When Stössel learnt this, he said to the commanding officer:

'You have got too many crosses in your company: I shall not give you any more.'

Despite many gallant actions done by the sappers at later periods of the siege, and the recommendations made to him, Stössel kept his word: not a single cross was given to the sappers. With regard to the question of rewards in general, space does not permit of a description of the general system of their disposal by Stössel, but to give some slight insight of his methods, the following extract of a letter written to his relations by an officer when a prisoner of war in Japan is quoted. After describing his feelings and the hardships he and his companions had undergone, he continues:

'And to all this is added the knowledge of the insults heaped upon us by the bitter injustice shown to many in the bestowal of rewards. Many unworthy officers who have done nothing to deserve good of their country have been plastered with orders by General Stössel, who wished to help them on. In the majority of cases these were either officers of high rank who were intimate with him, were with him in the China campaign, or were liked for " family reasons." Others were recommended by their immediate commanders more than once, but the reward lists were either lost in the office of the Officer Commanding the District or were purposely overlooked by General Stössel. In the Fortress at the end, counting those who had been recently promoted, there were fourteen General Officers. Of these, those who had already got the Cross of St. George of the fourth class received that of the third class, and those who had not got the fourth class were given it. There was *only one* General Officer who remained without this order for bravery, and he, need I say, was General Smirnoff, the Commandant!

'The private soldiers were also shamefully treated. Many of those who did countless gallant deeds and were recommended for rewards went to Japan as prisoners of war, having received nothing. Apparently these recommendations received no notice in Stössel's office. The case of Colonel Jerebtsoff, who commanded the only Sapper Company in the Fortress, is also noteworthy. At the beginning of the war he met with much opposition from the other Engineers in his endeavours to get materials, etc., for his company. During the siege he lost 12 officers and 350 men out of his company, of which 5 officers were killed and 2 died, and 100 men were killed. Work was carried on constantly, day and night, from April 14, and from July 1 to the surrender of the Fortress under constant fire. From September 28, during one and a half months, he supervised the sapping and mining works on his portion under incessant fire, and on November 26 went out and worked for four and a half hours under a heavy fire, losing an officer and six men. In short, he did an immense amount of work and showed the greatest gallantry. He was recommended by General Kondratenko in August, after the fighting at Green Hills, for the Order of St. Stanislav, second class, and by Colonel Grigorenko, after the assault of November 26, for the Cross of St. George, fourth class;

but he received nothing save a medal of the Order of St. Anne, third class, which he had won in peace-time! And why? Simply because he was a quiet, modest officer, asked for nothing for himself, and thought only of how best to do his duty and look after those under him. And he was one of many!'

CHAPTER XL

THE FALL OF ERH-LUNG-SHAN AND THE LAST COUNCIL

It is not easy to arrive at the truth about the fall of Erh-lung-shan Fort. There are many different accounts, and the loss of this fort is still the subject of keen discussion between various officers. Therefore, to enable the reader to form his own judgment, the evidence of two of the senior men in the Fortress who did not agree is quoted. One is General Smirnoff and the other Gun-Captain Direnkoff. Their evidence is amplified by extracts from the Raschevsky-Schwartz diary. I begin with Direnkoff.

'At 7 p.m. on December 27 the Japs stopped their mining work under the glacis of the salient. This cessation of work did not attract much attention, as it was thought to be temporary. As a matter of fact, the enemy, having reached the desired spot, had stopped excavating in order to load and fire their mines. On this occasion they gave no indication of their intention, and kept on firing 11-inch shells and throwing grenades into the fort as usual. The night passed quietly, with no suspicion of what was to come, on our part. At 7.30 the next morning the first explosion took place, but it was a failure. At eight o'clock a single Japanese dashed out on to our parapet, then rushed back again. Five minutes later I was walking from the inner parapet, and had not quite reached the caponier when a second explosion took place, which shook the whole fort and the hill it was on. The Japs at once opened fire and began hurling a quantity of hand-grenades and bombs, while they set to work to raise a wall of sand-bags on this side of the ditch. Our losses from the explosion were about 100 killed and wounded, several being suffocated by gases in the caponier. The officer commanding sent word to Major-General Gorbatovsky:

'"The Japanese have blown up our advanced parapet. Our losses are very heavy. Please send reinforcements."

'Reinforcements arrived, amounting, I should think, to about 500 men. When darkness came on the enemy's artillery ceased firing, and only the occasional crack of rifles disturbed the silence. The officer commanding ordered the wounded, who were lying about everywhere, to be brought in, and this was finished by about 10 p.m. He then sent word to Gorbatovsky:

'"Erh-lung-shan is surrounded by Japs. What are your orders?"

'The General replied:

'"Do what you can. There are no more reserves to send you."

'The officer commanding then sent fifty men of the *Retvisan* to drive the Japs from the inner parapet, but the attempt failed and nearly all were killed. The Japs, in addition to occupying this, had crawled into the caponier. Three times our men attempted to turn them out, but were three times driven back. By nine o'clock the Japs had contrived to make a sand-bag parapet in it and to drag a machine-gun and torpedo-tube on to the fort. By ten the garrison was ordered to evacuate the fort. The officer commanding ordered us to take away the breech-blocks from the 37-millimetre guns, and on leaving the forts to give them to General Gorbatovsky, which we did. When we left the fort about 100 men were still in the caponier. I imagine our casualties must have been about 600 killed and wounded. The guns left to the enemy were: three 6-inch (all disabled), one Baranovsky, two field-guns (4-pounders), seven 37-millimetre.

'We also left 300 rifles, a lot of entrenching tools, and 2 unloaded spherical mines; of ammunition: 37-millimetre, 2,000 rounds; Baranovsky, 200 rounds. I don't know what 6-inch ammunition was left. The gunners, by some careless mistake, did not remove the breech-blocks of these guns. Of food supplies we left 30 sacks of biscuits, 400 pounds of bread, 1½ boxes of tinned meat, and a quantity of groats.'

General Smirnoff's evidence about this fort was as follows:

'At last, at 9 a.m. on the 28th, a big explosion took place on the parapet. The enemy opened a heavy fire on the retrenchment; this our men could not stand, and they took cover in the casemates underneath. About 5 p.m. some of the enemy reached the retrenchment, while another portion of them moved along the flank ditches. Though the garrison of the fort consisted of some 7 to 9 officers and 300 men, their *moral* was so affected by the example of Fort Chi-kuan-shan that the men would not obey their officers, who ordered them out of the casemates back on to the retrenchment; nor did the officers give an example to the men. I sent one company after another from the reserve to reinforce the garrison, and ordered Gorbatovsky to drive out the enemy; but the fresh troops became infected by the others: they were demoralized, and would not put their hearts into a counter-attack.

'When Gorbatovsky told me of this on the telephone, he, not wishing to make it public, sent Captain Stepanoff to report personally to me, and begged permission to abandon the fort, or else all the garrison would be killed. I forwarded this news to Reuss for information, and *did not give* Gorbatovsky the permission asked for, as I was waiting to see Stepanoff first; but before he had reached me Gorbatovsky received orders direct from General Stössel that the fort was to be abandoned. On withdrawing, our men rallied on the half-prepared position some 300 to 500 paces in rear, from Rocky Ridge to Fortification No. 3.'

From the Raschevsky-Schwartz Diary, December 28.

'At 7 a.m. the enemy began to shell intermittently Fortification No. 3 and Erh-lung-shan Fort, and their miners continued working. At 9 a.m. the noise of work in the mining galleries suddenly ceased, and two charges were exploded in the salient angles of the fort. At the moment of the explosion there was only the gun crew on duty in the casemate; the rest of the men were in their quarters in the gorge. Great blocks of the inner skin of armoured concrete were torn off by the force of the explosion and piled up in the exit, crushing several men. On the parapet, to left and right of the shelter, were two huge craters. To relieve the position to some extent, and to check the enemy's assaulting columns, our batteries were ordered to fire on the approaches in front of the fort; but what good could our fire do when in the Zaredoubt Battery there was only one serviceable 6-inch gun, on Laperoff Hill also only one 6-inch and a 40-millimetre battery, on Mitrofanieff's hill one 40-millimetre battery, and on Tumulus Hill four quick-firing field-guns? All these batteries, though under a heavy shell-fire, did what they could.

'About 11 a.m. the first message from Captain Bulgakoff, commanding the fort, was received by the staff of the section, reporting that the enemy had destroyed the parapet by the great explosion, and had seized it, that our men were panic-struck and were holding the retrenchment with great difficulty. Gorbatovsky then sent up a company at once from the reserves to relieve Bulgakoff, and to drive the Japanese out of the fort. However, despite this reinforcement, the garrison not only failed to hurl back the enemy, but lost the retrenchment. The officers tried to lead a counter-attack, but when, on going out from the retrenchment, the first men were killed, the remainder refused to go on, and bolted from the retrenchment into the quarters in the gorge. Taking advantage of the darkness, small parties of the enemy got round the flanks, threatening to surround the fort from the rear, to seize the gorge ditch, and cut off communication with the Fortress. The enemy's artillery continued firing all day. The communicating roads to the fort were destroyed, but were being repaired all the time by our sappers, especially at night. The abandonment of the fort was begun in the afternoon and finished about two in the morning. On leaving the fort Captain Bulgakoff gave orders to pour kerosene over the bed-boards and set light to the men's quarters and light the long fuses of the mines. At 2 a.m. Gorbatovsky ordered me to go to Fock in the morning and give him my opinion as to the necessity of holding Fortification No. 3 to the end.'

The general opinion of the officers in Arthur was that the loss of Erh-lung-shan Fort was due principally to the bad *moral* of the garrison, caused by the General's demoralizing influence and the example he had set by Fort Chi-kuan-shan.

At 6 p.m. on December 29 a meeting—the last meeting—of the Council of War took place in the District Staff Offices. All the senior commanders in the Fortress were present:

1. *Captain Golovan*, Chief Staff Officer 7th East Siberian Rifle Brigade.

2. *Lieutenant-Colonel Dmitrevsky*, Chief Staff Officer 4th East Siberian Rifle Division.

3. *Colonel Khvostoff*, Chief of the Fortress Staff.

4. *Colonel Reuss*, Chief Staff Officer of the Kwantun District.

5. *Lieutenant-Colonel Nekrashevitch-Poklad*, commanding 25th Regiment.

6. *Colonel Petrusha*, commanding 28th Regiment.

7. *Lieutenant-Colonel Handurin*, commanding 15th Regiment.

8. *Colonel Semenoff*, A.D.C., commanding 26th Regiment.

9. *Colonel Savitsky*, commanding 14th Regiment.

10. *Colonel Griaznoff*, commanding ———* Regiment.

11. *Colonel Mekhmandaroff*, commanding 7th East Siberian Rifle Artillery Division.

12. *Colonel Irman*, commanding 4th East Siberian Rifle Artillery Brigade.

13. *Colonel Grigorenko*, commanding the Fortress Engineers.

14. *Rear-Admiral Wiren*.

15. *Rear-Admiral Loschinsky*.

16. *Major-General Gorbatovsky*, commanding the eastern front.

17. *Major-General Biely*, commanding the Fortress Artillery.

18. *Major-General Nadein*, temporarily commanding 4th East Siberian Rifle Division.

19. *Major-General Nickitin* (no special appointment).

20. *Lieutenant-General Fock*, lately commanding 4th East Siberian Rifle Division, now in command of the land defences.

21. *Lieutenant-General Smirnoff*, Commandant of the Fortress.

22. *General Stössel*, A.D.C.

* Omitted by Author.—A. B. L.

It was evening, and the town and front were quiet. The collected members conversed and exchanged opinions in a low tone while waiting for the meeting to commence. Every one was naturally much interested in what was coming, and most guessed why General Stössel had summoned all the senior commanding officers. At last it began. The meeting is recorded for clearness in the following form:

Stössel. 'Gentlemen, I have called you all here to give me your opinion frankly with regard to the actual state of the Fortress and the steps which should be taken in future. When the meeting is over I will read you this paper' (in his hand was a letter).* 'Let us commence with the juniors. Captain Golovan, what is your opinion on this question?'

Golovan. 'We must certainly hold out to the very last.'

Dmitrevsky. 'The food is very bad. We have little ammunition now left. I do not see that we can expect anything by continuing the defence.'

Nekrashevitch-Poklad. 'We have no ammunition. Scurvy is on the increase, and the hospitals are full. We have few men to garrison the Fortress works. Under such circumstances, there is little use in carrying on with the defence.'

Petrusha. 'We have held out till now, and we can hold out longer; and then—God's will be done.'

* This paper appears, from an independent source ['The Siege and Fall of Port Arthur,' by Major-General Kostenko, President of the Military Court of Port Arthur during the siege], to have been the copy of a telegram to the Tsar which Stössel had despatched to the Tsar *before* this council meeting was held. According to Kostenko this telegram was: 'We cannot hold out more than a few days; am taking measures to prevent a street massacre'; and in his opinion Stössel did not read it out at this council meeting after the feeling of the members had been so strongly declared against surrender, because he was afraid of being arrested for having sent it.—A. B. L.

Savitsky and Griaznoff. 'It is very difficult to hold out longer. Everything is going badly.'

Semenoff. 'We must hold out at all costs. My troops are in excellent fettle and the best of spirits.'

Mekhmandaroff. 'We must continue the defence.'

Stössel. 'You must surely know, Colonel, that, having got possession of Erh-lung-shan Fort, the enemy command the neighbouring batteries and works, and can from there shell us. Can you guarantee that the enemy won't mount guns there?'

Mekhmandaroff. 'I cannot guarantee that, but I will swear that I will put any of their guns out of action as soon as they are mounted. As long as we hold on to Rocky Ridge the loss of Erh-lung-shan does not make our general position in any way critical. We can hold out easily for some time. We still have a number of splendid rear-guard positions. We can, and I consider we ought to, hold out—in fact, to defend ourselves to the last moment.'

Irman. 'In any case, we must hold out in the same way as we have already held out. Why, up till now one might say that we have really only been holding field positions, not permanent ones. We can easily hold out longer.'

Grigorenko. 'We *must* hold out. Let us look at the question on a broader basis. To do the best, I consider we ought to reduce the garrison of all points not being attacked—*i.e.*, Liao-tieh-shan and Signal Hill—and send the troops thus released to the threatened points.'

Fock. 'No, no. Liao-tieh-shan is the keep—it mustn't be touched.'

Reuss. 'As the fleet has ceased to exist, Arthur's rôle of affording a sanctuary to it is over. It is quite unnecessary to the army operating in the north, as that army has concentrated now in great strength. A further defence can only end in a street massacre, which is to be deprecated.'

Wiren and Loschinsky. 'The place *must* be defended to the bitter end.'

Gorbatovsky. 'If the Fortress is to fall or to capitulate, we must postpone the day as long as possible. We must fight to the last.'

Biely. 'I fail to understand what Dmitrevsky means by saying there is no ammunition. We have plenty to repulse two more big attacks—102,000 shells of our own and 100,000 still available from the fleet, with 8,000,000 rounds of small-arm ammunition. From an artillery point of view, I do not consider we are at all in a critical position. The defence ought to be continued.'

Nadein. 'I also agree. We must continue to hold out.'

Nickitin. 'We must certainly hold out to the last. If our position is bad, that of the enemy is not particularly happy. A further defence is possible, and should be successful, as we have a series of excellent positions, and in the New Chinese Town a number of excellent buildings for the troops.'

Fock. 'A short time ago I was in the trenches. My God! what did I not see? The suffering, the wounds, the sickness—never shall I forget the sights. Who is better or more noble than the private soldier? Who can equal him in gallantry, unselfishness, and endurance? We should not let him die for nothing. We should not let him die unless something is gained thereby. The losses will be greater now if the Japanese mount guns in Erh-lung-shan——'

Mekhmandaroff. 'I have already guaranteed that I will not allow them to bring a single gun into action there.'

Fock. 'Think of the wretched men—hungry, worn out——'

Smirnoff. 'I have heard everything that has been said

on the subject, and I consider it my duty to state that, according to regulations, there should be in every fortress secret instructions in which the *raison d'être* of the fortress in the theatre of war is defined. According to these instructions, the Commandant is to be the judge as to the extent to which the fortress has done its duty—fulfilled its mission. Unfortunately, such instructions do not exist in this fortress. One of the objects of this fortress—to afford a refuge and protection to the fleet—ceased to exist when the fleet was destroyed. The other object—to co-operate in the strategical plans of the main army by keeping employed the Japanese army now laying siege to us—is not finished. No matter what the opinion on the question may be, the Regulations for the Guidance of Commanders of Fortresses definitely require them to hold out till all strength and means are exhausted, which with us is far from the case. Thus we must continue the defence. The scheme of defence conforming to actual circumstances should be as follows: So long as possible we should hold the Chinese Wall, as from behind it we can throw hand-grenades and fire mines. To strengthen our fighting line we must weaken Liao-tieh-shan and Signal Hill.' (Fock shook his head and tried to interrupt.) 'I am sure that we can hold on to the Chinese Wall for a fortnight. Then we will fall back on the second line—*i.e.*, Tumulus Battery, Vladimir, Mitrofanieff, and Nameless Hills. This line has one defect—that it won't be possible to keep the supports and reserves near it, owing to the scarcity of cover. We must therefore regard it as a rear-guard position; but, all the same, we shall be able to hold the enemy on it for a week. Finally, there is the third line on Stonebroken Ridge, running from the left to the northern portion of the town wall, and from the right to Big Hill. It is at present well fortified, and has directly in rear of it a number of buildings, in which the supports and reserves can get cover. Thanks to the strength of this position, we should be able to hold on in it for at least three weeks. By that time our supplies will be running out, and then—not till then' (raising his voice) —'can the question of the Fortress's life be discussed.'

He finished.

Every one remained silent; no one liked to speak. The Commandant had spoken what all knew to be the truth.

Stössel continued: 'In my opinion the second line is extremely weak, and it is in no way important. Well, gentlemen, I see that all of you almost are in favour of a further defence, and we will accordingly carry on. Russian soldiers could not act otherwise. I am extremely grateful to all of you for coming to such a resolution.'

The meeting broke up, and the news of the conclusion reached and of the opinions of individual members was soon spread abroad.

CHAPTER XLI

THE FALL OF FORTIFICATION NO. 3—THE FAILURE OF THE DEFENCE AND MEDICAL ORGANIZATIONS

THE garrison no longer showed the same steadiness that it had shown in the many desperate fights in the beginning of December. This was certainly owing to the example of Fort Chi-kuan-shan. The men's spirits seemed to have gone, and it was too late for the officers to stop the hæmorrhage from the moral wounds caused by Fock. A passionate desire for life was everywhere noticeable, and any attempt to persuade the men that it was their duty to die was now useless.

Early in the morning of the 31st Gorbatovsky was summoned by Fock to confer with him. The latter was, as usual, dilating on the splendid qualities of the men, and the pity it was to make them suffer needlessly, when a great pillar of smoke suddenly shot up from Fortification No. 3, followed by a tremendous explosion.

'I must go back, sir, and I will return at once and let you know what has happened.'

'Yes, come back as soon as you can.'

Gorbatovsky then went off. Without waiting for a report from him, Fock there and then, in the presence of Captain Rodionoff, of the Engineers, wrote out his orders for the abandonment of Fortification No. 3, and sent them off by (I think) a sailor. There was no reference, no word to the Commandant, or even to Stössel. Comment is unnecessary; such action speaks for itself.

What had happened is best seen by reference to the diary:

'*December* 31.—About 6 a.m. General Gorbatovsky was summoned by General Fock to the third line of defences to confer. At 9 a.m. three successive explosions took place in Fortification No. 3. After a few minutes a telephone message came in from the work to say that the enemy had exploded two charges in the corners of one of the faces. At the moment when the garrison, led by its commanding officer, Captain Spredovy, dashed out of the quarters in the gorge casemate, in order to get out into the interior of the place before the Japanese could seize the parapet, a third charge was fired, which had been laid in the gorge itself. This charge destroyed the gorge casemates, and buried the commanding officer and 140 men under the débris. The fall of this mass of stuff caused the hand-grenades heaped up in the casemates to detonate and set off four mines, laid under the foundations. The wounded and remnants of the garrison were thus shut up in the casemate, with only one small exit into the gorge ditch, through which they had to crawl. Not being able to get into the interior of the work, the garrison could do nothing to hold the position. The enemy perceived this at once, quickly got into the interior of the work, and seized the gorge, where they brought machine-guns. About 10 o'clock we saw a white flag on the fortification. It is not known who raised it. General Stössel and the Fortress Commandant were informed, and within a quarter of an hour the following order was received from General Stössel:

'" In view of the difficulty of getting out of the Fortification, the remainder of the garrison may surrender; those who can escape may try to."

'This order was transmitted by telephone to the work, whence a list of those alive and wounded was telephoned back. The telephone was then cut to prevent the enemy hearing what we said. It was thought that, having seized the fortification, they would try and storm Tumulus Battery. General Gorbatovsky, therefore, ordered the garrison of this battery to be reinforced by one company of infantry, and a company of sailors to be sent into the trenches of the second line from Laperoff's battery along Vladimir and Mitrofanieff Batteries. About eleven o'clock the enemy's fire ceased. Gorbatovsky decided to hold the second line, having Tumulus Battery on the left flank and Eagle's Nest on the right. He told the Commandant of this, and asked leave to carry it out at night. . . .'

From Stössel's order and subsequent dispositions on that day it is clear that he had no idea of the relationship between the second and third lines. Among other things he ordered the left flank of the second line to be held, while part of the third line was held (Stonebroken Ridge and Big Hill). From this it was plain that Stössel had never seen the second line of positions, and had never been on the hills near.

After the fall of Erh-lung-shan Fort the besiegers opened a heavy fire on the north-east front from Tumulus Battery to Eagle's Nest. At 1 p.m. on January 1 they delivered an attack from the fort on Rocky Ridge. Our troops having lost heart, and being badly demoralized, gave way; but our gun-fire checked the enemy's assault, and the position remained in our possession. However, despite the very strict and definite orders given by the Commandant that the Chinese Wall from Rocky Ridge was to be held at all costs (it was quite possible), as soon as dusk came on, the abandonment of this wall and Rocky Ridge began under Fock's orders. The retirement was executed without any interference from the enemy, and we were able to take with us all except the heavier guns. At five o'clock on January 1 our troops were distributed along the second line—Tumulus Battery, Vladimir Battery, Mitrofanieff Hills, Eagle's Nest, the portion of the Chinese Wall behind Chi-kuan-shan Fort, and Kuropatkin Lunette.

The enemy having now arrived at such a position, it seems a fitting moment to mention in what directions the organization of Port Arthur as a fortress had most failed.

By this time most of the many grave defects in the original conception and subsequent execution of the material defences of this stronghold had become only too painfully clear, though it had not needed the test of bitter experience to make the more glaring errors obvious. There were terrible faults in the original tactical arrangement of the defences and in the details of the works themselves.

The main line of permanent forts, the girdle, was much too close to the objects to be protected—*i.e.*, the dockyard and town. The positions fortified by us were so close that, before capturing these positions, the enemy were able to bombard the place, damage our fleet, and demoralize the population. Some points of vital importance were entirely unprovided with permanent works—*i.e.*, 203 Metre Hill, Angle and Long Hills—and were left for an improvised fortification, which was carried out in a scrambling way after the place had been completely invested. So little had these three positions been considered important that until after May 18 no paths to them had ever been made. Accepting the main line originally chosen, such as it was, there were further defects in the forts themselves. They were in many cases badly sited. On the eastern front the enemy had commanding positions within two miles (Ta-ku-shan, Sia-gu-shan), from which the interior of our defence could be seen and fired into, and our communications shelled. This seriously hampered the movement of troops and the transport of munitions. They were also badly designed for their sites, having no good field of fire and much dead ground in front of them. It is not enough to say they were ill-concealed—they were ingenuously conspicuous. As regards armament, our long-range heavy guns, designed to fight the enemy's siege artillery, were placed right in the front, by which all the advantages to be obtained by their ranging power was thrown away. They naturally drew a concentration of the enemy's fire, and were soon rendered useless. They were a positive curse to the works in which they were placed, for they attracted a fire on to these works, to which they could not efficiently reply. In design many of the forts failed. They were not defiladed; they had no covered communications and no proper shelters. The parapets were feebly revetted with stones and sand-bags, and not having sufficient traverses, could be swept by enfilade fire. The concrete was not covered with earth, but was fully exposed. Lastly, such as they were, our forts were not finished and ready by the time they were wanted.

The faults in the choice of position and ground were largely due to the fact that the scheme was originally a paper scheme, worked out on the map instead of on the ground. When the local engineers saw things on the ground, it was too late for any alteration—the scheme had been approved and confirmed. The paucity of works, their half-finished condition, and the absolute lack of many essentials, however, were all due to a cheese-paring, misplaced economy. Money was scarce for the vital defences of Arthur, while millions were being poured out on the palaces and wharves of Dalny, on a well-equipped harbour, which was eventually to help the Japanese.

Let us now turn to the medical organization of the

Fortress. Did that correspond to the needs of the besieged Fortress? What influence had that on its fate?

At the beginning of the war, in spite of the growth of the garrison, there were the following hospitals: (1) A mixed hospital of 400 beds; (2) the Reserve Hospital No. 1, 200 beds; (3) the Port Hospital, 40 beds; (4) two small civil hospitals. Of course, this quantity of hammocks could not possibly suffice to meet the needs of a garrison 50,000 strong. If to the garrison be added the fleet, the civilian and native population, the number of beds appears yet more absurd. According to the field service regulations, the proportion of beds to strength of troops should be 1 to 8; the proportion existing at the commencement of the war was 1 to 100! In March was opened the Naval Hospital, 200 beds, increased in July to 500; in April Reserve Hospital No. 6, 210 beds; in May three reserve hospitals, 630 beds; in June three reserve hospitals and a mobile hospital, 630 beds. After the fortnight's assaults in August, when all the hospitals were filled with wounded and were threatened with dysentery, Reserve Hospital No. 11 was opened, with 1,200 beds, in the naval barracks.

Although, when once the war had started, it was daily to be expected that the enemy might land and Port Arthur be thus completely cut off, from the moment the first shot was fired the equipping of the hospitals with medical and other appliances was carried out at snail's pace. During the three months when the Fortress was in direct communication with the capital, no single additional bed was added—that is, omitting the Naval Hospital and the *Mongolia*, opened within two months of the beginning of the war for a special purpose. The former was arranged for during peace-time and the building had already been finished. It was only with the arrival of the new Commandant and the Sanitary Inspector of the Fortress, Civil

Councillor Subotin, that the organization of the medical service was gradually placed on some sort of footing. Their efforts were not particularly fruitful, because, instead of immediately giving effect to the urgent representations and applications of the Commandant, the authorities in the north spilt seas of ink, and continued thus to spend their time till we were cut off. At the beginning of the strict investment (after the fights on the advanced positions) there were only 2,500 beds in the hospitals under the Military and Naval Departments, and in the three hospital buildings taken over by the Red Cross there were only 500 beds, or a total of 3,000—one-third of the proper number. During the period of the strict blockade the number of beds increased. According to official statistics, another 1,500 were added; but this addition can only be taken as nominal, as there were practically no reserves in the medical store depôts at the beginning of the war, and it was impossible to procure any locally. But still, accepting these official figures, during the worst period in Arthur 4,500 sick and wounded could be tended. The minimum figure of sick at the end of the siege, which cannot be disputed, was 15,000; the actual number was more like 18,000. To show how these 'extra' 10,000 to 12,000 suffering soldiers found shelter or relief means the unveiling of the most revolting picture of the siege. About half of these 'extra' cases were distributed *somewhere* in the hospitals above mentioned, and the remainder were put in hastily-run-up sheds—little cemeteries of living beings. In these during the last month of the siege there were sometimes as many as a thousand sick men crowded together, under the charge of one medical man, often a surgeon, who could only be a helpless spectator of their sufferings.

Just glance at one of these 'infernos' in the month of December. Outside it is freezing; inside, in spite of the musty and sickening stench, the cold is intense. On all sides is filth, nothing but filth, and on it and amongst it crawl millions of greasy grey lice. The silence is only broken by the sighs and groans of the sick and the hungry —for all in here are both sick and hungry. Death, the Liberator, is also here. He is in every corner, at the doors, at the windows, crawling along the floors and on to the bed-boards; he envelops everything—and waits. At the front a man dies suddenly, and all is over. In the hospitals Death is fought. But here, here, everything is in his power—he only has to wait. Second after second, minute after minute, hour after hour, men pass into eternity, into oblivion. There are hundreds of cases of scurvy. They lie side by side on the floor, on the bed-boards, underneath them, just as they were placed when they came in—some in great-coats, some in tunics, some in miserable boots, some barefooted. The faces are shapeless, swollen, and distorted, and upon the yellow skin are large dark blue bruises. The swollen gums, covered with hideous sores, project out of many grinning mouths, and show the lack of teeth, which are continuously falling out. . . . Here, far away from their friends and relations, forgotten by all, in horrible, complete consciousness, they are silently waiting the end.

And to think that much of this suffering might have been spared these men had the Medical Service been properly organized, had the highest authorities done their duty, instead of busying themselves with writing orders. Things would not have been so bad even if Stössel had confirmed the resolution of the Council of War about the killing of horses on December 8. Feeding the garrison on horses' flesh and white bread would at once have checked the growth of disease; and there were more than 3,000 horses and 3,000,000 pounds of flour in the Fortress.

The hospitals which existed in peace-time and the hospitals which expanded before the strict blockade answered their purpose fairly well. Those which were opened after the commencement of the strict blockade were far from doing so. They had no linen, nor beds, nor medical supplies, to say nothing of a sufficient quantity of trained nurses or doctors. The most disgraceful in this respect were Reserve Field Hospital No. 2, of 1,200 beds, opened for infectious cases and Mobile Field Hospital No. 5 (4th Division, General Fock), situated on Tiger's Peninsula. What could be expected from hospitals opened after the August assaults, when there was nothing left in the place with which to equip them? For the 1,200 beds of No. 2 only four doctors were told off. This hospital was renowned throughout the Fortress for its horrors: there is no need to describe them. A commission was appointed, which found the internal organization and arrangements of the hospital so revolting that the Hospital Inspector was immediately removed, and in his place was appointed M. Menshoff, who had recently been Chief of the Police in Dalny. Of 3,500 patients received into it, 1,500 died. Mobile Hospital No. 5 was little better.

The system of opening a hospital extension on the day of a big attack was hopeless. It led to the sudden concentration of the sick and wounded in the hospitals nearest to where the attack was taking place, and where there was most congestion and appalling confusion. The wounded sometimes received no medical assistance for days together, as the personnel, working as it did for twenty-four hours in the twenty-four, could not cope with such a big influx, and they were carried from one hospital to another, often dying on the road. Meanwhile, the other hospitals, situated some way off from the locality attacked, did not take their share, owing to this inefficient organization.

Many of the doctors made desperate efforts, but when dealing with masses like this individual efforts were drops in the ocean.

Subotin was the Fortress Sanitary Inspector, immediately subordinate to the Commandant, and he did his best; but there was no independent central organization in the Medical Service of the Fortress, which could have looked ahead and taken steps to distribute the sick properly in the hospitals during attacks. The Medical Service was dependent on the combatant authorities, whose hands were much taken up with fighting. What was required was a central administration, which could have foreseen what might happen and have controlled the arrangements. The officer in charge should have been invested with high rank and great authority, and should have had a properly trained personnel. Scurvy first made its appearance in the Fortress at a very early date: as early as April it appeared among the crew of the *Pallada*, but, thanks to timely and energetic measures, it was then stamped out. Unfortunately, no material preventive measures were taken against its recurrence, with the exception of vague suggestions as to better food and to add green food to the rations, though where better food could be got or vegetables could be bought was difficult to say. The scurvy cases increased from hundreds in October and thousands in November to 10,000 in December. The hospitals were so full of it that men were afraid of going into them, and at the end of the siege preferred to remain on duty, even when sick.

Of 18,000 sick and wounded reported on the day the garrison marched out, 6,000 only were wounded; the balance were cases of scurvy. There were really more, as many men only slightly ill were doing duty. Dr. Kefel, of the Naval Hospital, on making an inspection of the men on one section of the right flank on December 11, found that 21 per cent. of these on duty had scurvy. Exactly a fortnight afterwards, on his inspecting the same section, he found 40½ per cent. suffering from it. These were the same men, for they had not been relieved.

It was pointed out in his report on this that: 'If the spreading of scurvy increases in the above arithmetical progression, then in every fortnight we shall have 200 more on the sick list out of every thousand in the fighting line, and in one and a half months there will be no men left fit for duty. . . .

'If extreme measures are immediately taken, and we make use of all the meat, white bread, and antiscorbutic diet available, we may hope that those who are now well may not catch it, that the slight cases will not become worse, and that the worse cases will do tolerably well. Therefore there are before us two alternatives: to keep our food-supply and have, after a month and a half, not a single serviceable soldier, or to have eaten up our supplies of provisions at the end of six weeks, but during all that time to have kept the garrison in fighting strength. The strategist, not the arithmetician, can decide which is the more advantageous choice to make for the Fortress.'

When this report was laid before General Stössel, with a proposal to increase the ration, he replied: 'There cannot be so many men as this ill in that section. It is nonsense; there are not half that number there.' And so the question remained undecided. It was only at the very end that an order was given for a slight increase.

To the question, 'Was it possible to have avoided this epidemic of scurvy, and could we have checked it with what we had in Port Arthur?' the answer is undoubtedly 'Yes!'

How exactly this could have been done is a harder question to answer. From the moment we were cut off from the north the rations of the garrison were gradually cut short, and by November, when the men were physically and morally weakened, the rations were reduced to the minimum. Instead of bread, biscuits were issued, which could not really be counted as rations for scurvy cases, as to these they were as useful as stones.

The progress of the disease might have been checked if (1) a probable period of resistance had been thought out and fixed; (2) if rational use had been made of all sources of supply—horses, mules, cats, dogs, and flour. In the beginning of December more than 2,000,000 pounds of excellent flour was received. Had 3 pounds of white flour been issued per man, it would have lasted for three months. Half a pound of horse-flesh per man would have lasted for six weeks, though the number of horses for transport purposes would, of course, have been limited.

The first was not done, thanks to the chaos resulting from the harmful interference of Stössel and Fock.

The second was decided on at the council of December 8 (at which, by some incomprehensible oversight, the Sanitary Inspector of the Fortress was not asked to attend), but was not confirmed by Stössel.

CHAPTER XLII

THE LAST DAY BUT ONE

THE dawn of January 1, 1905, ushered in an anxious day. All the roads near the forts were now so much under rifle and machine-gun fire that movement on them soon ceased. In the Staff Office of the section it was expected that the enemy would at any moment commence to pound and then storm Eagle's Nest, which was now the key to the position. Sure enough, about nine o'clock the bombardment commenced, shell after shell with clockwork regularity striking the top of the hill. The staff of the section went from their usual observation-place to the dressing station, from which an excellent view of the rearward slope of Eagle's Nest could be seen, and which had a telephone. At noon Captain Galitsinsky, who was in command of the work, began sending in alarming messages to the effect that the enemy, by repeated rushes, were successfully concentrating in force in front of the position, evidently with a view to an assault, and asked that he might be reinforced. The assault soon began, but made at first little progress in face of the garrison's steady fire. General Gorbatovsky, commanding the section, kept the Commandant regularly informed of the progress, and urged that our guns should increase their fire. Our fortress guns poured in a fairly heavy fire, but not so heavy as the circumstances warranted, as we had but few howitzers, which alone could have been effective. Galitsinsky continued anxiously to report the critical condition of the position. Gorbatovsky never left the telephone, talking all the time with either Fock, Biely, or the Commandant: he kept on begging for reserves to be sent up, saying that without reinforcements he could not guarantee the issue. Suddenly some infantry were seen running back from Tumulus Hill, and it was ascertained that the enemy, having climbed a spur in front of Eagle's Nest, had enfiladed some of our trenches. The men in them wavered and then ran. The presence of mind of Captain Stepanoff alone restored order and averted a panic. A party of fifty sailors were sent up to Galitsinsky, followed by a second party somewhat later, and the fight waged hotly, our men with difficulty holding their own.

At midday, while the issue of the fight was in the balance, Rear-Admiral Loschinsky received the following letter, No. 2,544 of January 1:

'The state of the Fortress is becoming so critical that its further resistance cannot be guaranteed. If it becomes necessary to surrender, it is essential that the most important papers and standards be sent away. I am, therefore, directed by General Stössel to ask you whether it will be possible to send a destroyer at any moment to Chifu on board which an officer could be despatched with such papers. If this can be arranged, the destroyer ought to keep under steam ready to depart, as it will be impossible to foresee the precise moment when she will be required. I have the honour to inquire if this can be done?

'REUSS.'

Loschinsky replied to the effect that a destroyer would be kept always ready, and, to ship articles more conveniently, would lie under Electric Cliff. The *Statny*, under Lieutenant Baron Kasinsky, was told off for this. While this took place the Commandant was occupied issuing orders for the defence of the north-eastern front, and it never entered his head that anyone was then thinking out arrangements in case of a surrender. He was not told of the letter sent to Loschinsky, although the latter, in his capacity of Commander of the coast defences, was immediately under him.

Meanwhile the assault on Eagle's Nest continued, and about 2.30 p.m. the telephone from it ceased to work. Everyone at the dressing station was busy with his glasses watching the top of the hill, which was shrouded in clouds of bursting shrapnel, when, to our intense surprise, Galitsinsky, the commander of the place, suddenly arrived.

'How? What's happened? Why?'

'I was the last to leave. None of our men are there now.'

He looked exhausted, dishevelled, overcome.

The staff were much perturbed, for the loss of this important tactical point decided the fate of the north-east front. Any minute the Japanese might force their way along the valley and commence a massacre. Our guns concentrated their fire on the position that a few hours before had been ours; but soon Lieutenant Malchenko could be discerned riding along the road past our position with a large white flag!

When he was seen, someone laughingly said:

'Looks as if he were taking our New Year greetings to Nogi.'

But he was not armed with empty greetings. Alas! he was taking to Japan an unexpected New Year's gift. He was the bearer of the following letter from General

Stössel to General Baron Nogi, dated December, 1904 (no day of the month):

'Being acquainted with the general state of affairs in the theatre of war, I am of opinion that no object is to be gained by further opposition in Port Arthur, and so, to avoid useless loss of life, I am anxious to enter into negotiations for a capitulation. If your Excellency agrees, I would ask you to be so good as to appoint accredited persons to negotiate concerning the terms and arrangements for surrender, and to appoint a spot where they may meet my representatives.'

The despatch of the *parlementaire* had been decided on directly General Fock had brought word of the capture of Eagle's Nest, and Colonel Reuss had been immediately summoned to translate the above letter into English. No meeting of the Council of War was held. There was no attempt made to persuade Stössel to alter his decision to surrender. The Commandant was not even informed of the intention to despatch a *parlementaire*.

The decision to give up the Fortress had really matured on the day of the last meeting of the Council of Defence, for General Stössel had that day despatched a telegram to the Tsar, in which he reported that the men had become worn out, and that the Fortress could not possibly hold out more than a few days.*

In this he was undoubtedly influenced by the desire to save the lives of his close friends. If any of them had opposed the despatch of the *parlementaire*, and had informed the Commandant of it, Stössel alone would never have dared to do it. But he was supported, and so risked ignoring Smirnoff and proposing the surrender.

Simultaneously with the despatch of the *parlementaire*,

* The text of this message has been quoted.—A. B. L.

Rear-Admiral Wiren, commanding the battleship and cruiser division, received the following letter from Colonel Reuss:

'A letter has just been sent by a *parlementaire* from General Stössel to General Baron Nogi proposing to begin negotiations for a capitulation; there is, therefore, only to-night for you to do what you consider necessary to your ships!'

Admiral Wiren, distinguished and gallant officer that he was, was thunderstruck at such tidings, and immediately went off to Admiral Grigorovitch, to whom it was also news. Thence he went to General Biely, and even to the Commandant, who were both equally thunderstruck at what he told them. From them he went to Stössel, where the information of what had been done was confirmed.

The troops, who very soon heard of it, no longer remained troops. It was absurd to count on their obedience. And is it to be wondered at? They had fought long, obstinately, doggedly, dying and suffering awful agonies. They had been accustomed to expect death, and now—now—what did they not hear? Their hopes rose. They longed for life. They did not wish to die, and no power on earth would have again made them exchange these hopes for death. After the news of the despatch of the *parlementaire*, it would have been impossible to inspire 30,000 worn-out men, whose minds had already been poisoned by the fatal doctrine of some of their leaders, with the idea that the Fortress should be held to the last, and the senior commanders recognized this. When the Commandant went to the Admirals, and a council was held, with him in the chair, to consider what had best be done to avert a shameful surrender, they all came to the inevitable conclusion that there was not the slightest hope of counting on the obedience of the troops, already demoralized and knowing all about the negotiations. The arrest of Stössel, Fock, Reuss and others would have caused dissension in the garrison, perhaps a mutiny, and the last state of the Fortress would have been worse than the first. The Commandant and Admirals accordingly wisely refrained from taking any active steps, in order to avoid the awful scandal, which would only have increased the shame surrounding the surrender, and would have availed nothing.

Admiral Wiren issued orders for the ships under his command to be disabled by charges being exploded in their most vital parts (engines, boilers, etc.), but though every precaution was taken, the last demolitions were only brought off by the morning of January 2. The *Sevastopol* on that morning was tugged out by the *Silacha* to a depth of 30 fathoms, and her Kingston valves* were opened, with the result that she heeled over to starboard and quietly foundered. It was impossible to blow up the large number of guns in the Fortress as well as its munitions of war, as, according to the terms of the capitulation, all the forts, guns, ammunition, etc., were to be handed over intact. During the afternoon and night several guns were destroyed and much ammunition was buried; but General Biely, by Stössel's direct orders, strictly forbade this, as the enemy had said they would make reprisals if the guns, etc., were found destroyed. Some obeyed, others did not. Certainly most of the Artillery spent the night destroying their weapons and equipment.

From the Raschevsky-Schwartz Diary, January 1, 1905.

'The firing gradually slackened, and about 6 p.m. ceased. Deathly silence took the place of the constant noise of firing and roars of explosions, even the whistling of bullets overhead ceased. Tired and anxious, we went to the dressing station, where we bolted some food, and

* Valves which control the sea-water inlets of a ship.—E. D. S.

then went to the New Chinese town to the staff quarters of the section. We had scarcely lain down to snatch a little rest, when a mounted scout arrived with a letter from General Fock, in which he ordered Gorbatovsky immediately to carry out his orders, and abandon the third defensive section, for which he gave no reasons. He added that the section up to Fortification No. 2 was also to be evacuated. [On December 22, Fock, realizing the importance of this section, had ordered me to draw up a scheme for strengthening its defence. I had done this on the 23rd, and had carried the work out in two days.] Nothing was left for us but to obey the orders, and orders to this effect were accordingly issued by eight that evening. And so the whole of the north-eastern front and almost half of the eastern front was in the enemy's hands. The Fortress could no longer hold out, as all roads to the town were in the hands of the Japanese, and from Zaliterny Battery they could demolish the town at leisure. It is inexplicable how anyone understanding the great importance of this section and of B Battery could have ordered their abandonment without a fight.

'At the same time a second message was received, in which it was said that the Japanese had agreed to the negotiations, and had ceased firing, requesting that we also should cease. The horrible day gave place to a warm, quiet night, and the unusual silence seemed uncanny. Suddenly explosion after explosion rang out from the harbour—our battleships being blown up. It was the last straw. . . .'

The letter referred to above, in which General Gorbatovsky was ordered immediately to carry out instructions with regard to the abandonment of the third defensive position and the portion up to Fortification No. 2, is now in his possession. The abandonment of these positions was in no way warranted by circumstances, and to carry out such a retreat without fighting was most demoralizing to the troops. The negotiations for a capitulation were still before us, and had we retained something 'up our sleeve,' we could have bargained obstinately and have threatened to hold out longer, in order to obtain better terms. This threat would not have been an empty one.

At dark two huge conflagrations burst out from Eagle's Nest, lighting up the whole north-east front. Port Arthur lay silent—more silent than it had been for five long months — while the tongues of flame seemed to lick the low clouds which brooded over the Fortress and its triumphant foe. The silence was short-lived, however, for soon several muffled explosions from the direction of the harbour and the forts showed what Wiren was doing to his ships and the artillery to their guns. Another fire broke out near the harbour, and the town lay bathed in its blood-red glow. From the summit of Quail Hill the picture of Port Arthur on its last night—last night as a portion of the Russian Empire—was tragic enough. The place seemed to shudder at each dull explosion, as if it knew that it was near its end. Its former owners, having once more bought it at the cost of thousands of lives, were standing on the threshold of their great holiday and of the long-coveted prize.

CHAPTER XLIII

THE END

ALMOST before dawn next morning, on the eastern front near Signal Hill, was sounded the last note in the titanic struggle for Arthur. Some volleys rang out on the quiet air, died away into independent firing, then stopped. Boom! boom! went two guns, and then all was silent. It appeared that the Japanese, thinking that Signal Hill was only held by outposts, decided to seize it under cover of night. They advanced without even taking the usual military precautions. Unfortunately for them the hill was held by a company of infantry, which, having noticed their approach, allowed them to get within short range, and then poured volley after volley into them. Twenty dead and eighty wounded were left on the ground. They wavered, and our men charged with the bayonet. The fight continued for some moments, costing us five wounded and one killed.

At daybreak all the hills on both sides swarmed with men who had recently been foes: they stared at each other fascinated. The two great masses of men differed but little from each other. Both had come here to die, to die without a murmur and obediently. The only difference was that on the one side they died for duty and for an object understood by all, knowing their own superiority; on the other they died for the same reason, but feeling their inferiority. The latter it was who drank the bitter cup. Their

ADMIRAL WIREN.

To face page 330.

one hope now was that they should be spared the fate of being taken prisoners of war. Negotiations were being carried on that day, and, of course, those responsible would spare them the shame of imprisonment. But no! They had to drain the dregs.

A carriage was seen driving from the District Staff Office; it proceeded quickly round the central Mandarin Road to the village of Siu-shuing, the place appointed for the meeting. In it was Colonel Reuss, who was escorted on horseback by Colonels Khvostoff, Dmitrevsky, Captains Schesnovitch, Golovan, Student Lebedeff (interpreter), and Malchenko. Before they started, General Stössel, in the presence of Fock, told them all that he had given all instructions and full authority for the conclusion of the capitulation confidentially to Reuss, and that Reuss had also been given a letter for General Baron Nogi. Stössel, Fock, and Reuss were nervous; they were also, it seems, in a great hurry, for no lawyer was asked to look over the terms of capitulation, nor was one present even when the terms were signed.

The Commandant, holding aloof from any participation in the surrender, sent the following cipher telegram to the Commander-in-Chief, dated January 2, No. 1,300:

'General Stössel has entered into negotiations with the enemy for surrendering the Fortress without informing me, and in spite of my opinion and that of the majority of the commanding officers.'

Reuss, with his companions, soon reached the appointed spot. They were met by the Chief of the Staff of the Japanese Army, who handed to them the proposed text of the agreement,* written in English. He gave them an hour in which to think it over, and went away. Reuss then read the contents aloud to the others. Golovan

* The text of this capitulation was drawn up two years before by one of the most able Japanese lawyers.

began to protest; he was cut short. 'They are the victors; we must submit to their demands.' After a short conference and passionate protests from Khvostoff, Golovan, and Schesnovitch—as a matter of fact their protests were waste of breath, for Reuss alone had plenary powers, the others being only there for show—Reuss agreed to make three alterations: (1) That the garrison should not be made prisoners of war; (2) that officers should be permitted to take their orderlies with them; (3) that the allowance of baggage should be increased. The Japanese returned punctually within the hour, and took away the text of the capitulation with the alterations for consideration. After a quarter of an hour they returned, and said definitely:

'We only agree to the second alteration. Will you sign?'

Reuss pondered for a moment, then said:

'I will.'

I will not bore the reader with the terms of the convention, which are now well known, or the procedure of signing. No sooner was the shameful document signed than Reuss sent a Japanese messenger to Stössel with a note, saying:

'The capitulation is signed, and, in accordance with it, the destruction of all property must be immediately stopped.

Stössel at once replied:

'I have done everything; tell the Japanese.'

The news of the surrender being an accomplished fact soon spread among the garrison. Our men seemed suddenly to change their natures, all discipline went to the winds, and rioting commenced. Some, throwing their arms away, went straight down to the town, which became one vast scene of drunkenness and orgy. The shops and stores were looted, and wholesale robbery was the order of the day. The crowd broke up everything they could, amongst other things the library of the *Novy Kry*. The officers, seeing that it was hopeless to try and cope with their men, hid from the maddened crowds.

And now a few words as to General Stössel and how he took the surrender. When the riot was reported to him, he at once became alarmed, and asked for a hundred Japanese soldiers as a guard over his house and property. Nogi sent the men, fully armed and equipped. Fearing that matters would become serious, Stössel sent the following note to Smirnoff:

'The strictest steps must be taken at once to deal with the looting which has commenced. I would request you to be so kind as to send out patrols. Reuss tells me that the terms of the surrender are honourable. Please excuse pencil.'

It is difficult to understand what was in his mind when he wrote that note. Was he laughing at the Commandant, or had he gone off his head? As soon as Irman heard of the surrender he went to Smirnoff.

'Is it true, sir, that the Fortress has been surrendered?'

'I know nothing about it. Stössel has done everything without reference to me. Go and ask him.'

Irman went at once to Stössel, and having ascertained that the Fortress had been given up, he asked leave to go to Chifu on a destroyer: he wished to break through to the army in the north. But Stössel flatly refused permission, saying:

'Good heavens! what are you talking about? What are we to do with all the gold vases? How am I to get them away? Why, the Japanese might get them; we must save them.'

'If you want to make certain that the Japanese don't get them, sir, I should throw them into the sea,' was Irman's answer.

Stössel was referring to the gold vases, goblets, spoons, etc., looted from the Pekin Palace which were kept in Arthur. The gold plate had been kept under special arrangements in the quarter-guard of the 12th Regiment, but when this corps left for Manchuria the plate was left behind. On the evening of January 3 a mysterious cart arrived at the quarter-guard, and disappeared in the dark of the night.

Some of the questions put to Stössel later at the Commission of Inquiry, and his replies to them, may help to show how he was occupied at this time. When asked by Major-General Roops why he, contrary to all military regulations, took out of Arthur some thirty-eight cartloads of his own property, he replied:

'I did it with the permission of the Emperor of Japan.'

On being asked why he did not share the fate of the garrison and go into imprisonment, he answered:

'I was ordered not to by Her Imperial Highness the Tsarina.'

He had indeed received a telegram from the Empress in which she had said she would be glad to 'see him in Russia.' The Emperor and Russia did not at that time know what Stössel was!

When he was asked by the Commission why he surrendered Port Arthur on his own responsibility, and did not summon the Council of War to consider the question, he said:

'There was no time for that. I forestalled the Japanese, and did not give them the possibility of breaking into Arthur; I was thus able to prevent a street massacre.'

And this was the cry of all the whole Stössel clique before the Committee of Inquiry.

One extract from the diary and I have finished:

'*January* 2, 1905.—On the way to the rendezvous of the Japanese Commission appointed to take over, we met an officer of the Japanese General Staff who greeted us in Russian. Ribnikoff at once recognized him to be a man called Ito, who had been in Arthur for several years as a watchmaker!'

Small wonder they beat us!

So it ended—so ended Russian Port Arthur. From its loss—from this mighty struggle, this long-drawn-out nightmare of suffering, this death of all our aspirations—new hope is born to our nation, a hope of better days.

Salus patriæ. Suprema lex est.

CONCLUSION[*]

As this book leaves the hands of the printer, the columns of the daily press are conveying to the world the terms of the indictment of the chief characters mentioned in it for their share in the surrender of the Fortress of Port Arthur to the Japanese. As this constitutes an official confirmation of much that I have written, I include it in my book, so that the reader may be in a position to judge if the title of my work is justified.

This indictment, I may add, has been drawn up by three separate Commissions, composed of the highest Government officials and experts in military law.

OFFICIAL INDICTMENT.

Lieutenant-General Stössel, of the retired list, is charged as follows:

1. In that he, having on July 3, 1904, received an order from the Commander-in-Chief of the Army in Manchuria to hand over command of the Fortress of Port Arthur to its Commandant, Lieutenant-General Smirnoff, and to leave the Fortress, disobeyed, and, remaining in the Fortress, retained command of it—an action provided for under Article 255, Book XXII., of the 'Military Code of 1869,' third edition.

2. In that he, in defiance of Order No. 339 of April 27, 1904, by the Viceroy in the Far East, did interfere with

[*] Written by the author in October, 1907. This was the official indictment then published, and contains the main charges upon which the officers stood their trial.—E. D. S.

the powers and duties of the Commandant of the Fortress, thus undermining the latter's authority, shaking public confidence in him, and so diminishing the defensive capabilities of the Fortress. The following are instances of such interference:

- (a) Granting permission over the Commandant's head, and against his orders, for supplies to be taken out of the Fortress.
- (b) Appointing Civilian Counsellor Riabinin to the charge of the Medical Department without making him subordinate to the Commandant of the Fortress.
- (c) Transferring the Dalny Hospital, in opposition to the Commandant's orders and to the detriment of the public service, to a site selected by himself.
- (d) Removing the Chief of the Fire Brigade, Weykanen, from duty.
- (e) Sending the Gendarmerie to Liao-tieh-shan.
- (f) Closing the printing-offices of the *Novy Kry*, and ordering the arrest of M. Nojine, who was on the staff of that journal.
- (g) Stopping work on the second and third lines of defence.

   Provided for under, etc.

3. In that he did not in time take proper steps to increase the quantity of supplies in the Fortress, as follows:

- (a) By not supplementing the reserve of vegetables, although this was quite possible.
- (b) By not arranging to requisition horses, in accordance with the Mobilization Regulations, and to increase the number of cattle in the Fortress.
- (c) By not sanctioning the Commandant's request

that the rations of horse-flesh might be increased, a course which was absolutely necessary to maintain the strength of the worn-out garrison.

  Provided for under, etc.

4. In that he, during the siege, received and read certain 'Memoranda,' written by Lieutenant-General Fock, which were composed in a derisive and offensive spirit, and of a nature calculated to undermine the authority of, and bring odium upon, several of the Commanders, subvert discipline, and lower the *moral* of the garrison; and, in spite of their harmful influence upon the defence, took no steps to prevent their publication and circulation among the troops.

  Provided for under, etc.

5. In that he, for his personal ends, sent reports to the Commander-in-Chief of the Army in Manchuria on May 27 and 31, and to the Viceroy on May 30, referring to the battle at Kinchou, in which he, in contradiction to the actual facts and to the actions of himself and those present, asserted that 'In this warm corner we fired every shell we had got,' and that 'we retired in perfect order on Nangalin,' and drew up these reports in such a manner as to make it appear that he, General Stössel, had in person acted with great energy and directed operations, while—

 (a) During the battle at Kinchou, he—General Stössel—remained in Port Arthur, and personally took no part in the action.

 (b) There was a large quantity of ammunition at Nangalin Station for the quick-firing guns, as was known to all the artillery units.

 (c) The retirement on Nangalin was carried out in

great haste and in complete disorder—so much so that certain units rushed through and broke down the wire entanglement obstacle.

Provided for under, etc.

6. In that he, for his own advantage, and in order to place the actions of his subordinates in the most favourable light, on May 28, 1904, reported to the Commander-in-Chief of the Army in Manchuria that the force under Lieutenant-General Fock 'was falling back gradually towards Wolf's Hills'—a statement directly opposed to facts, as the retirement of the force direct on to Wolf's Hills (the last of the advanced positions) was effected in complete disorder and in great haste along a hilly road, blocked with transport and by the inhabitants of Dalny retreating to Port Arthur.

Provided for under, etc.

7. In that he, for his own advantage, and in order to represent himself as taking a part in various actions (which did not take place), on June 14, 1904, reported in writing to the Commander-in-Chief of the Manchurian Army as to his own great activity in the conduct of the defence, in which report he stated, in opposition to facts: '. . . I always make a point of being in every possible engagement . . .'; while from February 8, 1904, to June 14—*i.e.*, up to the date of his letter to General Kuropatkin—not a single engagement with the Japanese took place (except the battle at Kinchou, in which he—General Stössel—took no part) but the bombardments, during which the whole population of Port Arthur were in equal danger.

Provided for under, etc.

8. In that he, in the hope of justifying the prearranged surrender of the Fortress to the enemy, on December 29, 1904, reported to the Tsar in a telegram that: 'By the

capture of Fort No. 3 the Japanese have become masters of the whole north-east front, and the Fortress can only hold out for a very few days. We have no artillery ammunition . . .'—a report which was not in accordance with the facts, as at the Council of War held on that day (December 29), when the members by a large majority declared themselves in favour of holding out to the last moment, both Major-Generals Biely and Nickitin declared that there was sufficient ammunition in hand for a further defence.

    Provided for under, etc.

9. In that he intentionally, improperly, and with false statements recommended :

 (a) Lieutenant-General Fock for promotion to the Third Class Order of St. George for the battle which he lost at Kinchou, and in which he displayed complete incompetence ;

 (b) Major-General Nadein for promotion to the Third Class Order of St. George for the same battle, in which he in no way distinguished himself ;

 (c) Major-General Reuss for the Fourth Class of the same Order, this officer himself asserting that he had done nothing whatever to merit such a reward.

    Provided for under, etc.

10. In that he, while in command of the District, and being the senior officer in a fortress which was being besieged by the Japanese, and of which the Commandant was subordinate to him, decided to surrender the Fortress to the enemy, and, in order to do so, in spite of the opinion of the great majority of the Council of War held on December 29, 1904, in favour of the continuation of the defence (which was in every way possible), and without, in accordance with the Regulations, convening a

fresh Council of War, did between 3 and 4 p.m. on January 1, 1905, despatch a *parlementaire* to General Nogi, commanding the besieging army, proposing to enter into negotiations for the surrender of the Fortress, although all means of defence had not been exhausted, as the fighting strength of the garrison and the amount of war material and of supplies permitted of a continuation of it.

In that he, after this, agreed to the proposal of Lieutenant-General Fock, commanding the land defences, to abandon Little Eagle's Nest, Kuropatkin Lunette, and B Battery without a fight, which action greatly diminished the power of resistance of the Fortress.

In that he, on the following day—January 2, 1905—authorized Colonel Reuss, his Chief of the Staff, to conclude definitely the capitulation without giving him any precise instructions as to the terms to be insisted upon on our side, in consequence of which Colonel Reuss signed, in the village of Siu-shuing, to terms which were disadvantageous and derogatory to the dignity of Russia, in which action General Stössel himself failed to perform his duty according to his oath and to the honour of a soldier.

In that he, having surrendered the Fortress to the enemy, did not share the fate of the garrison by accompanying it into military confinement.

Provided for under, etc.

Major-General Reuss is charged as follows:

1. In that he, while Chief of the Staff of the Kwan-tun District, and being aware of General Stössel's intention to surrender the Fortress of Port Arthur to the Japanese at a time when the fighting strength of the garrison and the quantity of munitions of war and of supplies assured the possibility of a continuance of the defence, concurred in this intention, and assisted General Stössel in the execution of it—for instance:

(a) At the meeting of the Defence Committee on December 8, 1904, and at the Council of War on December 29, 1904, exaggerating the critical state of affairs, and declaring that further opposition was useless, and that the Fortress should be surrendered.

(b) Prematurely composing and despatching at General Stössel's direction on January 1, 1905, a letter to General Nogi, commanding the Japanese besieging army, in which proposals were made for negotiations for a capitulation.

(c) On the following day, January 2, 1905, without demanding definite instructions from General Stössel regarding the conditions to be insisted on for surrender, going to Siu-shuing village—the place appointed for the negotiations—and raising no objections to the demands put forward by the Japanese representatives, signing that same day to the capitulation of the Fortress upon terms disadvantageous to Russia and derogatory to her dignity, and by such action co-operating with General Stössel in the surrender of the Fortress to the enemy.

Provided for under, etc.

Lieutenant-General Fock is charged as follows:

1. In that he, having received categorical instructions on February 27 and May 19, 1904, to make an obstinate defence, even to a defence with the bayonet, at the Kinchou position, not only with the 5th East Siberian Rifle Regiment, but with the 13th and 14th Regiments, which were close at hand, and disregarding these orders and the fact that General Stössel had himself undertaken the defence of Inchenzy Bay, which was in rear of the position—

(a) When the battle had begun on the morning of May 26, 1904, instead of taking command, did go away to Inchenzy Bay to select a position there for the 15th Regiment, in case the Japanese should land there, and did not arrive at the attacked position till 2 p.m.

(b) Did only send one of the four regiments present at Kinchou into action, and thus did cause its separate destruction.

(c) Did not only fail to make any use of his reserves during the battle, but did stop two battalions which were going up into the fighting line, under orders from General Nadein.

(d) Without having exhausted every means of defence, and without having recourse to the bayonet, did telegraph to General Stössel in Port Arthur, in order to induce him to order a retirement, as to 'the critical position,' and the complete lack of gun ammunition, there being at the time a large quantity of ammunition at the station of Nangalin.

(e) Having, in consequence of this, received instructions from General Stössel to retire at dusk, did commence the retirement in daylight, thus causing many casualties, and ceding to the Japanese the fortified position at Kinchou, without having made use of all the means at his disposal for its protracted defence.

Provided for under, etc.

2. In that he, during the battle of August 21, 1904, having received an order from his immediate Commanding Officer—the Commandant of the Fortress—to send two battalions of the 14th East Siberian Rifle Regiment to the advanced forts on the north-east front, did not at once obey the order, but entered into an untimely argument

with the Commandant, and did not himself accompany the last unit of the reserve under his command.

Provided for under, etc.

3. In that he, having no official position in the defence from August 22, 1904, to December 16, 1904, and going round the positions on his own initiative, under the pretext of assisting the defence, but really in a cowardly desire to prove himself superior in bravery, knowledge and ability to the other commanders, did allow himself to discuss affairs and to issue 'Memoranda,' in which he not only offensively criticized the actions of those who were not under his orders—accusing them of incompetence and cowardice—but also spread abroad the idea that the defence of the forts and fortified positions should not be carried to such a length as to cause many casualties, and did act in such a manner that his views and 'Memoranda' became known to the garrison at large (including the soldiers), by which he shook the belief of the troops in the necessity for, and the possibility of, holding the defences to the very last.

Provided for under, etc.

4. In that he, having on December 16, 1904, taken over the duties of Commander of the Land Defences of the Fortress of Port Arthur, and finding it impossible to hold Fort No. 2 any longer, did report this fact personally to the Officer Commanding the District, and did not report it to the Commandant of the Fortress, to whom he was directly subordinate, and having received General Stössel's permission on December 18, 1904, did order that this fort should be abandoned and blown up without informing the Commandant.

Provided for under, etc.

5. In that he, while Commander of the Land Defences of the Fortress, and being aware of General Stössel's

intention to surrender the Fortress of Port Arthur to the Japanese before all means of defence had been exhausted, as the fighting strength of the garrison and the amount of supplies and munitions of war assured the possibility of a continuance, concurred in this intention, and assisted General Stössel in the execution of it. For instance :

> On December 1, 1904,* reporting to General Stössel that it was necessary to send a *parlementaire* at once to General Nogi with proposals to capitulate, and then, after its despatch, upon his own responsibility, and in spite of the orders of the Commandant, ordering, under threats, General Gorbatovsky, who was in command of the defences on the east front, to abandon Little Eagle's Nest, Kuropatkin Lunette, and B Battery without a fight, which works were accordingly in the evening abandoned by our troops, he—Lieutenant-General Fock—knowing full well that by these dispositions of his he had placed the defence of the Fortress under most disadvantageous conditions should the negotiations for surrender be for any reason broken off, and had enabled the Japanese representatives to demand from us most disadvantageous and degrading terms of capitulation.
>
> Provided for under, etc.

Lieutenant-General Smirnoff is charged as follows :

1. In that he, suspecting, after the surrender to the Japanese of Fort No. 2, the existence of an understanding between Generals Stössel and Fock to reduce the Fortress to such a state as to justify capitulation, and in despite of the responsibility resting upon him under the terms of Article 57 of the ' Regulations for the Guidance of Com-

* ? January 1, 1905.—E. D. S.

manders of Fortresses,' did not immediately deprive General Fock of his command, did not take energetic action to prevent the above-named officers carrying out their plan, and confined himself to despatching a telegram to the Commander-in-Chief, in which he requested that he might be either given full power as Commandant or relieved from all responsibility as such for the future defence of the Fortress.

Provided for under, etc.

2. In that he, having learned on January 1, 1905, of the despatch by General Stössel of a letter to General Nogi containing proposals for negotiations for surrender, in spite of Article 69, Book XXII., of the 'Military Code of 1869,' third edition, and Article 57 of the 'Regulations for the Guidance of Commanders of Fortresses,' did not convene a meeting of the Committee of Defence, did not insist that General Stössel should act in accordance with Article 62 of the above 'Regulations,' and did not carry out the resolution of the Council of War of December 29, 1904, to continue a protracted defence of the Fortress.

Provided for under, etc.

APPENDIX I

General Fock's Memorandum *re* the Surrender of Fort No. 2. [Chi-kuan-shan.]

In order that General Fock's motives may not be misunderstood, the Memorandum written by him, in which he essayed to clear himself of the charge of wrongfully abandoning Fort No. 2, is reproduced. It needs, however some elucidation, both for the sake of clearness and accuracy. Those who are not well acquainted with Fock's proceedings in Port Arthur, both as a General and as an individual, and with all the circumstances of the defence, might possibly misunderstand this document, as the authors possessed a great power of persuasion, both with pen and speech, and even now has a considerable number of adherents and advocates.

Memorandum.

'Fort No. 2 was abandoned on December 18, 1904, with General Stössel's permission and by my order. Next day I had a conversation on the subject with General Smirnoff, who said:

'" Why did you surrender the fort ? I would have sent you as many reinforcements as you wanted; I have some 30,000 in the Fortress. By abandoning it you have undermined the root of my principle—that no fort should pass into the enemy's hands except after the death of all its defenders."'

In saying this General Smirnoff was quite in the right. Fock did not reinforce the garrison either in time or sufficiently, although quite able so to do. The whole essence of the defence at the end consisted in the use of mobile reserves for the reinforcement of threatened points. It was by his intelligent anticipation of Nogi's tactics and his skilful movement and employment of reserves that Smirnoff was able so long to check the attack.

'... Later, when giving evidence before General Roop's Commission, I was asked:

'"Did you take any steps to prevent the example of Fort No. 2 being followed, and to ensure that the principle that a garrison should resist to the last should not be forgotten?"

'I was amazed at such a question, and that a principle, of which I had never before heard and which is not to be found in any text-book on tactics or field-service manual, should be assumed by the Commission to be an irrefutable axiom, to ignore which was a crime.

'But I was still more astonished a short time ago when, in a paper submitted by General Smirnoff to the War Minister and circulated amongst officials and other educated men, I saw the following:

'"The surrender of Fort No. 2 struck at the root of the principle that a fort 'dies, but does not surrender'—a principle preached and reiterated by myself and all those in command. By the example of the surrender of this fort the garrisons of the others were shaken in their belief that forts are 'holies of holies,' only to be captured after the death of the whole garrison defending them, and were led to consider them as just ordinary fortified positions which can be freely abandoned as soon as their defence becomes difficult. This was proved by the abandonment within ten days of Fort No. 3."

'Only when I became aware of this Note of General Smirnoff's did I understand the drift of the question put to me by the Commission; it was not hard then to see the connexion between the two. It was evident, therefore, that in this important question, as in those which had preceded, the Commission was being guided more by this memorandum of the late Commandant of the Fortress than by the desire for an impartial inquiry into facts.'

Though well on in years, General Fock apparently did not know, and was astonished to hear, that 'forts die, but do not surrender,' that 'the bones of a regiment should surround its fallen colours,' that 'a gun must be fought till not a man is left,' etc. Fock did not know this; he had not seen it laid down in any official text-book!

Naturally he did not and could not know it. Knowledge of the sacredness of duty is not acquired by the perusal of manuals and regulations any more than an honourable feeling is acquired by reading books of a high moral tone. The duty and honour of the citizen soldier has no written code as its guide, but only the long, brilliant list of great deeds extending from far-off olden times to the present day. Upon these legends, matured by time, nations, their armies, and individuals are brought up. A sense of duty and honour is not obtained by reading, but is imbibed with the mother's milk and developed by later teaching. I doubt if there could be found in any European army (naturally not in the Japanese, where officers and generals are brought up on the ethics of the chivalrous spirit ' Bushido ') a general officer who would be surprised to hear that a fort should not surrender. How could a Russian general be ignorant of it? Surely such an assertion is a stain on all the general officers of the Russian army!

No, it is not so. For General Fock's ignorance of the rudiments of military duty one must seek deeper reasons. He was, it appears, in the *Gendarmerie*—where the duties were somewhat different to those of the army—for almost five years. Their atmospheres are totally opposed: the work of the one is to fight an external foe: of the other to fight an internal enemy.

One amongst the many surprises so liberally provided for us by the old régime was Fock's sudden reappearance in the army and arrival in the Far East as Officer Commanding the gallant fighting 4th Division, as the friend and adviser of General Stössel, and, indeed, as the sole individual to work out Arthur's destiny. The defence of a fortress is soldiers' and not gendarmes' work.

'. . . The specific charge against me was framed as follows:
'" In that he, while in command of the Land Defences ordered the abandonment of Fort No. 2 without obtaining the Commandant's permission, and without even letting him know of his intention—an act in which he exceeded his powers, and one which is legislated for by Articles 141 and 145, Book XXII. (third edition), S.V.P., 1869."

'This charge is curiously worded. I was accused of exceeding my powers, and yet the Commission was at the same time well aware that I did not abandon the fort of my own freewill, but with the permission of General Stössel, who, being senior to General Smirnoff, had appointed me to command the Land Defences and issued orders to me direct. Consequently there can be no question of my exceeding my powers.'

According to the exact sense of the regulations on the subject, the Officer Commanding the Land Defences is directly subordinate to the Commandant of the Fortress, and has absolutely no right to abandon forts without his sanction, or without that of the Defence Committee. If General Stössel, having usurped the Commandant's authority, interfered with the defence, and his interference was detrimental to the defence, then Fock should not have obeyed his orders, even though proceeding from the senior officer. On the contrary, he should by every means within his power have endeavoured to counteract such detrimental influence in the same way that Kondratenko did during his lifetime: he should have consulted the Commandant with regard to everything, and have carried out his orders alone. The fact was that Stössel issued all his orders at Fock's instigation, and did nothing without him. He knew so little of what went on at the front that he would never have decided to issue any order himself, and especially such a weighty order as the abandonment of the first fort.

'... However, though the legal accusation of itself falls to the ground, I might perhaps be considered morally guilty of abandoning the fort. The above-quoted Articles of War might be strained, and it might be thought something was wrong about the defence of the fort and its abandonment.

'This prevents my confining myself merely to a straightforward answer to the charge and compels me to ask, "Could the fort have held out longer or not?"

'On going before the Commission for the first time, I was asked:

'"Why did you not defend the fort, and why did you abandon it without a fight, without even waiting for General Gorbatovsky?"

'I never expected the Commission to accuse me of such a thing, and I was so agitated that I could not reply calmly. How could I keep cool when I heard the defenders of the fort so unjustly accused by General Roop, the very officer whose words, twenty years ago, had been law to me and all other combatant officers, when for hours together we used to listen to his appreciations and criticisms of manœuvres? He still spoke as well as ever, weighing every word, but spoke with a sarcastic smile; and now that I have read or heard the evidence of all the General Officers who have been examined, I understand that it is possible even for him to have been led astray.

'The accusation levelled by General Smirnoff against the brave garrison was supported not only by General Officers who took no part in the defence and had not seen it, but even by General Nickitin, to whom the state of the fort was so well known that he refrained from accompanying General Kondratenko along the forts after the Japanese had mined the parapets. (It is to this that we owed his presence in our midst.) As to General Mekhmandaroff, he even asserted that after the explosion of three mines he could still see sentries standing by the parapet. And General Irman, who was at the time on the western front, based his statement on that given by Mekhmandaroff. The evidence given by the other officers was of equal value.

'But however varied the evidence, it all pointed to one thing—that the garrison failed to do its duty, that it did not crown the crater in the parapet. This being so, I should point out that it is usually the attackers who crown craters. At Sevastopol our sappers certainly distinguished themselves by themselves crowning the craters of the unsuccessful attack, but they had not been charged with some fifty hundredweight of pyroxyline, as was the case in Fort No. 2.'

Thus to divert the blame on to the garrison of the fort in order to parry the blow against himself was not creditable. The men did their duty gallantly to the last; they fought till they were ordered to withdraw; they did everything possible, and were in no way to blame for the surrender and had no need of Fock to defend or praise them. If they had not been able to crown the crater by five o'clock, it was Fock alone who was to blame; firstly for having weakened the garrison, secondly for not reinforcing it in time.

'The evidence of the Generals above mentioned was, on the whole, so absurd and so little supported by facts that it does not merit serious attention.'

The evidence of the Generals was founded on facts. They were men who throughout the siege were rarely absent from the attacked front. They were men of honour, whose names are the pride of the army; but this is no reason for treating their evidence as undeserving of attention.

'. . . That of General Gorbatovsky, however, is different. According to him he went to the fort at 11 p.m., and finding the men leaving it, drove them back, sent for Captain Kwats, who was in command, and threatened him with a court-martial for abandoning it on his own responsibility, and only then found out that the withdrawal was being carried out in accordance with orders from me. This evidence is plausible, and upon it the charge is probably based; for how is it possible to disbelieve the testimony of a General who was in command of the eastern front?

'To judge from it, one would think that the abandonment of the fort came as a complete surprise to him; that he thought it wrong, and, that had he himself been in the fort, it would never have been evacuated. I was unable to rebut this evidence at the time, and to assert that the abandonment was not a surprise; besides, no one present would have believed me. Fortunately for me, however, I was not caught tripping. I asked to see the telephone messages referring to that time, and in going through them came on one which I, and doubtless General Gorbatovsky also, had forgotten. This message clears me of his charge, and throws much light on the part taken by him in the abandonment of the fort; it was from him to the Staff of the Land Defences, and was dated 9.35 p.m., December 18, 1904:

'"From Fort No. 2 it is reported that heavy casualties are occurring from grenades thrown by the enemy. We have not been able to reoccupy the parapet. I therefore propose to avail myself of your permission to blow up the casemates, and I have ordered the garrison to hold out until the sappers have got the mines ready. As a precautionary measure, and to cover the garrison during the retirement, please move a company, temporarily, from the main reserve to the Icehouse. I am just going myself to Colonel Glagoleff to give the necessary instructions on the spot."

'Consequently, at 9.35 that night General Gorbatovsky was not only not opposed to the surrender of the fort, but himself gave orders for it to be abandoned; while at 11 p.m. he was, according to his evidence, horrified at his own order, saw that it was wrong, and talked of courts-martial.

'I hope that a study of all the papers similar to these produced before the Commission will acquit me of the charges preferred against me by General Roop's Commission.'

Quite true! That message was sent by General Gorbatovsky, but only after a telephone message had been received from Fock at 7.40 p.m. to the following effect:

'General Stössel has given orders that the casemates of Fort No. 2 are to be mined at once, and then, if the Japanese do not withdraw from the fort—*i.e.*, from the parapet—the garrison is to leave the fort, and the casemates are to be blown up. The enemy are not to be allowed to establish themselves on the parapet, which must be fired on by the guns and the torpedo tube. In view of Captain Stepanoff's report, to the effect that before sunset he and Colonel Mekhmandaroff could see from Big Eagle's Nest only one Japanese officer and three men on the parapet, laying sand-bags, I leave it to you to hold on to the fort as long as you think necessary. In giving this order, based on my report, General Stössel came to this decision only because he thought that under present circumstances no other course was possible. At sunset a sailor came to me and reported that by the explosion of a bomb thrown by the enemy we had had fifteen casualties.'

As the reader can see for himself, it was impossible to tell from this how Fock meant to act or what he meant to do. Knowing from experience that anything might be expected from him, and that directly after the explosion of the mines during the day he had called the fort lost, Gorbatovsky decided to make all arrangements for a well-organized retirement, and so to avert a possible panic and consequent dash through by the enemy. It was only for this reason that he sent the telegram quoted above by Fock, but he gave no order for the fort to be abandoned.

In reply to his message to Fock, sent at 9.35 p.m., he at once received the following from Colonel Dmitrevsky, Chief of Fock's staff, despatched at 9.40 p.m.:

'General Fock fully concurs in your opinion about Fort No. 2. He trusts that you will see that the repairs to Kuropatkin Lunette are energetically carried out.'

And this was immediately followed by a message to him from Lieutenant Kondrasheff, dated 9.45 p.m., December 18, 1904:

'General Fock, commanding the Land Defences, wishes you to see that all the ammunition and other stores are carried away from Fort No. 2, and that the bridge is destroyed.'

When General Gorbatovsky received these messages he went to the fort. Orders had already been received from General Fock to abandon it, and the withdrawal had begun before his arrival. He had gone to find out the exact state of affairs on the spot, and on reaching it after 11 p.m. he met the retreating garrison. It was such a surprise to him that he 'fell upon' Captain Kwats, threatened to have him tried by court-martial for abandoning the fort without orders, and was in reply informed that it was being left upon an order received direct from Fock.

'However, in order to give a more accurate description of the state of affairs, I will describe the fighting just as I saw and reported it. I described the fight in March to General Roop's Commission, but what I said was doubted.'

Unfortunately, a knowledge of the true state of affairs at the withdrawal from the fort shows that Roop's Commission had formed a true opinion of Fock's account.

'According to General Smirnoff, I so demoralized the men, that on December 18, when the explosion took place, no volunteer could be found among them to crown the crater.

'... I am ashamed, not on my own account, but on account of the gallant defenders of the fort, to read Smirnoff's slander concerning them. For what did he take Captain Kwats, the commanding officer, and the men? Had it been necessary for the garrison to be on the parapet, Kwats would have had no difficulty in finding volunteers even at that critical moment. He need only have shouted, "Follow me—advance!" and they would have dashed after him. As I have said above, my evidence as to the fall of the fort is considered by many to be untrue, and more credit is attached to the evidence of General Mekhmandaroff, who said he saw a man on the rampart after the explosion, etc.'

To say that Fock demoralized the troops would only be to repeat what has frequently been said. In Arthur no one doubted it. It is in vain that he sheds tears for the garrison; it is his own conduct that is questioned, not the gallantry of the men. That Kwats did not dash forward and take men with him to crown the craters is Fock's fault. It required much presence of mind, and the garrison was much upset.

'After the explosion, which took place at noon, the fort was subjected to a heavy fire, and our men ran to the retrenchment and held it. To this timely occupation of the retrenchment I ascribe the death of many of the Japanese "forlorn hope." Having jumped up on to the parapet and seen that we were there to meet them, they hesitated for a moment, but this moment was long enough for them to be wafted into eternity. They were buried under the falling débris of the explosion.

At the same time the Japanese guns opened fire on all our near batteries; and when these were silenced, whole regiments of the enemy stormed the parapet, but were repulsed with case shot and rifle-fire. A few men only reached the craters, whence they began throwing grenades, while we, from the glacis and caponier, fired torpedo-heads and bombs.'

The storming by whole Japanese regiments is pure imagination on the part of Fock, who was at the time at least four miles from the scene of action. Mr. Norregaard,* who watched the attack, says that, after the destruction of the first party of stormers by the falling débris and the fire of our batteries, the Japs busied themselves clearing the approaches to the fort and did not assault till evening.

'The heroic garrison were almost all annihilated, when a reserve of sailors was sent up to the fort. I regret that I cannot say to what ship they belonged or what officers were with them; I can only say that from first to last they were heroes.

'They had to go from the Chinese Wall through Kuropatkin Lunette, and what was this lunette like by now? Stones, planks, sand-bags, corpses were all jumbled together in the trenches, and at the entrance of that communicating from Fort No. 2 there was not a vestige of a parapet. These men at first ran along the trench, and then, seeing that it was filled up, jumped out to right and left, and under a murderous fire doubled along in the open, officers in front. They rushed to where it entered the fort, which was full of killed and wounded. Some crossed the bridge, others went down into the ditch, jumping from heap to heap.

'They entered the fort in order to fill the thinned ranks of the defenders, and seventeen of them were at once blown up by a mine. With their arrival one might have felt confident that the fort would not easily be seized by the Japanese; but darkness came on and the shouts of " Banzai " could still be heard, mingling into one continuous and increasing roar.

'The wounded now came back less frequently, but those that came told of horrors. From what they said I understood how difficult it was to cross the ditch, and that few would succeed in doing it; and so, fearing that all means of access would be closed, I asked for the bamboo ladders to be sent up, which had been taken from the enemy on November 26, when they tried to storm Fort No. 3.

'The position of the garrison got worse and worse. To get an order taken we had to call for volunteers and offer the Cross

* 'The Great Siege,' by B. W. Norregaard.—E. D. S.

of St. George to those who succeeded in carrying it. It was clear to me and to every one else present that the fort could not be held longer under such conditions, and so I thought it my duty to withdraw the remnants of that gallant band at night. I reported this to General Stössel and asked his permission to abandon the fort; he agreed.

'I then ordered Colonel Glagoleff to hold on till night, when, after removing everything possible in the way of supplies, he was to withdraw the men and blow up the fort.

'At 11.30 p.m. the garrison moved out of the fort, which was blown up at 2 a.m., and retired on Kuropatkin Lunette. It had held out for four months, despite the Japanese having seized the caponier in October, and established themselves in the ditch. Military history contains few instances of such a dogged and prolonged defence.

'Next day General Smirnoff had the above quoted conversation with me. In reply to his question as to why I had surrendered the fort, etc., I said:

'"I did not need your men; they would only have hampered me."

'He seemed surprised at this answer and asked, "Why?"

'"Because," I said, "the men would never have reached the place, and then what should I have done? They wouldn't have gone because they couldn't have done it."

'"Ah, your men are wasters—runaways!" said he, and then began to talk of them in his usual manner.

'I quoted a few instances from history to him—among them some of Austerlitz—in order to show him that some things always had been and always would be; and I finished my remarks by saying:

'"It was a pity that you were not taught psychology at the Academy."'

No one denies that the fort was in a very bad way, but such conditions are only to be expected in war where the path to glory is not strewn with roses. As soon as the situation became critical the garrison should have been reinforced, and this Fock did not do. He had decided during the day that the fort could not be held, and for this reason abandoned it.

In repeating his conversation with Smirnoff he perverted the facts, which were, as I have already described in detail in a foregoing chapter. Since he touched on the question of psychology, it would be interesting to know what kind of psychology he himself understood—that of police-work service or of war? Smirnoff certainly did occasionally call the men 'runaways' in conversation with his intimate friends, but he was far from thinking that the troops could be disobedient. In saying that 'the men would never have reached the place, and then what should I have done?' Fock was himself accurately describing the very demoralization of which he was accused of being the cause. During Kondratenko's life there had been no suggestion of such a spirit.

'After this I felt it was useless to attempt to persuade Smirnoff of anything, for the simple reason that both he and Colonel Khvostoff look upon every one who was not a General officer or an officer of the General Staff in the same way that our great-grandmothers looked upon their serf-handmaidens.'

What General Fock meant by this I really cannot tell.

'Our great-grandmothers said and believed that it was impossible for Palashka to fall in love. In the same way General Smirnoff and Colonel Khvostoff believed that the common soldier had no instinct of self-preservation, and that such need not therefore be taken into consideration. It need only, they thought, be reckoned with in Generals and General Staff officers, who alone have a right to possess it.

'Colonel Khvostoff preached this doctrine to General Nickitin in the following words: "Officers of the General Staff are of great value to the Empire, and they should, therefore, take care of their lives."'

'From General Smirnoff's words, "It undermined the root of the principle which I have always insisted on," it is evident that General Stössel did not harass General Smirnoff as much as the latter sometimes makes out. Moreover, all who went through the siege would like to know in what way Smirnoff insisted on the observance of this principle. Principles can be driven into men by orders, speeches, and examples. He did not do it in his orders, for such as he issued were generally taken up with the transfer of nursing-sisters from one hospital to another. And he was wise, for such orders can only be written by leaders like Tsar Peter, Suvoroff, Napoleon, who are well known to their men. He did not attempt it by speeches; for where, when, and to whom could he speak? Church parades were few, and were rarely attended by more than twenty to thirty men per regiment. For a new, unknown man like General Smirnoff there was only one way left—"example"; but this method was out of date, and its uselessness was shown by Gustavus Adolphus, Nakhimoff, Korniloff, Istomin, and therefore it did not find favour with him!

'All this proves that he did not inculcate his principle to

the garrison of Arthur, though undoubtedly future generations will know of it through the medium of Roop's Commission.'

It is perfectly true that Smirnoff did not take to speechifying. Together with Kondratenko he worked at the fortifying of the place while General Stössel was haranguing the troops at church parades and writing long orders and detailed telegrams. This principle was not published in orders, as it was well understood by all good officers. Of this there could be no two opinions. Generals Smirnoff, Kondratenko, Gorbatovsky, Irman, and Tretiakoff, who stood at the head of their troops in Arthur, supported by their fearless example—fighting desperately for every inch of ground entrusted to them—and not by their words, this principle, which according to Fock was incomprehensible and silly.

The next generation will know through this Commission how well the garrison of Arthur lived up to that principle, and it will, at the same time, know on whom the responsibility of surrender rests.

'He reproaches the garrison of Fort No. 3 for not hurrying out of the casemate when the explosion took place, though I, and all those at Big Eagle's Nest, saw them fighting for a long time, throwing hand-grenades and stones from the retrenchment.

'But it is odd that he should make such charges against anyone when he himself not only made no haste, but did not attempt to leave his quarters when the explosion took place in Fort No. 3 and Fortification No. 3, and when the Chinese Wall, Rocky Ridge, and Big Eagle's Nest were being stormed. That he did not leave his quarters and was practically a stranger to his troops is borne out by the fact that when, after the surrender, the Japanese were taking over the garrison as prisoners, and he began talking to some of the men, they made rude remarks, and were heard asking their officers "who is that General?" As it was the first time that the majority of officers had seen him, they had to reply: "I don't know; wait, I'll ask." Only after inquiries were they able to tell their men, "That is General Smirnoff, the Commandant of the Fortress."'

Fock, of all people, accused Smirnoff of staying in his quarters, and of being a stranger to the men! In the foregoing pages I have shown by facts what Smirnoff was to the Fortress, what he did for its defence, and how he was thwarted at every turn. As far as is in my power I have tried as clearly and truly as possible to draw the picture of the hopelessness of his position. Fock, suddenly appointed Officer Commanding Land Defences, was indeed the autocrat of the Fortress, for Stössel was to all intents and purposes his subordinate, and Smirnoff was ignored. Having telegraphed to the Commander-in-Chief, Smirnoff awaited the reply, and till it came he was powerless to do anything, for like a wise man he did not want to make bad worse. But had it come, and had it been favourable to him, he would soon have got everything right. Smirnoff invested with authority would have saved Arthur's honour. Very possibly so many sound men, and so many cripples, would not have returned to Russia, so many decorations would not have glittered on the breasts of officers, and the number of widows and orphans might have been greater; but there would have been no need for any Commission such as that of General Roop. The highest tribunal of the nation would have judged those responsible for the lost campaign, but Arthur would have fallen, and not been surrendered.

'I shall be now believed, perhaps, if I say that no one in Arthur knew of the above-quoted principle, and no one heard tell of it from Smirnoff. I only heard it at General Roop's Commission. When asked, "Did you take any steps to prevent the example of Fort No. 2 being followed, and to ensure that the principle that a garrison should resist to the last should not be forgotten?" I at once understood that the defence was degraded to the level of simple treason, and that they were trying to mock me. Was it not mockery indeed to ask me such a question? The Commission knew that the garrison abandoned the fort not of their own free will but by my order. To this insult I replied as follows:

'"No steps were taken or could be taken by me, as the fort was abandoned by my order."

'It would have meant I was to take steps against myself—cunning question indeed. I am satisfied with the defence of that fort; nay, proud of what constitutes one of the most brilliant pages of the defence, and will be quoted as an example. By it one principle was taught, namely, that no soldier will leave his post without orders, and that the officer in supreme command will never sacrifice lives needlessly.

'I wrote this in February or March, before any of us had seen the translations of the books by English authors on the siege of Port Arthur.

'My description of the fighting does not in the least agree with that of either Norregaard or James,* and no wonder, as I wrote of what happened under my eyes, and they only wrote what they heard from survivors of the horrors of that day. I was not credited, because with us every one wished, and still wishes, only to believe what will besmirch the fair name of Arthur. This was why only generals were examined by the Commission.'

He was insulted by the question put to him by the Commission, and in his reply stated that in defending that fort he had inculcated the principle that 'no soldier will leave his post without orders, and that the officer in supreme command will never sacrifice lives needlessly'!

To teach this principle in field warfare is right and proper. But in fortress warfare, when the enemy are pressing on the line of defences, when they are storming the forts, when the fall of one fort may bring on the fall of others, and so lead to greater complications, when there is nowhere to retire to (we had the third line made by Smirnoff, but it was ignored by Fock), a fort must indeed 'die and not surrender.' Thus alone can the spirit and strength of the men in the other forts be kept up.

'But I will return once more to the discussion of General Smirnoff's principle. This dogma could only be instilled into the fresh minds of children, and could not be suddenly introduced during war, for, after one fight the bravest troops in the world would refuse to believe in it. The more experienced and braver a man is, the dearer he wants to sell his life.

'But General Smirnoff called the troops "wasters" and "runaways" because they did not remain in the wrecked lodgements upon an order issued by him from his snug room, but ran into others that were whole, and continued fighting. That commanding officer who inspires confidence that he will allow no one to perish needlessly will alone be loved by his officers and men, and may God spare them from feeling that any General is sacrificing their lives for such a principle as that for which I was called to answer.

'But it deserves to be examined that we may thoroughly

* 'The Siege of Port Arthur,' by D. James. Translation from English by Captains von Schwartz and Romanovsky: 'Voenny Sbornik.' 1906. No. 11.

understand on what lines we are to act in the next war. If the matter is clearly settled one way or the other it may in the future spare commanders, who may find themselves in the same position I was in, the horror, the torments to which I have been subjected in hearing the reproaches levelled at me by such a weighty Commission—reproaches which did not touch only me, but also the heroic defenders of the fort.

'My acquittal, I feel, is due to the fact that the principle was announced by Smirnoff, and not by Suvoroff or by the Tsar Peter, whose nature would have precluded the enunciation of anything so vague, so abstract.

'The birth of pure theory amongst us is synchronous with the arrival upon the scene of a certain type of General, whose influence and work I can best describe indirectly, by quoting a remark made upon its results: "We are ourselves to blame for everything. Where the General was, there were no men; where the men were, there was no General." This was said by a lieutenant-colonel at a conference between the Army and Navy, when remarking on a communication of Lieutenant-Colonel Galkin's, of the General Staff.

'Such are the Generals—the originators of principles similar to that announced by General Smirnoff. The Japanese Generals were different. It is true that their Commander-in-Chief and Generals Commanding armies, like Oyama, Nogi, and others, did not command battalions and companies; but the subordinate Generals led their troops—even scouting parties—in the attack, as we more than once witnessed in Arthur. I mention this because, when I once spoke of Japanese Generals sitting in the advanced trenches, some of our Generals, hearing of the gallantry of the Japanese men from Smirnoff, told me that I was incorrect, and that "the wonderful Japanese soldier did not need the presence of a General." But in action things were different. Even "the wonderful Japanese soldier" required to be set an example by his General. Our—according to many —very ordinary soldiers were grateful even for the fleeting presence of a General whom they only saw passing by.

'Put into simple language, the question asked me by the Commission, as to what steps I had taken to see that the principle that "the garrison of a fort should resist to the last" was not shaken, means that a Commander must not allow a single man to come out of a fort alive.

'(a) If regulations permit the surrender of a *fortress* under certain conditions, how can they be construed to forbid the abandonment of a *fort*, when its defenders might be useful in defending other works of the same fortress?

'(b) Is it desirable that a unit told off to the defence of a fort should go to it feeling like men who went across "the Bridge of Sighs" in Venice?

"Was it possible for me to literally carry out this principle in practice?

'Fort No. 2, according to Norregaard, for some hours resembled a "witch's cauldron," vomiting fire, smoke and flames from the bursting of countless shimose shells, hand-grenades and torpedoes. Behind the sand-bags our handful of men were repelling with rifle and machine-gun the numerous assaults. The Japanese cut off their communication with the Fortress; reinforcements were not received, and the number of defenders dwindled. The enemy pounded them continuously, and the hours of the fort were numbered.

'Such was its state at the moment when I had to decide whether to save that handful of brave men, or to sacrifice them for the sake of General Smirnoff's "principle."

'I preferred the first alternative—not from feelings of humanity, but because I could not take the other; every one else in my place would have done the same. To judge my action fairly, it must be borne in mind that I was not sitting before a green-topped Committee table when I had to make this decision, nor in General Smirnoff's comfortable quarters, but was near the Chinese Wall.* Far from being in comfort and security, I was at a place that would have suffered the next blow after the fall of Fort No. 2.

'How I should decide this question was vital to the men—if I should become their executioner or would act as they expected me to. It was by no means immaterial to me either; for I should be judged by my action, and upon it would depend in the future how others fought.

'Though General Smirnoff never left his quarters during the fight, it did not prevent him reporting it as follows:

'Page 33. "At 11 p.m. I knew that Fort No. 2 had already been abandoned by our troops and its casemates blown up. This was done by Captain Kwats, who had only been appointed to command it that day, under instructions from Lieutenant-Colonel Glagoleff commanding the section, who was acting on orders received from General Fock, without even waiting for the arrival of General Gorbatovsky, who was in supreme command on that flank.

'Page 34. "Meanwhile General Stössel, feeling that it was a very bad business, issued an order, dated December 27, No. 961, based on untrue reports made to him by Captain Kwats and Colonel Glagoleff, in which he made out that the whole shameful affair was a great exploit. . . . Ten days later the example of Fort No. 2 was followed by the abandonment of Fort No. 3, which forced the Council of Defence and myself to the conclusion that there was an understanding

* General Fock was at the time in his quarters, a long way from the fighting.

between Generals Stössel and Fock to reduce the Fortress in the shortest possible time to such a condition as would justify a capitulation."

'As regards General Smirnoff's opinion that the abandonment of Fort No. 2 was due to treachery on the part of General Stössel and myself, I am silent; but I cannot allow him to call its surrender shameful. This opinion of his bears witness to the fact that between him and the defenders of Arthur there was about as much in common as between the baby and the mother who said, "Divide it," when Solomon had ordered half of the baby to be given to each mother.'

The principle of the non-surrender of a fort should be instilled into all soldiers from the day they join. A good soldier knows that he must be the first to lay down his life for his country in war, and remembers during the whole of a campaign that success is founded on a clear appreciation of the principle of self-sacrifice by all, from Commander-in-Chief to private soldier.

War is a death summons.

Death is the soldier's crown.

Every soldier—that is, in the true sense of the word, one who is willing to die in the struggle—sees in death the highest end of his calling. By this feeling he exalts the *moral* of his comrades to an extent which ensures victory in the end.

Under the circumstances of modern war it is more than ever necessary that this spirit should be instilled into the individual as well as into the mass, for the surroundings of a modern battle are more harrowing than they were in old days. Success in war will be to that side in which this feeling is most deep, which is best equipped, and which possesses the most skilful and heroic leaders.

APPENDIX II

Extracts from the Official Report on the Kwantun Fortress Artillery, by Major-General Biely, lately Commanding the Fortress Artillery in Port Arthur (submitted after the Capitulation).*

When hostilities commenced at Port Arthur, neither the engineer nor artillery preparations for defence were completed, and had hurriedly to be carried out. To make clear how some of the artillery positions came into being needs some explanation.

In 1902 a special Committee sat, by order of the Officer Commanding the District, in order to work out a defence scheme for the district and for Port Arthur itself. After inspections of the ground, carried out in 1902 and 1903, this Committee decided to allot artillery units to the following places:

(a) Yinchow: some fortress artillery, in the old Chinese fort at the mouth of the Liao-ho, to protect the entrance.

(b) Dalny and Talienwan: some field batteries, to protect the mine fields in Talienwan Bay.

(c) Kinchou: twelve batteries, to check the enemy's invasion of the peninsula through the narrow neck between Khinoeze (Hand) and Kinchou Bays.

The advanced positions of Nangalin and Wolf's Hills were noted for field batteries. Plans were made for artillery emplacements immediately in front of the Fortress on Pan-lun-shan ridge, on the height near the temple of Miaosan.

On General Biely's recommendation it was proposed to supplement our own artillery by the following guns, taken by us from the Chinese in 1900: One 28-centimetre,† two 24-centimetre, two 21-centimetre, four 120-millimetre, two

---

* Figures are given exactly as in the Report.
† For table of British equivalents see p. 385.

150-millimetre, twenty-eight 87-millimetre, more than twenty 75-millimetre, and ten 57-millimetre. We had enough ammunition, spare parts, and gear to render the greater part of these guns useful, and work upon their repair and preparation was started. For the 120-millimetre, 87-millimetre, and 57-millimetre, a supplementary order for shells, fuses, etc., was in 1903 placed in Germany (with Krupp). However, when war broke out some of these guns were not ready owing to deficiency in accessories, etc., and so were not mounted in position, but were placed in reserve; but the 87- and 75-millimetre guns for Talienwan Bay and the Kinchou position were allotted.

General Biely, foreseeing that an enemy, by taking up a position with their ships behind Liao-tieh-shan, would be able to shell the harbour and town with impunity, suggested that one 28-centimetre and two 24-centimetre Chinese guns should be mounted on the top of that hill. This was not agreed to by the Committee, as they considered such an operation by the Japanese fleet to be improbable, and because they were alarmed at the difficulty and cost of the proposal. Similarly, the Committee rejected his recommendation for mounting these guns elsewhere on the shore front—for instance—in the group of batteries on Cross Hill.

Later, after the outbreak of war, the Viceroy gave orders that a 28-centimetre gun should be mounted on the Kinchou position; but this was not done, as it was not ready up to the time we abandoned this position. As will be seen later, this gun, as well as others, were afterwards got up into position on Liao-tieh-shan and Cross Hill.

In 1902 also, as soon as the scale of armament had been settled, General Biely laid great stress upon the early provision of a proper fortress-telephone system, of observation stations, of accurate maps of the neighbouring ground, and of all the apparatus necessary for accurate shooting and fire observation; but, from various causes not under his control, matters hung fire till the end of 1903, when authority was obtained to raise the required sum by selling a quantity of the Chinese artillery. Orders were then at once placed with Krupp, Kunst and Albers, and others, for such articles as could not be procured in Arthur, whilst other material, such as telephones, wire, insulators, etc., were bought locally. By the time war broke out this material had not arrived, which prevented the installation of a new telephone system.

The destruction of our fleet had naturally not been anticipated in the original defence scheme; and the idea of mounting naval guns on shore to supplement the land armament only took shape after the *Cesarevitch*, *Retvisan*, and *Pallada* were damaged on the night of February 8, 1904, and thus condemned to a prolonged inactivity. The first proposal was to mount four of the *Retvisan's* 6-inch Canet guns on Liao-tieh-shan, where, since the middle of March, two 6-inch (68 cwt.) fortress guns had been in position. The arming of this hill had been shown to be necessary when the enemy's ships from behind it shelled Tiger's Tail Peninsula, and our ships in the western basin on March 10, 22, 23, and April 15. After these guns had been mounted and high-angle fire from our ships in the western basin had been started, the enemy's fleet ceased this bombardment. The armament of the Fortress was naturally much strengthened by the addition of these guns.

Their allotment to batteries was decided by circumstances. The 6-inch and 120-millimetre guns, being powerful and having long range, were placed on those points whence they could best attack the enemy's siege guns. The 47-millimetre, 37-millimetre, and other smaller guns, were placed in the first line in the intermediate works and in the trenches between them, principally with a view to repelling assaults. Except the $2\frac{1}{2}$-inch Baranovsky, these guns only had common shell, but their accuracy, rapidity of fire, and the abundance of stores for them, made them suitable for this purpose. The 75-millimetre guns were told off to the first and second lines as auxiliary armament against the enemy's nearest siege and field batteries.

This system of allotment of naval guns was not very strictly adhered to, for it was felt that they were only lent temporarily, and would have to be returned directly the ships' repairs were completed. For this reason, and owing to the anxiety to mount them as quickly as possible on account of the enemy's rapid advance, the 6-inch Canet guns were mounted on separate batteries, newly built for them, and on such of the forts and positions as were completed. It was not sound; and later, when the Japanese began to pound the forts containing these guns, they were at once silenced, and it was very difficult to remove and replace them. It was in some cases impossible owing to the destruction done by the enemy's fire—for instance, when the bridges over the ditches were damaged.

The fortress howitzers were not mounted in accordance with the authorized armament table, though the character of the ground rendered them essential. The 6-inch howitzers were of little use, having only a short range; for this reason General Smirnoff ordered eight 9-inch coast howitzers to be mounted in two batteries on the land side. They were taken from the coast batteries, where they had been quite idle, and were mounted in rear of the first line, from which position they did excellent work against the enemy's siege batteries, approaches, and places of concentration. They were of the greatest use up to the end of the siege.

For the twenty 6-inch (43 cwt.) guns (latest pattern) which arrived in the Fortress in March and the twenty-one carriages (1877 pattern) new batteries were built. The carriages had to be adapted to the guns, but it was a very difficult operation and not successful, and they were continually under repair.

On the land front new batteries were being constructed right up to the end of the siege, to take either fresh guns from the fleet or repaired Chinese guns, and whenever the plan of defence was changed the guns again had to be moved.

Most of the heights round Port Arthur on which the forts and batteries settled on by the Committee (which had drawn out the scheme for the armament of the Fortress) were placed were sloping on the outer side, while on the inner they ran sharply down into deep ravines. It was, therefore, almost impossible to site these batteries to shoot well and yet to keep them concealed. If they were placed near the top, there was very little ground in rear of the guns, and they were visible; if they were placed further back and down the rear slope, all idea of shelling the approaches up the front slope would have to be given up. This was the reason why permanent batteries and fortifications were placed on open ground where they were visible to the enemy, and why guns were mounted in the open on the permanent forts.

The reserve of guns was originally intended to be organized by units of artillery, but in April it had to be broken up to arm new points. Later on another reserve was formed of guns from the unattacked left flank of the western front and from the central wall.

The Chinese wall, which played such an important part in the defence, merits some description. Along the line of old Chinese batteries, from A up to Tumulus Battery, the Chinese had built a continuous mud wall—a dense mass of clay revetted with stone—14 feet thick at bottom, and 2 to 4 feet thick at top. It was $10\frac{1}{2}$ feet high, and had a banquette all along the inner side; the outer had a slope of about 45°. Where the roads from the town passed through it had traversed openings and gun emplacements. There were three such openings on the eastern front—at A Battery, Wolf's Battery, and in the ravine between Fort Erh-lung-shan and Fortification No. 3. Before the war no one dreamed of this wall being of use, and not only was it not kept in repair, but in places stones and earth were taken from it. It eventually proved most valuable; it is doubtful if we could without it have managed to repulse so successfully some of the assaults. When the eastern front was manned, General Smirnoff had the wall repaired and loopholed; splinter proofs and barbettes for the guns were built, and small guns for repulsing attacks were mounted. It was frequently hammered by the enemy's guns, even by their 11-inch howitzers, but little real damage was done to it, and to the end the enemy could not drive us back from it or breach it beyond repair. Only a small portion of it near Fort Erh-lung-shan was abandoned just before the capitulation, and this was done by General Fock's order, but was not really necessary.

The following tables bear witness to the state of the Fortress on the outbreak of hostilities :

TABLE I.

Showing the Authorized Armament as laid down by the Committee in 1900, and the Guns actually in the Fortress on January 14, 1904.

Nature of Guns.	Number.	
	Authorized.	Actuals.
10-inch of 1877	10	5
9-inch of 1877	12	12
6-inch quick-firing Canet	20	20
6-inch of 1877 (of 68 cwt.)	37	30
6-inch of 1877 (of 43 cwt.)	38	18
42-line	28	24
Heavy guns of 1877	12	12
Light field	233	146
57-millimetre coast	24	28
57-millimetre caponier	84	14
11-inch howitzers of 1877	10	10
9-inch howitzers of 1877	32	32
6-inch field-howitzers	26	24
3-line machine-guns	48	38
Total	614	413*

TABLE II.

Showing Allotment of Guns on Works on January 14, 1904.

In consequence of the conversions and alterations in progress, the coast batteries alone had their armament. There were eighteen† coast batteries—Nos. 1, 2, 3, 4, 5, 7, 9, Artillery, Tiger's Tail, Nos. 12, 13, 14, 15, 17, 18, 19, 20, 21. Two were being finished and armed—Nos. 6 and 16.

* By this table, the armament was 201 guns short of its proper number, and of the 413 only 110 were mounted.

† This does not exactly agree with the map supplied by the author.—E. D. S.

The armament mounted consisted of:

	Mounted.
10-inch guns	5
9-inch guns	12
6-inch Canet	15
6-inch (68 cwt.)	12
57-millimetre coast guns	28
Heavy	4
11-inch howitzers	10
9-inch howitzers	24
Total ready for action	110

	Being Mounted.
6-inch Canet	5
9-inch howitzers	8
Total	13

On the land front only two batteries were armed:

B Battery, 6-inch guns of 68 cwt.	4
G (Sapper) Battery, 6-inch of 68 cwt.	4
Total guns ready for action	8

Fort 1 and B (Jagged) Battery and D Battery were under construction.

There were, therefore, only eight guns mounted on the land front.

The remaining guns were distributed in parks, according to sectors or sections, near the batteries for which they were allotted—*i.e.*:

Section 5: for Fort 1 and the intermediate batteries between Battery 21 and Fort 1. The park near batteries 19 and 20 (four 6-inch of 68 cwt., eighteen light on wheeled carriages, and eight machine-guns).

Section 6: for Fortification 1, Ta-ku-shan Hill, A and B Batteries, Fortification 2, Fort Chi-kuan-shan and Big Hill. The park near the Ice House in front of Big Hill (six 6-inch of 43 cwt., six 57-millimetre caponier, twenty-two light guns on wheels, six light guns on pedestals, eight 6-inch field howitzers, four machine-guns).

Section 7: for Eagle's Nest, rear caponiers of Redoubts Nos. 1 and 2, Fort Erh-lung-shan, Fortification at head of

Water Supply Redoubt, Fortification 3. The park near the barracks of the 7th Company (four 6-inch of 43 cwt., twenty light on wheels, four heavy, two machine-guns).

Section 8: for C and G Batteries (Jagged and Sapper), Fort 4 and Fortification 4. The park near G Battery (eight 6-inch of 43 cwt., six 57-millimetre caponier, 24 light on wheels, four machine-guns).

Section 9: for Forts 1 and Chi-kuan-shan, D Battery and Salt Battery, Fortification 5, and Redoubts 3, 4, and 5. The park near D Battery (six 6-inch of 68 cwt., two 57-millimetre caponier, six 42-line, six machine-guns).

In Store and in Reserve: In the park in the Chinese arsenal, 56 light guns on wheels; sixteen 6-inch field howitzers, eighteen 42-line guns, fourteen machine-guns, four heavy guns.

Thus it was intended to mount another 244 guns and 38 machine-guns on the batteries and intermediate works so soon as these were sufficiently advanced to receive them.

The central magazines, being merely Chinese brick buildings, were in no way shell-proof; but of the numerous section magazines required to store ammunition, spare parts, etc., for the decentralized supply, only four had been built and taken over from the engineers in February, 1904 (two on the sea front, Tiger's Peninsula and Battery 17; two on the land front, Big Hill and C Battery).

TABLE III.

The following were the shells in the Fortress on January 14, 1904:

Guns.	Shells.
10-inch	790
9-inch	2,889
6-inch Canet	4,951
6-inch (68 cwt.)	17,512
6-inch (43 cwt.)	10,459
42-line guns	10,925
Heavy guns	2,409
Light guns	41,227
57-millimetre coast	24,078
57-millimetre caponier	3,210
11-inch howitzer	2,004
9-inch howitzer	7,819
6-inch field howitzer	11,981
Cartridge cases for machine-guns	957,615

TABLE IV.

Taking all cartridges, fuzes, spare parts, and other accessory stores into consideration, the following were the rounds per gun in the Fortress on the outbreak of war:

Guns.	Rounds per Gun.
10-inch guns	158
9-inch guns and howitzers	243
6-inch Canet guns	247
6-inch guns (68 cwt. and 43 cwt.)	583
42-line and heavy guns	370
57-millimetre coast guns	860
57-millimetre caponier	230
Light field guns	282
11-inch howitzers	200
6-inch field howitzers	500

In the artillery magazine there were for the 3-inch quick-firing field artillery guns:

Cartridge cases	6,957
Double action fuzes	8,479

Of small ammunition there were:

	Cartridges.
3-line rifle	12,621,176
3-line revolver	14,512
4, 2-line revolver	5,357
4, 2-line Berdan	41,635
Chinese	2,122,050

Since the date of our taking over Port Arthur, particularly during the disorders in China in and after 1900, the diplomatic sky had never been really clear, and at times the political barometer alternated between the 'set fair' and 'storm.' In 1903 it was first very unsettled, and then kept steadily falling, which caused us to think seriously of fortifying Port Arthur, not as heretofore, by talk and correspondence, but by deeds.

General Vernander, head of the Engineer Department, rendered no material assistance. He only greatly delayed matters, which had been practically decided on, by fresh proposals and fiddling with details; but the visit of General Kuropatkin, the War Minister to the place in 1903, gave a great impulse to affairs. After being three weeks in Port Arthur he made himself acquainted with all the details on the spot, inspected all the proposed fortifications, gave great encouragement to us, and ordered certain changes to be made. The most important result of his visit, however, was that he changed the order of building the different works laid down by the original authors of the scheme of defence, in accordance with their actual requirements and importance, and gave orders for us to set to work at once simultaneously on all the most important.

Amongst other things, he thought it advisable to strengthen the summit of Ta-ku-shan by building a block-house for 100 men with two or four quick-firing guns in a caponier for flanking the approaches to the main line of works and to the hill itself. He also thought the height near the temple behind the village of Siu-shuing should be strengthened to cover the approach into the valley of the Lun-ho, and to command the village. A block-house with two guns was to be placed on the near peak west of Fort 4, that the foot and slopes of the hills, on which this fort was built, might be shelled, and a trench was to connect up fort and block-house. He considered the interval between Fortification 5 and Fort Erh-lung-shan too great, and said an intermediate work should be made on the summit of the height in front of Fort Erh-lung-shan. To distribute the defence beyond this Fort by occupying Angle Hill and points D and E (High and Long Hills), he did not conceive to be possible without greatly weakening the garrison. But the sudden outbreak of war compelled us to diverge from much that had been intended.

In an order of the Viceroy's, dated February 9, 1904, the Fortress was declared to be in a state of siege, and three days later the reserve men began arriving. According to the artillery mobilization scheme, three weeks was supposed to be sufficient for this arm to be ready for war. But the Committee of Defence of the Kwantun District, to which this scheme was submitted, expressed the opinion that the mobilization would take two months. It was indeed lucky for us the enemy did not attempt a landing in Pigeon Bay the night of the torpedo attack; but they were cautious and none too certain of themselves at that time, and probably thought us stronger than we were.

At all events, for three months they took no decisive action on land, which enabled us, firstly, to mobilize the garrison, receive reserves, munitions and supplies, to look round and to draw up a scheme for the fortification and defence of the Fortress on land, and partly also from sea; and secondly, to get some knowledge of, and be able to appreciate the worth of the enemy and of ourselves. In the fights at Kinchou and on the advanced positions the enemy did not exhibit any extraordinary bravery or superiority over us. On the contrary, what was shown up was our inability to engage them and drive them back.

Our field force, under General Fock, having made a slight attempt to meet the enemy on the position before Kinchou, quickly withdrew on to the prepared position itself, and then, having lost this in sixteen hours, and lost all its guns of position and batteries at Dalny and Talienwan, retired more than hurriedly towards Arthur, and occupied a strong (in the topographical sense) but long position along the hills—Khelaza, Upilazy, Kuen-san. But the force retired from here also on July 30 to the Fortress works, not defending the position on Wolf's Hills, which had to a certain extent been fortified, and which it had been decided to hold.

All the schemes for the defence of Kwantun in general, and of Port Arthur in particular, which had been made out in peace-time, had to be abandoned or altered at the outbreak of war, and all those who drew up these schemes and were helping to carry them out left the district which was destined to be the arena of a long and bloody struggle. The brilliant ten months' defence was due to the fresh actors who appeared on the scene and the plans made out by them. During part of January and all February the arming of the land works and of two coast batteries (6 and 16) was energetically and incessantly carried on, chiefly by night. The work was often interrupted by the enemy's bombardment and attempts to block the harbour.

The following guns were received in January and February:

6-inch guns (43 cwt.)	20
6-inch field howitzers	2
87-millimetre Chinese guns (selected)	20
From the Fleet: 2½-inch guns	15
3-line Maxims	25

In February the following were sent to the fort at Yinchow:

1 officer, 72 men.
4 6-inch guns (43 cwt.).
8 light field guns.

By March the land works had been armed as follows:

Fort No. 1.

6-inch guns (68 cwt.)	4
Light guns	4
Machine-guns	4
Rocket troughs	3

Open Caponier No. 1.

Light guns	4

Fortification No. 1. (Danger Hill).

Light guns	4

A Battery.

6-inch guns (43 cwt.)	6
Light guns	4
Machine-guns	1
Rocket troughs	3

Fortification No. 2.

6-inch field howitzers	2
Light guns	4

B Battery.

6-inch guns (68 cwt.)	4
Light guns	2
Rocket troughs	3

Fort No. 2 (Chi-kuan-shan).

Light guns	4
Machine-guns	3

Open Caponier No. 2.
Light guns 4

Little Eagle's Nest Battery.
42-line guns 3

Kuropatkin Lunette.
6-inch field howitzers 4
87-millimetre Chinese field guns ... 4

Redoubt No. 1.
Light guns 4

Redoubt No. 2.
6-inch field howitzers 4

Ravine Trench.
Light guns 2

Fort No. 3 (Erh-lung-shan).
6-inch guns (43 cwt.) 4
Light guns 5
Machine-guns 2
Rocket troughs 4

Bridge Battery.
Light guns 2

Fortification No. 3.
Light guns 5
Machine-guns 2
Rocket troughs 6

Tumulus Battery.
42-line guns 2
6-inch field howitzers 4
Light guns 4
Machine-guns 1

Cemetery Battery.
42-line guns 4
Light guns 2
6-inch howitzers 2
Machine-guns 1

Lower Jagged Battery.
6-inch field howitzers 2

C (Jagged) Battery.
6-inch guns (43 cwt.) 4

G (Sapper) Battery.
6-inch guns (68 cwt.) 4
Machine-guns 2
Rocket troughs 2

Fort No. 4.
Light guns 6
Machine-guns 2
Rocket platforms 2

Battery near Fort 4.
6-inch field howitzers 4

Fortification No. 4.
42-line guns 3
Light guns 5
Machine-guns 2
Rocket troughs 2

Tea Trench.
Light guns 2

Rear Redoubt.
Light guns 2

Rear Battery.
6-inch field howitzers 4
Light guns 2

Fort No. 5.
Light guns 5
Naval Baranovsky guns 2
Machine-guns 2
Rocket troughs 2

Pigeon Battery.
Light guns 2
Baranovsky guns 1

D Battery.
6-inch guns (68 cwt.), all round fire ... 6

Lateral Battery.

Light guns	2
Rocket troughs	2

Flank Battery.

Baranovsky guns	2

Redoubt No. 3.

Light guns	2

Fortification No. 5.

42-line guns	4
Light guns	4
Baranovsky guns	4
Machine-guns	2
Rocket troughs	3

New Battery.

6-inch (43 cwt.) guns	4

Timber Redoubt.

Light guns	4
Machine-guns	2

Advanced Battery.

Light guns	2

Fort No. 6.

42-line guns	4
Light guns	4
Machine-guns	2
Rocket troughs	3

Salt Battery.

Light guns	4

White Wolf Battery.

Light guns	4
Rocket troughs	2

By the Lighthouse on Liao-tish-shan.

6-inch guns (68 cwt.)	2
Baranovsky guns	2

Sent to the Bays—Pigeon, Louisa, Ten Ships, Shaopingtao Lun-wan-tun, and Takhe.

Baranovsky guns	4
Machine-guns	3

On the Redoubts of the Central Wall.

By the slaughter-house	2 light guns
No. 1 (Artillery)	2 ,,
No. 2 (Engineer)	2 ,,
No. 3 (Sapper)	2 ,,
No. 4 (Powder)	2 42-line guns.
Between Batteries 20 and 21 ...	10 light guns

SUMMARY.

Thus, by March 14 there were mounted ready for action on the land front:

6-inch guns (43 cwt. and 68 cwt.) and 42-line guns	60
Light field guns	126
Baranovsky guns	15
87-millimetre Chinese field guns ...	4
6-inch field howitzers	24
3-line machine-guns	30
Total	259

On the sea front, the following guns taken from the ships had been mounted opposite the entrance to the inner roads:

Lighthouse Battery	2 120-millimetre guns
Golden Hill Battery	2 120-millimetre guns
Electric Cliff ...	2 37-millimetre guns
Battery 16 ...	5 Canet guns
Total ...	11

Total on sea front and in Bays:

Guns	37
Machine-guns	3

Grand total in Fortress:

Guns	362
Machine-guns	33

Of ammunition, all batteries on the land front had 200 and on the sea front 200 or 300 rounds per gun ready. There were also 50 rocket troughs on the former.

The whole perimeter of the Fortress with regard to artillery was divided as follows:

(a) *Sea Front.*

Section 1	Sectors 1 and 2
Section 2	Sectors 3 and 4

(b) *Land Front.*

Section 3	Sectors 6 and 7
Section 4	Sectors 8, 9, and 10
Section 5	Sectors 11 and 12

Kinchou.

The following were sent to and mounted on the Kinchou position in February:

42-line guns	2
6-inch field howitzers ...	6
Light field guns	16
Chinese 87-millimetre quick-firing guns	12
Chinese 87-millimetre guns ...	8
3-line maxims	6
Rocket troughs	8

}44 guns

Ammunition was sent to bring up the number of rounds per gun as follows:

	Rounds.
42-line, light, and 87-millimetre non-cartridge guns	200
6-inch field howitzers	155
87-millimetre cartridge guns ...	140
Rockets	400

To fight the guns at Kinchou, a provisional company was formed of 4 officers and 392 non-commissioned officers and men. In February the Port Arthur Sortie Battery of eight 3-inch quick-firing guns and a provisional field battery of four 57-millimetre Chinese guns were also organized.

APPENDIX III

Showing the 'matériel' and 'personnel' landed from the fleet for the land defence of Port Arthur.

Order No. 70.

IN continuation of Order No. 32 of August 20 by Rear-Admiral Prince Ukhtomsky, temporarily in command of the Pacific Ocean Squadron, the following is the detailed list of fortifications, showing the numbers and distribution of naval guns, searchlights, and *personnel* in them:

THE 'RETVISAN.'

Names of Batteries.	Guns.	Search-lights.	Personnel.		
			Guns.	Search-lights.	Mines.
Battery No. 20 ...	1 24-cm.	—	18	—	—
Takhe Pipe ...	6 37-mm.	—	12	—	—
Fort No. 1 ...	3 47-mm., 6 37-mm.	1 90-cm.	21	10	—
Between Dragon's Back and No. 19 ...	4 47-mm.	—	12	—	—
Between Dragon's Back and No. 1 ...	1 37-mm.	—	2	—	—
Takhe Cliff ...	2 47-mm.	—	5	—	—
To the right of Fort No. 1 ...	2 47-mm.	—	5	—	—
To the left of Fort No. 1 ...	2 47-mm.	—	4	—	—
Open Caponier ...	—	1 40-cm.	—	6	—
Dragon's Back ...	2 6-inch	—	12	6	—
A Battery ...	2 47-mm., 7 37-mm., 1 2½-inch	1 40-cm.	21	6	—
Fortification No. 2 ...	4 47-mm., 2 machine-guns	1 40-cm.	21	6	—
Fort No. 2 ...	2 47-mm., 4 37-mm.	—	10	—	—

APPENDIX III

THE 'BAYAN.'

Names of Batteries.	Guns.	Search-lights.	Personnel.		
			Guns.	Search-lights.	Mines.
Fort No. 3	12 37-mm.	1 75-cm., 1 40-cm.	19	9	7
Fortification No. 3	2 6-inch, 1 47-mm., 8 37-mm.	—	28	—	—
Tumulus Battery	2 75-mm., 4 37-mm., 1 120-mm.	1 75-cm., 1 60-cm.	27	13	—
Quail Hill	2 6-inch, 1 120-mm.	1 40-cm.	20	6	—
Rocky Ridge	1 120-mm., 10 75-mm., 2 47-mm., 2 37-mm.	—	60	—	—
Above Chinese Town	4 47-mm.	—	16	—	—
Slope of Big Hill	4 47-mm.	—	16	—	—

THE 'POLTAVA.'

Names of Batteries.	Guns.	Search-lights.	Personnel.		
			Guns.	Search-lights.	Mines.
Cemetery Hill	4 75-mm., 4 47-mm., 4 37-mm.	—	39	—	—
B Battery and under	1 120-mm., 2 47-mm.	1 75-cm., 1 60-cm.	11	13	3
Fort No. 4	4 75-mm., 2 47-mm.	1 40-cm.	39	4	2
Intermediate Battery	2 75-mm., 2 47-mm., 2 37-mm., 2 machine-guns	—	37	—	—
Fortification No. 4	2 75-mm., 4 37-mm.	—	14	2	—
Obelisk Battery	1 6-inch, 8 47-mm.	—	32	—	—
Council Battery	2 9-pounders	—	13	—	—

THE 'PERESVET.'

Names of Batteries.	Guns.	Search-lights.	Personnel.		
			Guns.	Search-lights.	Mines.
Fort No. 5	2 6-inch, 2 75-mm.	1 75-cm., 1 40-cm.	28	11	—
Pigeon Battery	2 75-mm., 4 37-mm.	—	30	—	—
Triangulation	1 6-inch of 1877	—	15	—	—
Fort D (? D Battery)	1 6-inch	1 75-cm.	13	6	—

APPENDIX III

THE 'PALLADA.'

Names of Batteries.	Guns.	Search-lights.	Personnel.		
			Guns.	Search-lights.	Mines.
Fortification No. 5 ...	4 75-mm., 4 47-mm., 10 37-mm.	—	62	—	—
Wooded Hill	2 75-mm., 4 47-mm., 4 37-mm.	1 60-cm., 1 40-cm.	44	7	—

THE 'POBIEDA.'

Fort No. 6	2 47-mm.	1 40-cm.	9	6	—
White Wolf	2 37-mm., 2 2½-inch	1 60-cm.	—	6	—
Salt Hill	4 75-mm., 4 37-mm., 1 2½-inch	—	28	—	—
Battery at entrance ...	1 120-cm.	—	—	—	—
Battery No. 9 ...	—	1 60-cm.	—	9	—

THE 'SEVASTOPOL.'

Liao-tieh-shan Light-house	4 6-inch, 4 37-mm. 4 2½-inch	1 75-cm.	45	7	2
Liao-tieh-shan Top, 218 and 200 ...	1 21-cm., 2 6-inch, 3 37-mm., 2 2½-inch	1 75-cm., 1 60-cm.	54	15	—
Grand total			852	142	14
				1,008	

WIREN,
Rear-Admiral.

Note.—TOTAL OF GUNS (WITH BRITISH EQUIVALENTS).

Calibre, etc.	Equivalent.	Number.
120 millimetres	4·7-inch	5
75 ,,	3-inch	38
47 ,,	Small quick-firing	60
37 ,,	,,	91
6-inch	6-inch	17
2·5-inch	2·5-inch	10
24-centimetres	9·4-inch	1
21-centimetres	8·2-inch	1
9-pounder	9-pound	2
Machine	Machine	4

CIRCULAR

by the Officer Commanding the Division of Battleships and Cruisers in Port Arthur, November 17, 1904.

No. 241.

In continuation of Order No. 70 and Circular No. 205, the following guns have been taken over by the Kwantun District authorities:

From the	Mounted on	Guns.
Retvisan	Fort B	2 47-mm.
Peresvet	Rear Battery	3 37-mm. and 1 75-mm.
Poltava	Sapper Battery	1 75-mm.
Pobieda	Battery No. 1 (Tiger's Peninsula)	2 47-mm.
Pallada	Big Pigeon Bay	1 47-mm.
Bayan	Hill in rear of Fortification No. 3	3 47-mm.

APPENDIX IV

THE following pages will give some idea as to the real state of the Fortress as regards Supplies, Munitions of War, and Men, when the surrender took place.

SUPPLIES.

This table, drawn up by the Fortress Intendant, shows the amount of food in the supply depôts exclusive of what was in possession of private firms:

To the Commandant of the Fortress.

TABLE SHOWING THE AMOUNT OF SUPPLIES IN THE PORT ARTHUR SUPPLY DEPÔTS ON DECEMBER 31, 1904.

Supplies.	Depôts.				Total.	Number of Rations.	Men, 32,213; Horses, 3,258. Amount of Rations in Days.
	1	3	4	5			
	lbs.	lbs.	lbs.		lbs.	lbs.	Days.
Flour	784,320	—	40,680	—	825,000	437,569	13½*
Groats and rice	145,720	—	77,360	—	223,080	} 693,120	21½
Do., broken	—	—	5,600	—	5,600		
Millet	—	—	2,360	—	2,360		
Tea	—	—	86,720	—	86,720	5,550,080	172½
Sugar	48,960	—	—	—	48,960	391,680	12
Biscuits	—	—	866,280	—	866,280	495,017	15
Dried vegetables	—	—	124,000	—	124,000	2,976,000	92
Salt	652,040	—	13,040	—	665,080	5,804,335	180
Preserves	—	—	154,120	—	154,120	—	—
Oats	—	127,280	—	—	127,280	} 114,406	35
Beans	—	1,245,600	—	—	1,245,600		
Cattle, 3.							
Sheep and goats, 9.							

* In addition to this, 422,000 pounds of flour and 1,201,600 pounds which arrived in the *King Arthur* are still in hand.

(Signed) CAPTAIN DOSTAVALOFF,
Fortress Intendant.

No. 9,953.
PORT ARTHUR.
   December 31, 1904.

Munitions of War.

As regards the stores in the Fortress, the following extracts from a letter from Major-General Biely, Commanding the Fortress Artillery, to Major-General Reintal, Inspector-General of Artillery, shows the true state of affairs:

'The unexpectedness of the surrender of the Fortress, and the rapidity with which we were all sent into imprisonment in Japan, prevented me from finishing a detailed report of the work done by the artillery in the Fortress during the siege, and sending it, as I intended, to the Artillery Department. The conditions of my imprisonment stopped my doing so afterwards. Up till now not a single artillery commanding officer who knows the actual state of the artillery in the Fortress on the day of the surrender, and can report the true state of affairs, has returned to Russia. Meanwhile, however, a Royal Commission has been appointed to investigate all the circumstances of the capitulation. The details furnished to this Commission about the artillery which I have happened to read in the papers, and in particular those communicated by such a witness as Major-General Reuss, are on the whole highly coloured, presumably with a view to belittling the artillery service generally and showing an insufficiency of reserve stores. Judging from this and from what he has said to correspondents, General Reuss apparently has some other object in view than that of informing the public of the true state of affairs in the Fortress. It is not my intention to join issue with him in the columns of a daily paper, but if such evidence is believed, without proper inquiries being made of those who had to do with these matters, a false impression will be gained. At the Council of War convened by General Stössel on the afternoon of December 29, 1904, at which twenty-five commanders and officers were present, some members expressed the opinion that the defence could not be continued, basing their arguments on the absence of necessary artillery stores. At the time I protested against the matter being represented in such a wrong light, and I did not conceal my surprise that members should dare to assert things in my presence of which they apparently either had no knowledge or which they were purposely perverting. I based my statement on figures which

I had in my hand at the time, and I insisted on my opinion, which was entirely opposed to that which had just been expressed. I pointed out that, in regard to artillery stores, the Fortress had a sufficient quantity for the struggle, and was in a state to be able to repulse another two assaults—perhaps more—and that if there were also sufficient food-supplies, then, in my opinion, the defence ought to be continued till they were exhausted. No one attempted to contradict me. On the contrary, I was supported by all the artillerymen, by my senior assistants at the Council (Irman, Mekhmandaroff), and by the Intendant of the Fortress, and a general conclusion was come to that the defence was to be continued, a portion of the defence line alone being reduced. . . .

'During the last days, up to January 1, when we were informed that a proposal for surrender had been sent to the enemy, things were in much the same state, especially with regard to munitions of war. If we look at the figures, we find that there were, counting the naval reserves, as many as 180,000 shells. Of these there were about 1,000 rounds of 9-inch, bigger calibre, and howitzer; 6,800 rounds of 6-inch and forty-two line. Of light and 57-millimetre coast quick-firing (put ashore) there were 1,800. Of 57-millimetre, about 2,000. Of 75, 57, 47, and 37 millimetre (for the naval guns mounted on the batteries) there were about 150,000. For 3-inch quick-firing field artillery, about 4,000. In round numbers, not counting the 3-inch quick-firing field-guns, there were about 14,000 rounds of shrapnel and 10,000 rounds of common.

'Although the guns were less in number and worse in condition than they had been, yet they were quite serviceable. The casting of shell for 6-inch and 42-line guns, the preparation of fuses, of pyroxyline shells, and the fusing of shell, were in full swing; we were turning out 100 shells a day, and hoped to do more.

'I consider generally that the tales in the papers about the deficiency of shrapnel, the unserviceability of the shells and guns, of the lack of fuses, etc., are exaggerations, told on purpose to put things in a light to justify the defence being cut short. The question of surrender was one for the decision of the highest authorities, but I imagine they did not lack for irrelevant and incorrect reports. The papers can, of course, say what they like, but at a formal investigation official reports and more responsible and competent evidence will, it is hoped, be taken, and not that of those who allow themselves to be interviewed. . . .

'To get at the true position of affairs as regards the artillery in Port Arthur, it is not sufficient to look merely at figures; it is necessary to understand them. In this respect General Reuss is quite at sea, and it would have been better if he had not meddled with that of which he knows nothing and understands less. It is true that the want of powder, quick-firing fuses, and range-finders was felt; that naval shells were spoilt and had to be remade; that naval common shell burst badly, etc.; but steps were taken to cope with all this, and the artillery service did splendid work. . . .'

Garrison.

As regards the garrison of the Fortress, General Smirnoff, its Commandant, gives the following details:

'The strength of our troops on the day of the surrender was as follows:

'On the defences of the Fortress:

'Bayonets (infantry and sailors) ...	12,500
'Artillery	5,000
'Engineers	500
'Non-combatants in army	1,000
'Total	19,000'

There were 15,000 sick and wounded in the permanent, 5,500 in the extemporized hospitals. Total, 20,500 sick. As 24,000 men marched to the village of Chilindzui as prisoners, 5,000 of these must have been able to walk.

This led to a curious contretemps, for in the terms of surrender it had been stipulated that not more than 9,000 men would march out. The Japanese had accordingly made arrangements to handle and ration that number, and were quite nonplussed when they found that the 9,000 had increased to 24,000. While they were making the necessary arrangements to deal with these 15,000 extra mouths the exodus was stopped, and Smirnoff spent these last three days in his old quarters.

INDEX

AIDE-DE-CAMP to the Czar, Stössel and Semenoff appointed, 181
Ammunition, small arm, deficient, 4; blank, fired from big guns, 7; runs short at Battle of Kinchou, 72; estimate of expenditure of (up to September 21), 196; waste of, 201, 219; amount available (December 8), 271; list of guns (on outbreak of war), 369
Angle Hills, 106, 135; Japanese attack repulsed, 158; loss of, 166; anger of Smirnoff, 166
Armament of the Fortress, 369 (Appendix II.); list of guns, authorized and actual, 369; allotment (in sections) of guns, 369
Artillery, Kwantun Fortress, report on the, by Major-General Biely, 364 (Appendix II.)
Artillerymen, Russian, endurance of, 64
Askold, the, 153
Assaults, the great August, 183; of October 30, 119, 220; repulsed, 221; of November 24, 239
Attack of blockers fails (March 25), 29; on Green Hills (July 26), 113 *et seq.*; of August 19, 164; and subsequent days, 183

B Battery, storming of, 220; state of, 230; assault of, November 24, 239
Bayan, the, in action of April 12, 34; sinking of, 256
Bazilevsky, General, 194
Biely, General, 1, 29, 175, 199; at last meeting of Council of Defence, 304; his opinion, 307; his report (after the war), 364
Big Eagle's Nest, storming of, 322; loss of, 324
Boevoy, the, loss of, 110
Bogdanovitch, his absurd congratulations to Stössel, 18 :
Bombardment (naval) of February 9, 7; March 10, 21; April 15, 36; October, 26 to 29, 219, 220, 221
— (land), fears of, 105; commences August 7, 140; system of, 148

Bomb-proofs constructed by inhabitants, 105; Stössel discourages, 106
Borodatoff, Lieutenant, death of, 110
Boyarin, the, 6
Butusoff, Colonel, in the defence of Green Hills (July 26), 117, 119; in the defence of 203 Metre Hill, 253; death of, 254

Capitulation signed, 332; its effect, 332, 333
'Caponier,' meaning of, xi (Preface)
Cattle allowed to be driven away, 40
Censorship of letters, 91; of press, 148, 163, 189
Cesarevitch, the, 96, 97, 153
Chinese make military roads, 24
Chinese Wall, the, x (Preface), 366 (Appendix II.)
Chi-kuan-shan Fort (Fort No. 2), bloody assault on (August 23), repulsed, 183; Japanese sap towards, 202, 210, 211, 213; mining operations, 210, 214, 215, 216; Smirnoff's inspection of the gallery, 217; fires the camouflet countermine, 217; Fock's memorandum on the surrender of, 347 *et seq.*
Chkheydsey's battery, 113, 119, 120
Civilians attempt to leave Port Arthur, 140
Confidence increases under Smirnoff, 26
Confusion on outbreak of war, 4
Coolies, Chinese, desert, 25
Council of Defence (see Defence)

Dalny, confusion at, 45, 49; docks and quays not destroyed, 49, 82; abandonment of the town, 81; retreat of the inhabitants, 82; effect of Stössel's action, 83, 89
Danger Hill, look-out station on, 164
Darkness in Port Arthur, 8
Defence, Council of, protests against surrender, 18; meeting of December 8, 265; Smirnoff's opinion at, 266; Fock's arguments, 268; final meeting (December 29), 303

Defences, general description, x (Preface); neglect of, 18; grave defects in the original scheme of, 313; Kuropatkin's modifications, 373
Diana, the, 153
Diplomacy, failure of Russian, 3
Drunkards, flogging of, 11
Drunkenness, 158

Egoroff's battery at Battle of Kinchou, 63
Electric Cliff, 7
Endrjievsky, Lieutenant, Stössel's treatment of, 192
Engineer officers—some did good work, 162; others did not, 164; responsibility of, for loss of life, 164; inactivity and inefficiency of, 194. See also Sappers
England, Russian attitude towards (before the war), 226
Erh-lung-shan Fort, bombardment of (September 28), 201; assault of October 30 fails, 223; state of, 230; assault of November 24, 239; anxiety about (December 15), 274; assault of December 18, 285; abandonment of, 288; Fock responsible for, 288; his disclaimer, 289; Smirnoff's message to Kuropatkin, 290; effect of its fall on the garrison, 310

Fleet, Russian, sortie of June 22, 96; disappointing result, 101; sortie of August 10, 152; its failure, 153; state of (after August 10), 262; retrospect of position of, 258-264
Fleet, Japanese, opens fire, 6
Flogging of drunkards, 11
Flug, General, 6
Fock, General: his influence over Stössel, 13; his opinion of Japanese troops, 13; his neglect to fortify Kinchou, 37; his blunders at Shanshilipu, 55; his behaviour at the Battle of Kinchou, 71; his idea of fortification, 106; his message as to retirement from Green Hills, 122; his behaviour there, 127; occupies Wolf's Hills, 129; delays sending reinforcements on August 21, 167; Smirnoff threatens to remove him, 169; removes him from his command, 171; his memorandum of November 3, 227; its effect, 229; urges retirement from 203 Metre Hill, 247; appointed to succeed Kondratenko, 280; reduces garrisons of the works, 283; 'the General of Retreats,' 285; at last meeting of Council of Defence, 304, 306, 307; orders Gorbatovsky to carry out abandonment of third position, 330; his memorandum on the surrender of Chi-kuan-shan (Fort No. 2), 347 *et seq.* (Appendix L)
Food, insufficiency of, 46
Foreigners, visit of the two, 202 *et seq.*; its result, 207
Fort No. 5, bombardment of, 197
Fort No. 6, construction of, 134
Fortification No. 3, assault on, 220; its fall, 310, 311; Fock's order to evacuate it, 310
Fortifications (of Port Arthur), dilatoriness in constructing the, 24; defects in scheme of, 313
Froloff, Lieutenant-General, opinion of Council of Defence, 265
Frontier Guards, the, not made use of, 48; in the defence of Green Hills, 117
Fuji, the, damaged by mines, 51

Garrison, its false sense of security, 13; takes to robbery, 22; mobilization of, 374
German Emperor's letter to his naval attachés, 161
Gilgenheim, Captain, German naval attaché, murder of, 161
Giliak, gunboat, as look-out, 26; in action of May 2, 41
Golden Hill, 7; opens fire on Takushan, 142; 11-inch howitzers on, 165; premature bursts of iron shells, 165, 176
Gorbatovsky, General, 1; his energy, 163; Fock accuses him falsely, 171; at assault of Kikwanshan Fort, 300 *et seq.*; at last meeting of Council of Defence, 304; decides to hold second line of defence, 312
Green Hills, value of, for defence, 88; loss of, 93; recovered, 94; fortifying of, 107; battle of July 26, 113 *et seq.*
Griasnoff, Colonel, at last Council of Defence, 304
Grigorenko, Colonel, Officer Commanding Fortress Engineers, 29; at the last meeting of the Council of Defence, 304, 306
Grigorovitch, Admiral, 1; his proposals opposed by Witgeft, 151; his work, 199
Guns of Fortress fail to co-operate in defence of Wolf's Hills, 132; list of, 375 *et seq.*
— naval, use of, 201, 366 (Appendix II.); list of, 381 *et seq.* (Appendix III.)
Gurko, Lieutenant-Colonel, sent to Kuropatkin from Stössel, 173

Hammer, Lieutenant, Aide-de-Camp to Smirnoff, 168
Handurin, Lieutenant-Colonel, at last Council of Defence, 304

Hatsuse, Japanese battleship, destroyed by mines, 50
Hill 113, key of the Suantsegan position, 126
Hill, 203 Metre. See Metre
Hospital, shell falls into, 253; organization in the Fortress, 315; deficiency of accommodation, 316; state of the (in December), 317
Howitzers (11-inch) on Golden Hill, premature bursting of shells, 165; use of generally, 367 (Appendix II.)

Investment begun, 156
Intelligence Services (Russian), badness of, 90, 92
— (Japanese), 92
Irman, Colonel, his gallantry at 203 Metre Hill, 253; present at the last meeting of the Council of Defence, 304; his opinion, 306
Itsukushima, the, damaged by mine, 186

Japanese nation, dissatisfaction of, at slow progress of siege, 177; action of Mikado's Government, 177; views of, before the war, 224
— officers in disguise in the Fortress, 9
— troops held in contempt at first, 12; ignorance of Russian army about, 13
Jerebtsoff, Colonel, commanding Sapper Company, 294; ordered to do the impossible, 295; his energy and gallantry, 297; unrewarded, 298

Karseladse, Prince, his telegram to Bogdanovitch, 19
Khvostoff, Chief of Fortress Staff, 5; arrives with Smirnoff, 23; his work, 29, 199; at last meeting of Council of Defence, 304
Kinchou, importance of, 8; realised by Smirnoff, 28, 37; Tretiakoff's efforts to fortify, 37, 47, 56; the confusion at, 58; battle of (commencement), 61 *et seq.*; (continuation), 67 *et seq.*; Fock's behaviour during the battle, 71
Kondratenko, General, 1, 18; Smirnoff's personal assistant, 23; his share in fortifying and arming the Fortress, 25, 29, 87; overruled by Fock, 108; on resisting an attack on Green Hills, 111; his anger with Fock, 112; at the attack on the Green Hills on July 26, 114; prevents deadlock between Stössel and Smirnoff, 199; persuades Stössel as to Fock's uselessness, 199; at the meeting of Council of Defence (December 8), 268; his last evening, 275; his death, 276

Kuen-san Hill, 89; abandoned, 93; attempt to recapture fails, 94; results of the loss of, 104; commands the Green Hills, 108
Kuropatkin orders Stössel to hand over command to Smirnoff, 174; inspection of the Fortress, 195, 364; his telegram as to relieving the Fortress, 209; refers to St. Petersburg as to recall of Stössel, 209; result, 210; informs Smirnoff of Stössel's official deceit, 282
— Lunette, 230
Kuteynikoff, engineer, repairs the ships, 22

Lao-tieh-shan Hill, 7; guns mounted on, 22; rapidly fortified after Smirnoff's arrival, 26; Fock and Smirnoff disagree as to strengthening (in December), 269
Laperoff, Colonel, at Battle of Kinchou, 68, 73
Letters, censorship of, 91
Liao-yang, the retirement from, 231
Lieutenant Burakoff, the, loss of, 110
Long Hill, Japanese attacks on (September 20), 195
Lopatin, Captain, sacrificed to save Fock, 93
Loschinsky, Admiral, 1; mines the shores, 14; draws up a scheme for mining Port Arthur waters, 20, 36; defeats attempt to block the entrance to the harbour, 41 *et seq.*; urges Witgeft to capture the damaged *Fugi*, 51; appointed to command, 187; at the last meeting of Council of Defence, 304; his opinion, 307

Machabelly, Prince, retakes Pan-lun-shan Redoubt, 167; circumstances of his death, 167
Mackalinsky, Prince, intermediary between Fortress Staff and navy, 148
Makharoff, Vice-Admiral, arrival of, to command the fleet, 20; his death, 35; his attitude towards England, 226
Malaieff, Lieutenant, heroism of, 23; his death, 34
Manchuria, the, capture of, 20
Medical organization of the Fortress, 315; neglect to equip hospitals, 316
Mekhmanaroff, Colonel, present at last meeting of Council of Defence, 304; his opinion, 306, 307
Menshoff, M., appointed Hospital Inspector, 318
Metre (203) Hill, 106; its great value, 106, 135, 156; state of, 157; furious attacks on (September 20), 195; assault of (September 21), 196;

fight for, 243 et seq.; Nogi determines to take it, 243; Stössel's apathy, 244; calls a conference and proposes retirement, 246; defence of, by Colonel Tretiakoff, 248; bombardment renewed (December 2), 250; truce to bury dead, 251; occupied by Japanese, 255; Kondratenko's mistake, 256; retirement of Russians, 257; effect of loss on the fleet, 260

Mickeladsey, Prince, in charge of police gendarmes, 38
Mine-layers (Japanese), the work of, 32, 38
Mines, land, 198
Mining (siege operations), 210, 213, 214, 215, 216
Mobilization scheme fo. Fortress, want of, 194; of reserves, 374
Mongolia, the, hospital ship, 193
Mount Samson, 62, 64
Munitions of war, report of General Biely, 386 (Appendix IV.)
Murman, Colonel, Stössel's treatment of, 223

Nadein, General, at last meeting of Council of Defence, 24; his opinion, 307
Nakamura, General, his order for assault of November 24, 240
Nangalin Heights, value of, 88; armed by the Japanese, 234
— railway-station, 76
Nan-shan, Battle of. See Kinchou
Naval engagement of February 25, 17; of March 22, 27
— guns mounted in the forts, 201, 262, 366 (Appendix II.)
— officers (Russian) want of training, 59; their differences with the army, 59; inefficiency of, 97, 154
Navy, Russian, want of reforms in, 153
Negotiations with Japan fail, 3
Nekrashevitch - Poklad, Lieutenant - Colonel, at last Council of Defence, 304
Newspaper censorship, 148, 163, 189
Nickitin, General: his duties, 226; at last meeting of Council of Defence, 304; his opinion, 307
Nogi concentrates two divisions to take Chi-kuan-shan Fort, B Battery, and Eagle's Nest, 183; fails to carry the position, 184; directed to capture Port Arthur at any cost, 236
Nojine, M. (the author): his treatment by Stössel, vii (Preface)
Novik, the, 4, 59, 153, 262
Novy Kry newspaper objects to publish Stössel's order of March 17, 83; publishes scurrilous allegory, 102; censorship of, 148, 163; publication stopped for a month, 189
Nurses' opinion of the war compared with the Boer War, 194

Officers (Russian) kept in ignorance of the topography of the Fortress, 8; their lack of care for their men, 126
Old Town, defences of, 8
Order of St. George, Third Class, bestowed on Stössel, 187, 188
Orphan Hill, Japanese attack on, repulsed, 157
Otvajny, gunboat, as look-out, 26, 42
Oyama, Field-Marshal, joins the besieging army (November), 236

Pallada, the, 96, 97; destruction of, 259
Pan-lun-shan Redoubt, Japanese capture, 166; retaken with great loss, 167; shelled on September 20, 195
Petropalovsk, the, blown up by mines, 35
Petrusha, Colonel, authorized to arrest anyone, 12; at last Council of Defence, 304; his opinion, 305
Petsivo, Japanese land at, 44
Pobieda, the, injured by mines, 35, 96; sinking of, 259
Poltava, the, sinking of, 259
Port Arthur, dilatoriness in constructing defences of, 24; cut off, 45; invested, 156; want of mobilization scheme for the Fortress, 194
Press censorship, 148
Proclamation left about by Japanese, 110

Quail Hill, 7, 259

Rafalovitch, Lieutenant, at 203 Metre Hill, 253
Raschevsky, Colonel: attack on his battery (August 23), 175; his opinion of Stössel and Semenoff, 181; his report of the expenditure of men and ammunition (to September 21), 197; his opinion of Fock's trench work, 200; extracts from his diary of the siege, 207, 209-211, 213, 214, 215, 223, 230, 233, 234, 238; his energy, 233; his death, 277
Radetsky, Colonel, at Kinchou, 65
Redoubts Nos. 1 and 2, desperate assaults on, 176, 179; finally captured, 182; strengthened by Japanese, 186
Retirement from Green Hills, 121 *et seq.*
Retreat from Kinchou to Port Arthur, 76 *et seq.*
Retvisan, the, damaged, 5; floated off the shoal, 20; sinking of, 259

Reuss, Colonel: at last meeting of Council of Defence, 304; appointed to conduct capitulation, 332; the terms agreed to, 332
Rewards for the garrison announced, 187; treatment of private soldiers, 297
Russian army: its ignorance of Japan, 13
— attitude towards England before the war, 226
— fleet driven in on February 25, 17
Rocky ridge, attack on, repulsed, 312; Fock orders its abandonment, 312

Sadikoff, Lieutenant, and his bullock battery, 55
Savitsky, Colonel, at last Council of Defence, 304
Sanshilipu occupied by Japanese, 49; General Fock's blunders at, 55
Schwartz, Captain, succeeds Rachevsky, 280; continues his diary, 283
Scurvy, 271, 317, 319, 320; neglect of preventive measures, 321
Searchlights, Japanese, during siege, 172; Russian withdrawal to Kinchou from, 56
Sebastopol, comparison of Port Arthur with, 113
Selinen, Colonel, deprived of his command, 19
Second line of fortifications, retirement to (January 1), 312; its works, 313
Semenoff, Colonel: conversation with Kondratenko, 111; at the attack on the Green Hills, 113; appointed Aide-de-Camp to the Czar, 181; at last Council of Defence, 304
Sevastopol, the, 99, 262; destroyed on surrender of Fortress, 328
Shell, 11-inch, introduction of, 206; some effects of, 230
Shao-pingtao, Japanese advance from, 92
Sia-gu-shan Hills, importance of holding, 88, 92; condition of, 139; loss of, 142
Sickness breaks out, 230
Siege, progress of the (last days of August), 179; Raschevsky's diary, 207, 209, 210, 211, 214, 215
Signallers from the hills to be shot, 15
Signal Hill recaptured, 207; final fight at (January 2), 330
Sappers: deficiency of officers and men, 293; ignorance of Stössel and his staff as to the capabilities of, 294, 295; neglected in rewards, 296
Sapper Company, the Kwan-tun, 293

Skridloff's battery, 113, 119, 120
Smirnoff, Lieutenant-General, 1; is chosen to supersede Stössel, 7; organizes Fortress Gendarmerie, 9; protests against surrender, 18; arrival at Port Arthur (March 17), 23; horrified at the want of preparation, 24; orders Kinchou to be fortified without delay, 28; his energy, 29, 30; is overruled by Stössel, 86; persuades the Council to occupy the outer position, 88; fails to assert his authority over Stössel as Commandant of the Fortress, 129; attempts to retake ..., 145, 155; drafts reply to proposal of surrender, 159; his coolness and courage during the attack of August 21, 170; his message to Kuropatkin about the district command, 173; his quarters shelled, 208; inspects the mine galleries and fires the camouflet, 217; attacked by Fock in the memorandum of November 3, 227; refused money to pay labourers, 235; speech to Council of Defence (December 8), 267 *et seq.*; action on the death of Kondratenko, 277 *et seq.*; his message to Kuropatkin as to Stössel's behaviour, 291; at last meeting of Council of Defence, 304; his speech, 307, 308; telegram to Kuropatkin, protesting against surrender, 331; his report of strength of garrison on the day of surrender, 388
Solomonoff's battery at Battle of Kinchou, 68
Sortie of fleet (June 22), 96
Spy, a Japanese, 335
Staff, disorganization of the Fortress, 5
Stereguschy, loss of the, 21
Stössel, General: his demeanour on February 9, 6; Viceroy decides to supersede him, 7; neglects to remove families, 8; wastes time constructing inner wall, 8; mismanages supplies, 9, 10, 91; allows rowdyism, 10; permits Chief of Police to flog drunkards, 11, 12; influenced by General Fock, 13; his 'signalling' fears, 14; freely criticized in the restaurants, 15; publishes 'no retreat' order (February 28), 17; 'a fighting infantry General,' 19; admits his ignorance of fortress warfare, 19; his farewell order of March 17, 23; ordered to remain in command of the land defences in the Kuan-tun district, 29; his extraordinary orders, 47, 48, 49, 61; derides the Naval Commander, 60; his behaviour during Battle of Kinchou, 70; sows dissension between the fleet and the army, 101; his greeting to the 5th Regiment

after the battle, 84; his decision to take the command of the Fortress out of Smirnoff's hands, 86; inspects the advanced position, 108; supports Fock against Kondratenko, 109; his account of the evacuation of Wolf's Hills, 133; ordered by Kuropatkin to leave Port Arthur, 133, 173; remains in Port Arthur, 136; on the Japanese proposal of surrender, 161; his action on receiving Kuropatkin's orders to hand over to Smirnoff, 174; his false telegrams to the Czar, 175; denounces the author as a Japanese spy, 180; the author's telegrams to St. Petersburg, 180; appointed Aide-de-Camp to the Czar, 181; prevents a sortie in force, 182; promoted to the Order of St. George, 187; his censorship of the *Novi Kry* newspaper, 189; his treatment of Lieutenant Endrjievsky, 192; his ignorance of fortress mobilization schemes, 195; his interference with Smirnoff, 199; his action with regard to the two newspaper correspondents, 204; and district order on the subject, 205; his quarters shelled, 208; orders Fortress to be mined in case of surrender, 218; wastes ammunition in order to justify capitulation, 219; orders work on the inner lines of defence to cease, 234; refuses money to pay labourers, 235; calls conference on retirement from 203 Metre Hill, 246; orders to Admiral on loss of 203 Metre Hill, 260; opinion on the minutes of Council of Defence (December 8), 272; attempts to isolate Smirnoff, 273; appoints Fock to succeed Kondratenko, 280; at last meeting of Council of Defence, 304, 309; his ignorance about the lines of defence, 312; despatches a *parlementaire* to negotiate surrender, 325; his behaviour after the surrender, 334

Strashny (Russian destroyer), sinking of the, 34

Subotin, Sanitary Inspector, 317, 319

Supplies begin to run short, 233; horse-flesh proposed, 270; amount available on December 8, 271; on December 31, 385

Supply branch, mismanagement of, 9, 38, 40, 46, 90

Suicides begin to occur, 207

Surrender suggested by Nogi, 159; discussed among Stössel's staff, 218; *parlementaire* dispatched to negotiate, 325; effect of the news, 326, 332

Tafashin Heights, 75

Ta-ku-shan Hills, importance of, 88, 92; position of, 123, 139; loss of, 142; attempt to recapture, 144; failure of, 147; second attempt fails, 155; omission of Velichko to fortify, 217; effect, 238

Telegraphy, wireless, not used, 157

Telephones (Russian), quite unreliable, 14, 145; use of, by the Japanese, 104; delay in working, 197

Temple Redoubt, 107, 108, 192; renewed attacks on, 195; capture of, 195

Trenches, Russian, defects of, 200

Tretiakoff, Colonel: his efforts to fortify Kinchou, 37, 47, 56; at Battle of Kinchou, 69, 71; applies to Fock for reinforcements, and is refused, 72; his heroism in holding 203 Metre Hill, 248

Truce, to find wounded, after November 24, 241

Unreadiness of Russia, 4

Urasovsky, Captain, death of, 33

Velichko on the importance of holding the advanced position, 135; his omission to fortify Ta-ku-shan, 217

Vershinin, Colonel, Chief Commissary, 9; opposes Stössel's orders, 11

Veselovsky, Lieutenant, death of, at 203 Metre Hill, 253

Viceroy, the (Admiral Alexeieff), orders on outbreak of war, 6; decides to remove Stössel, 7; orders as to removal of all families neglected, 8; arrives and assumes command of fleet (April 14), 36, 41; leaves for Mukden, 44; leaves for St. Petersburg, 231

Vladivostock, question of the fleet forcing its way to, 187; attempt of August 10, 152

War material, insufficiency of, 38

Water, source of supply, 196

'Water-supply' Redoubt, 106; Japanese efforts to capture, 166, 186, 192; its value, 192; renewed Japanese attacks on, 195

White flag sent out (January 1), 324

Wiren, Admiral, 1; to command battleships and endeavour to reach Vladivostock, 187; present at last meeting of Council of Defence, 304; his opinion, 307; receives news of surrender, 326; orders ships to be disabled (January 1), 327

Witgeft, Rear-Admiral, takes over command of fleet, 44; his lack of decision, 51; his incompetence, 59; his conferences as to fleet breaking out to sea, 150; opposes Loschinsky's proposals, 151; death of, 153

Wolf's Hills, importance of holding, 88, 92; Fock's division to occupy, 129; loss of (July 29), 131

Wounded, treatment of the, during retreat from Kinchou, 73 *et seq.*; none found after assault of November 24, 242

Yalu, news of the Battle of, 37

Yamoaka, Major, bearer of message about surrender, 160

Zabiyak, the, sinking of, 260
Zaredoubt Battery, attack on (August 23), 175
Zedgenidsey, General, death of, 277
Zeitz, Captain, in command at Golden Hill, 142

THE END

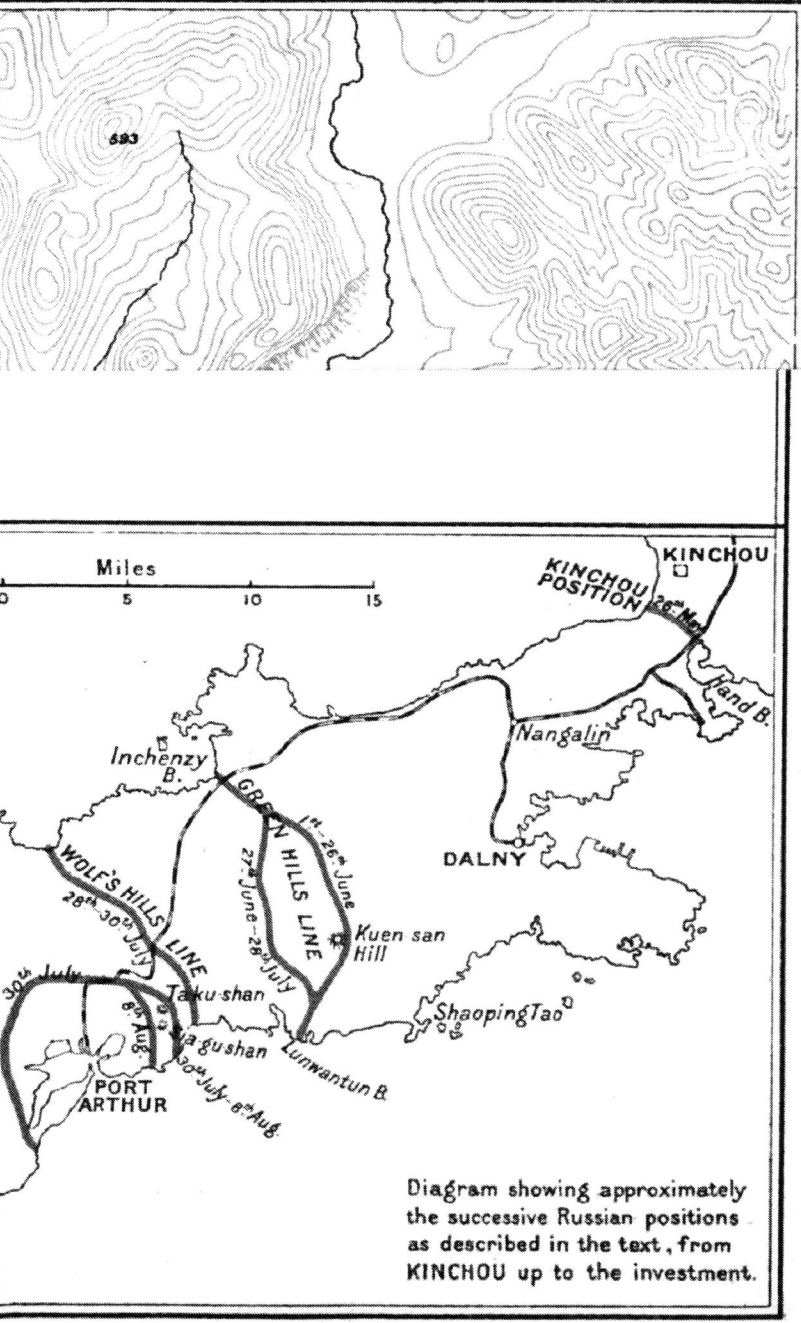

Diagram showing approximately the successive Russian positions as described in the text, from KINCHOU up to the investment.

Lightning Source UK Ltd.
Milton Keynes UK
UKOW022224050213

205888UK00008B/513/P